THE
COMING
DEATH

THE COMING DEATH

TRACES OF MORTALITY ACROSS EAST ASIA

RICHARD F. CALICHMAN

SUNY
PRESS

Published by State University of New York Press, Albany

For information, contact State University of New York Press, Albany, NY
www.sunypress.edu

Library of Congress Cataloging-in-Publication Data

Name: Calichman, Richard F., author
Title: The coming death: traces of mortality across East Asia / Richard F. Calichman, author.
Description: Albany : State University of New York Press, [2022] | Includes bibliographical references and index.
Identifiers: ISBN 9781438487298 (hardcover : alk. paper) | ISBN 9781438487304 (ebook) | ISBN 9781438487281 (pbk. : alk. paper)
Further information is available at the Library of Congress.

10 9 8 7 6 5 4 3 2 1

CONTENTS

Acknowledgments vii

Introduction 1

Chapter 1 Lines of Mortality in Kurosawa Akira's *Ikiru* 9

Chapter 2 Tsai Ming-liang and the Time of Survival 33

Chapter 3 From Culture to Finitude: The Question of Death in Takeuchi Yoshimi's Reading of Lu Xun 63

Chapter 4 Interlacings of Nothing: The Question of Death in Takeuchi Yoshimi's Reading of Lu Xun II 99

Notes 153

Bibliography 169

Index 175

ACKNOWLEDGMENTS

The gap between the moment of writing and the moment of publication means that one can never be sure that either the person who gives thanks or the people to whom thanks are given will in fact still be alive to read these words in print. It is for this reason that my gratitude is marked, in equal measure, by hope and fear. Among the many people to whom I owe thanks, I am especially grateful to Mayumo Inoue, Atsuko Ueda, Tarek El-Ariss, and Andreas Killen for their kindness in reading and commenting on various parts of the manuscript. Mayumo Inoue also generously arranged for me to travel to Tokyo and present certain parts of the work in the summer of 2019. I would like to signal my appreciation to him as well as to Professors Gōda Masato and Fujimoto Kazuisa for organizing talks at Meiji University and Waseda University.

At SUNY Press, James Peltz and Ryan Morris were instrumental in shepherding the work through to publication. I am indebted to them together with the two anonymous readers for the press, who treated the work with sensitivity.

Lastly, but in truth firstly, the book is dedicated to my parents, Murray V. Calichman and Linda Fox Calichman.

INTRODUCTION

At the time of this writing, hundreds of thousands of people have died as a result of the coronavirus pandemic, and these numbers show no signs of abating. The disease has exposed various forms of inequality, revealing that death, far from being democratic, preys especially upon those who society has rendered the most vulnerable. From the perspective of the living, the response to this horrific situation reveals the presence of death across the broad spectrum of time: we may wish to remain close to the dead whose lives now belong to the past; we may seek through our words and deeds to preserve life and reduce the number of dead in the future; and finally we may find ourselves gripped in the present by an anxiety that either we or our loved ones will fall victim to the disease and join the ranks of the dead. It seems that wherever we turn, from our everyday focus on the present back to the past and then ahead to the future, death is already there.

In this way, the historical specificity of our current time provokes fundamental questions about the relation between life and death. These questions demand reflection insofar as our initial response to death is typically one of disavowal. Death, in this account, is that which happens to others, and if it happens to me it does so only at the far extreme of my life, such that its presence remains quantitatively minor and otherwise unconnected to the sum total of experiences that will have preceded it. Death can be conceived in this manner because it is regarded as the very opposite of life. In order for life to be present, that is, death must be absent, and conversely death appears only at the site where life has disappeared. Yet these formulations raise the question of whether the relation between life and death is best understood on the basis of logic and its system of oppositions. At the very least, it seems that the act of

honoring the dead on the part of the living points to the possibility that
these two spheres may not be separated by such a pure and absolute gulf.

If life and death appear resistant to a thinking of logical opposition,
this is because each of these terms may be seen to partly inhabit the
other. Just as there can be death within life, so too might life be detected
within death. At issue here is the notion of animation, derived from the
Latin *animus*, meaning "breath" or "soul." This term is commonly used
to refer to life itself, but in truth life is less a fixed state than a kind of
movement or activity that can affect death as well. The act by which
the living remember the dead is one in which the latter can be said
to receive the animating gift of breath. This breath allows the dead to
be raised beyond the stillness of the grave and commemoratively take
their place among the living. However, the living must not be thought
to occupy a realm of perfect presence where they play the role of active
agents in unilaterally determining when and how the dead will be
mnemonically revived. For the fact is that death, too, possesses a kind
of breath that brings the living close to it. In constantly reminding the
living of the fate that awaits them in the future, the dead have the
ability to influence life and ensure that its presence and activity remain
diluted. In this way, the breath that is *animus* gestures toward a more
general form of life, one that serves as the common source from which
the division between life and death then comes to emerge.

The present volume views death above all as a question, and I have
sought to keep this inquiry open and resistant to those determinations,
based either in metaphysics or common sense, that might prematurely
limit its scope. Death is *not* that which happens to others, then, nor is
it something that happens to me only at the point of my extinction.
Moreover, death is *not* to be conceived in a logical or formal sense as
the strict opposite of life. To these negative assertions we may now
add another: the force of death is *not* restricted to the realm of the
organic. To be sure, death indiscriminately claims as its own humans,
animals, and plants, but there is no reason to draw the border between
life and death exclusively at the level of such concrete entities. Even
more abstract things, such as, for example, youth, love, or friendship,
come to suffer deterioration and death. In precisely the same manner as
humans, the phenomena of love and friendship that endow human life
with such value can suddenly emerge or be destroyed at any moment
in time. And, indeed, it is this reference to time that arguably provides
the key to approaching this issue of death. For the negativity of death

is indistinguishable from the negativity that enables all temporal movement. In order for time to live, so to speak, it must at each moment die to itself, since the radical difference that is time prohibits the survival of any moment as purely self-identical. In its broadest sense, death is thus to be reconceived as the past in which all present instants come immediately to be extinguished.

My insistence upon conceiving of death primarily as a question, one that unsettles many of its most traditional determinations, owes much to the work of Jacques Derrida. As Derrida comments with regard to Philippe Ariès, the historian most noted for his research on death:

> First, there is the semantic or onto-phenomenological type of limit: the historian knows, thinks he knows, or grants to himself the unquestioned knowledge of what death is, of what being-dead means; consequently, he grants to himself all the criteriology that will allows him to identify, recognize, select, or delimit the objects of his inquiry or the thematic field of his anthropologico-historical knowledge. The question of the meaning of death and of the word 'death,' the question 'What is death in general?' or 'What is the experience of death?' and the question of knowing *if* death 'is'—and *what* death 'is'—all remain radically absent *as questions*. From the outset these questions are assumed to be answered by this anthropologico-historical knowledge as such.[1]

Any approach to death must first self-reflexively take into account the methodological tools it uses to examine its object. Bypassing this initial step opens the possibility that certain conceptual prejudices embedded in one's methodology might unfairly predetermine the results of the inquiry. As Derrida suggests, the study of death from the perspective of the empirical sciences must presuppose that such essential issues of identity and ontology have already been resolved prior to research. However, death seems to throw a wrench into these assumptions. When considered in its relation to negativity—that which is irreducible to what "is"—death appears to refuse all attempts to presentify it in the form of an object. On the contrary, reflection on death leads directly to the realization that the operation by which objects are constituted on the basis of identity and ontology must itself now be rethought from the perspective of the negativity introduced by death. In other words, death is not simply an object to be treated by concepts more fundamental than itself; rather, death is itself conceptually bound up with a thinking of nothing and negativity that serves to expose the presentism intrinsic to empirical research.

Throughout this study I have tried to examine death from this more primordial perspective. In my account, the strange interweaving of death within life and life within death signifies that any fixed distinction between interiority and exteriority must now be reassessed. A consideration of death necessarily involves a thinking of negativity and time, and I believe that nothing is left untouched by this generalization of our understanding. What comes to be affected is not merely this or that particular object, but rather the entire edifice through which object constitution is enabled by the concepts of presence and identity. Here a contradiction might be perceived in my project insofar as I limit my object of research to the geographical site of East Asia as opposed to dealing with the problematic of death as such. As should be clear, however, such delimitation in no way implies that death may be fruitfully treated from a culturalist perspective that would seek to determine the particular characteristics of an Asian view of death in its distinction from, say, a "Western" approach.[2] On the contrary, my attempt to conceive of death in its generality means that all such claims of identity now come to be disturbed in the movement by which present entities are constantly subjected to the loss of themselves via the restless negativity of time. If death is narrowly seen as the mere opposite of life, then vital questions of presence and identity may easily be excluded from its scope. The aim of my work runs directly counter to this. By expanding the way in which we think about death, I propose, much of what appears to be the stability and fixity of life comes to be dissolved and open to remaking.

In this regard, the present volume can be said to form a pair with my previous book, *Before Identity: The Question of Method in Japan Studies*.[3] There I sought to demonstrate that the general forces of time and textuality are given insufficient expression within the identitarian framework of area studies. In order for such fundamental insights to appear, I believe the relation between object and method must be explicitly rethought along both conceptual and institutional lines. Here it is a matter of recognizing that particularism in its various forms—cultural, racial, ethnic, national, etc.—remains grounded upon a notion of subjective presence, one that disciplinary structures too often reinforce rather than dismantle, and that such subjectivity works to denude the relation between human and world of much of its inherent complexity. When, for example, a human being dies, the meaning (and loss of meaning) of such an event is poorly grasped by determining the individual on the basis of those particular identities bequeathed by society. In my reading, the occurrence of death rather comes to empty those identities of their significance in exposing a core vulnerability that is essential to one's status as a living being. While it is certainly true that Hegel's conception of the mediating relation between part and whole allows us to understand crucial aspects of the modern world and its forms of knowledge, there are nevertheless certain instances where valuable truths come to be obscured by this system. As a methodological principle, my analysis of the presence of death in the works of Kurosawa Akira, Tsai Ming-liang, Takeuchi Yoshimi, and Lu Xun avoids placing these figures within such a mediating chain of identity. My hope, however, is that this decision might allow these texts to come forth and engage us at their most foundational and disquieting level.

To be sure, the thinking of death never takes place in a vacuum. Thought must occur in a world whose materiality comes to the fore in the differential markings of ideas in time and space. Yet to acknowledge this materiality is not simply to yield to an empirical discourse in which issues of cultural identity have surreptitiously been resolved in advance. The following pages chart an itinerary that passes through such sites as Japan, Taiwan (via France), and China, but at no point are these particular areas allowed to conceal the general force that is the negativity of death. Of central concern here is the notion of priority, which sets in motion an operation of reversal that is in truth nothing more than a restoration. Grasped in its most fundamental sense of loss and disappearance, death shows its generality in taking place only by way of singular difference. This difference, significantly, *precedes* the relation between universal and particular that appears when area is determined as national culture, as this otherwise abstract universal comes to gain concreteness when content is added to its specific national forms. Hence the disturbance created by death cannot be so easily neutralized by anchoring its occurrence to such particular entities as, for example, Japan, Taiwan, and China. If death were considered in the particularist terms of Area studies, then it would leave untouched those forms of national identity in which it takes place. The negativity of death, in other words, would emerge only after the formation of these national entities in their positivity. The argument set forth in the present work contests such privileging of identity, for only in this way can the unsettling effects of death be considered in their proper generality.

In chapter 1, "Lines of Mortality in Kurosawa Akira's *Ikiru*," I examine various questions of death and mortality that arise in the Japanese filmmaker's 1952 work *Ikiru* (To live). This movie is unique in Kurosawa's oeuvre in presenting death as something that is both internal and protracted. Whereas the director's action films typically depict death as a sudden, spectacular event, abruptly ending life in an act of external violence, *Ikiru* instead focuses on an individual who is gradually forced to confront the fact of his own mortality in the form of stomach cancer. As Kurosawa shows, however, this individual does not exist in isolation but rather actively participates in a complex network of social relations that centers on the family and the state. These institutions, I suggest, maintain themselves on the basis of an awareness of the inevitability of death. In order for these entities as a whole to continue over time, that is, the mortality of the human beings that fulfill their constituent parts must be taken into account and utilized. In this way, the actual occurrence of individual death does not disable these institutions but, directly to the contrary, leads to their constant renewal and replication. Kurosawa introduces this vital point through the notion of succession. In parallel plotlines, he reveals how the imminent death of the protagonist provokes a battle of succession in his dual role as father and minor government official. As I argue, Kurosawa comes to resolve this tension between possible successors by determining individual death in far broader terms as meaningful for the social entity as a whole.

Chapter 2, "Tsai Ming-liang and the Time of Survival," considers the films of the Malaysian-Taiwanese director Tsai Ming-liang from the period 1992–2013. These diverse works, I contend, are tied together by a sustained thinking of the fragile border between life and death. For Tsai, this border is seen as all the more unstable since he determines death beyond its traditional biological meaning to include all instances of temporal loss and disappearance. Given the fact that the movement of time takes place through the permanent negation of what presently is, the question becomes how to retain for the future that which at each instant is irrevocably lost to the past. In this way, the relation between life and death comes to be conceived more generally as that between keeping and losing. Without exception, all of Tsai's works are devoted to this core project of keeping that which is otherwise condemned to disappear. Tsai intriguingly links this issue of life and death with the relation between space and time, and this determination allows me to investigate a certain hesitation or perhaps inconsistency that appears between his interviews and films. At issue here is cinema's ability to preserve that which is constantly threatened by the possibility of erasure. I then turn to Tsai's long-term collaboration with his principal actor Lee Kang-sheng and explore the complex dynamics involved in the manner in which this relation consciously repeats the famous partnership between the French New Wave director François Truffaut and the actor Jean-Pierre Léaud. Tsai's staging of these relations along the lines of filiation raises disturbing questions about the notions of rebirth and temporal order.

Chapters 3 and 4 shift the focus from cinema to literature as I provide an assessment of the Japanese critic and Sinologist Takeuchi Yoshimi's study of the founding figure of modern Chinese literature, Lu Xun. In chapter 3, "From Culture to Finitude: The Question of Death in Takeuchi Yoshimi's Reading of Lu Xun," I turn to Takeuchi's personal reflections on his 1944 work *Ro Jin* (Lu Xun) in order to grasp the mechanics of identification by which Lu Xun's death in 1936 allowed him to more openly confront the possibility of his own demise during the final stages of the Pacific War. Takeuchi is remembered today for his powerful thinking of modernity, but I claim that the notion of negativity that informed much of his sociopolitical insight must be partly traced back to Lu Xun's enduring fascination with death and its productively negative presence within life. Here it is a question of thinking death and negativity in a manner that exceeds their status as the logical opposites of life and presence. For Takeuchi, Lu Xun's notion of life is not to be understood along the lines of mere biological survival but rather as that which, while certainly distinct from death, nevertheless remains continually haunted by it. From Takeuchi's standpoint, it is primarily for this reason that Lu Xun merits the status of "thinker," as he calls him. For both these figures, the relation between life and death contains elements that offer themselves to psychological and historical analysis. My claim, however, is that the concepts of interiority and exteriority that serve to ground these perspectives in their mutual difference fail to account for the unsettling presence of death within life, thereby pointing to the limits of such empirical inquiry.

Chapter 4, "Interlacings of Nothing: The Question of Death in Takeuchi Yoshimi's Reading of Lu Xun II," extends my analysis of Takeuchi and Lu Xun with regard to their thinking of death and negativity. This extension is at the same time a broadening, however, as I now pursue

the chain that links the negativity of death with the notions of forgetting and darkness. In his reflections on Lu Xun, Takeuchi puts forward
a generalized view of negativity that he regards as foundational to Lu
Xun's literature. Such conception can be seen in what I call the "death
of death" in which, following Lu Xun's depictions, the individual flesh
that has already been deprived of life and yet remains as a trace of that
being comes subsequently to be extinguished by time. In this way, the
being is returned to the nothing from which it originally sprang. From
the perspective of the mourner, recognition that life cannot be kept yields
to a focus on material traces through which to remember the deceased.
Yet even these are susceptible to destruction, Lu Xun realizes, and this
acknowledgment leads in turn to the conclusion that the trace must be
spiritual rather than material if the deceased is to be truly kept. The
problem, of course, is that even spiritual traces in the form of memory
are themselves at any moment subject to loss in the possibility of forgetting. The chapter ends with an examination of Takeuchi's analysis
of the relation between light and darkness in Lu Xun. Here I connect
Takeuchi's assertion that all light is grounded in darkness with a certain
blindness that appears as an essential attribute of human praxis in its
distinction from knowledge.

CHAPTER 1

LINES OF MORTALITY
IN KUROSAWA AKIRA'S *IKIRU*

In Moscow I received word of Yama-san's death. It may seem strange that I should start writing about Yama-san from the point of his deathbed, but there is a reason.

—Kurosawa Akira[1]

INTRODUCTION

Of the many films directed by Kurosawa Akira (1910–1998) that depict the relation between life and death, his 1952 *Ikiru* (*To Live*) occupies a unique place. Tracing the final months in the life of a bureaucrat who discovers that he is dying from stomach cancer, the work urgently poses the question of what constitutes a meaningful existence. The forced reckoning with mortality as experienced by the protagonist serves to distinguish *Ikiru* from Kurosawa's other works in which focus is narrowed to the tragic event of death. In, for example, the 1949 *Nora inu* (Stray dog), issues of grief over those already dead and fear for those who may yet die soon give way to the far more banal if cinematically thrilling question of where the killer might strike next. In the 1954 *Shichinin no samurai* (*Seven Samurai*), similarly, the unsettling tension before battle, during which both warrior and farmer alike must confront the possibility of their own demise, is quickly overcome by the spectacular scenes of violence in their conflict with the bandits. Kurosawa reinforces this emphasis on the specific event of death in his 1963 crime drama *Tengoku to jigoku*

(*High and Low*). There the question of the fate of the kidnapped child is resolved midway through the narrative, thus redirecting the spectator's attention to the series of murders committed by the antagonist in his attempt to silence his accomplices.

It is not difficult to understand why Kurosawa chooses to represent death as primarily an act of violence as opposed to a necessary condition of all mortal life. In the visual medium that is cinema, reflection on human finitude does not easily lend itself to dramatic images. This is especially true for a master of action film such as Kurosawa, whose talent for choreographing the frenzied movement of people and animals was matched only by the ingenious mobility of his camerawork. And yet in *Ikiru* such intensity of movement seems to come to a halt in the protagonist Watanabe Kanji's attempts to comprehend the simple fact that he will die. Indeed, Kurosawa reveals that it is precisely to escape the thought of his imminent death that Watanabe turns to the pleasures of the red-light district, for there the constancy of distraction takes the form of heightened visual and auditory stimuli that are typically associated with the action genre. This opposition between the relative stillness of contemplation and the dynamism of action is ultimately reconciled by the protagonist's decision to devote what remains of his life to the larger community. In this way, a collective work will be created that continues to survive even after Watanabe's own individual self has been extinguished.

In the present chapter, I examine what I find to be the tension in Kurosawa between a thinking of death as grounded in its various social ramifications and one determined along the lines of the vulnerability of human finitude. Undeniably, *Ikiru* contains moments when death is presented as essentially indivisible from life, and this attention adds both emotional and philosophical substance to the work. Nevertheless, these instances eventually yield to a thinking of death as meaningful to the community of survivors, for whom the dead continue to live on in the form of memory. Here Kurosawa draws attention to the different dimensions of community whose work it is to honor the dead that it claims as its own. Most immediately, the protagonist Watanabe Kanji exists as part of a family, but this family itself belongs to the larger community that is the nation-state Japan, as represented by Watanabe's own work at the lower levels of municipal government. *Ikiru* reveals how the death of the individual comes to be mediated at these distinct dimensions of community. From this communal perspective, what must above all be preserved is the meaning of the death of its members.

In this sense, Kurosawa's film can be seen to powerfully illustrate the manner in which the dead come to be raised beyond the grave to the spiritualized level of meaning.

"TO LIVE" FINITELY

From the opening shot of *Ikiru*, the narrator announces in voiceover that the protagonist is suffering from stomach cancer. This message is visually conveyed by an X-ray image of Watanabe's stomach, which strikingly precedes our first glimpse of the character's face and general appearance. Indeed, it is only by means of a dissolve between these internal and external images that we come to understand that both the stomach and the cancer residing within it belong to Watanabe. Why does Kurosawa decide to open the film in this manner? A more conventional beginning would seek to place the spectator in a position of identification by first revealing the protagonist and then eliciting sympathy by informing us that this man has unfortunately been stricken with cancer. Yet Kurosawa suggests that it is the threat of death that must be considered primary. The message seems to be that human life only first makes its appearance because death is already at work, setting the stage for that life to unfold before its eventual disappearance. Whatever actions Watanabe might engage in throughout the course of the film, his conduct will be steadily accompanied by an awareness that each passing moment might be his last.

This message is consolidated by Kurosawa's refusal to conceive of life and death as purely distinct from one another. Watanabe, as the young Toyo nicknames him, is a "mummy" (*mīra*). That is to say, he is a man who, having mechanically performed the same menial tasks as a government servant for nearly thirty years, appears to be more dead than alive. The narrator's voiceover confirms this impression when he contemptuously introduces Watanabe: "This is the hero of our story. But it is simply too boring to speak about him now. For he is only killing time. He has had no time to live. In other words, it can hardly be said that he's alive."[2] In these lines, Kurosawa informs his audience that the notions of life and death are not to be restricted to their traditional biological meaning. To be sure, the question of organic life in its relation to death is central to *Ikiru*. But Kurosawa's point is that these notions are of such complexity as to exceed even this determination and that their various meanings are, moreover, vulnerable to contradiction. Thus

Watanabe leads an existence that is deemed unworthy of the name of life. Furthermore, it is only after he has died that his capacity to influence his colleagues and provoke animated discussion among them paradoxically appears to reach its zenith. In this manner, *Ikiru* sets out to disturb many of our most fixed assumptions concerning the difference between life and death.

Kurosawa provides a vital hint of this disturbance in the particular language that he employs. In the foregoing voiceover, the narrator refers in the negative to Watanabe's "time to live" (*ikita jikan*). From this speaker's perspective, Watanabe has unfortunately failed to understand the fundamental link between time and life. As a result, he has spent his days "only killing time" (*jikan wo tsubushiteiru dake*: literally, "crushing time"). This violence to time that stems from his misrecognition of the intimate connection between time and life is further suggested by Watanabe's actions as shown during the narrative commentary. In Kurosawa's description, "Watanabe again stifles a slight yawn and glances at his watch" (*Watanabe, mata nama akubi wo kamikoroshite chiratto tokei wo miru*).[3] Although these words appear at the very opening of the screenplay, they are, significantly, a repetition of an even earlier instance in which Watanabe displays this same behavior. There Watanabe is observed to "sometimes stifle a slight yawn and glance at his watch."[4] I call attention to these passages in order to trace out the subtle relationship that Kurosawa aims to establish between time, life, and violence. Watanabe is portrayed as continually looking at his watch,[5] and his association with time is accentuated by Kurosawa's own repeated use of this word "time" together with a variety of terms whose function it is to mark temporal movement, such as "now" (*ima*), "again" (*mata*), and "sometimes" (*tokiori*). Similarly, the double usage of the verb "to live" (生きた, 生きている) that appears in the voiceover is mirrored in the otherwise innocuous description of Watanabe's yawn, which is merely "slight" (生). Finally, the strain of violence that subtends these initial moments of *Ikiru* can be perceived not merely in the narrator's statement that Watanabe is merely "killing" or "crushing" time, but also in the particular verb used to represent Watanabe's attempt to "stifle" his yawn: かみ殺す, where of course 殺す means "to kill."

Why does Kurosawa seek to present the link between time and life specifically in terms of violence? At first glance, it seems that the intent is to remind viewers that the only life available is temporal life, and that the precariousness of such existence must be recognized as opposed to crudely suppressed and forgotten. This insight forms a major part of the reception of *Ikiru* among both general and critical audiences. At an even deeper level, however, the sustained focus on time in a film whose title means "to live" implicitly poses the question of the life of time itself. If Kurosawa's work teaches that life can only proceed by way of time, then how are we to conceive of time unfolding itself in the form of life? It is in this sense that a very different conception of violence comes into view. For one of the great paradoxes of time is that it can only live by violently negating itself. In order for temporal movement to be possible, in other words, each moment must come into being at the very instant that it disappears. Time proceeds by way of succession, in which an earlier moment comes to be overtaken by a later moment. Yet this transition does not take place merely externally, such that the preceding moment would be destroyed by the arising of the moment that immediately replaces it. In such conception, violence appears to derive from a position of exteriority, affecting a moment whose unity or integrity would then, however instantaneously, exist prior to that violence. Yet to claim that such unity is antithetical to the continual negation that is time is to in effect speak of time as originary violence. Here the change from a preceding to a succeeding moment must already be underway even prior to the formation of that earlier moment, whose existence is therefore entirely dependent on its reconstruction. Only by determining time as originary violence can we understand that time "lives" through the constant experience of its own death.

This conception of time and life as fundamentally mediated by violence is essential, I believe, if we are to grasp the dynamics behind Kurosawa's project of unsettling some of our most deeply rooted prejudices concerning the relation between life and death. The insight that death or negation exists most essentially *within* entities is found at the very core of *Ikiru* and serves to distinguish this film from nearly all of his other works. We can see this awareness, for example, in the debate that takes place during Watanabe's wake that occupies the second half of the film. This discussion centers on the important question of *shiin*, or the "cause of death" suffered by Watanabe. Here the deputy mayor is speaking with a group of reporters, who notify him of the rumor that Watanabe had committed suicide as an act of protest against the city government for failing to publicly acknowledge his efforts in the construction of the park. In his reply, the deputy mayor refers to three possible causes of death. Rejecting the first two, he identifies the third as the true reason for Watanabe's demise. On the basis of the autopsy results, it is asserted that Watanabe neither committed suicide nor froze to death in the park that he helped build; rather, he died because of stomach cancer. Or more precisely—and here we see the scrupulous attention that Kurosawa pays to this issue—he died because of the "internal bleeding as caused by stomach cancer," a conclusion that revises an earlier statement, subsequently rejected by the director and unused in the film, that Watanabe's death was due to "vomiting blood as caused by stomach cancer."[6]

Despite the deputy mayor's keen distinctions, it must be recognized that from a philosophical perspective all three causes of death that he names possess merely an external or contingent status. That is to say, there is no necessary reason that Watanabe's life be destroyed by either suicide, freezing to death, or stomach cancer (whether in the form of internal bleeding or vomiting blood). All of these things either may or may not occur; they are not essentially related to the issue of Watanabe's extinction. Such contingency opens the possibility for a quite different cause of death, one not enumerated by the deputy mayor but in fact plainly signaled by Kurosawa himself. This cause, which occupies a radically distinct level from the three explicitly mentioned, is that of finitude. Prior to Watanabe dying by this or that cause, the fact of his death is most intrinsically announced by his status as a living being. This, I would like to argue, is the true meaning of the notion of "living" as revealed in *Ikiru*. Temporal life is given because it carries its death within itself. It is for this reason that death can never strictly be opposed to or excluded from life. Here we glimpse the originary violence that operates at all times within human life. Just as time can only "live" on the condition that it continually die to itself, so too does Kurosawa suggest that Watanabe's death was in fact indivisibly bound up with his own life.

This message is most powerfully conveyed in a remark made by the subordinate Kimura during Watanabe's wake. Much alcohol has been imbibed by this point in the evening, and the bureaucrats' tongues are loosened. Noguchi, a fellow subordinate, claims that Watanabe's unusual zeal in building the park must have been motivated by the fact that he knew about his cancer and wished to complete the project before his death. Ōno, Watanabe's successor as citizens section chief, vigorously agrees, exclaiming that all those present would certainly act in the same manner if they, too, were faced with cancer. This comment angers Kimura, who uncharacteristically rebuts his superior: "But any one of us could drop dead at any time!"[7]

In order to underscore the significance of this statement, Kurosawa introduces an interval of shocked silence among the mourners. All stare aghast at Kimura, who has reminded them of an appalling truth. Kurosawa shoots this scene in a visually striking fashion: immediately after presenting the group collectively gazing at Kimura in medium shot, the director shifts to a series of six cuts in which the various petty officials are shown individually framed in close shot, their head and shoulders alone visible. Each looks desperately at Kimura, but the heightened anxiety of their expressions, which appear only momentarily before the shot cuts to the next, reveals that they are focusing less on him than on the fact of their own mortality as reflected in his words.[8] In terms of composition, this series of cuts is rare in the context of the long wake scene, for Kurosawa primarily shoots the bureaucrats as a group, tightly wedged together in the same frame. Indeed, it is to emphasize the contrast between Watanabe and his colleagues that Kurosawa mainly reserves his single framing of individuals to the photograph of the dead Watanabe as displayed on the altar. The series of cuts prompted by Kimura's abrupt reminder of finitude thus functions to contest the dominant spatiality of the scene, in which the dead is visually set apart from the living. These shots identify each of the petty officials with the deceased Watanabe, and in this sense they complement Kimura's message that the death suffered by Watanabe must be understood in properly general terms as a fate that awaits them all. Using both dialogue and image, Kurosawa reminds his audience of the incontrovertible fact of mortality in much the same way that Kimura has boldly recalled this truth to his colleagues.

This attention to finitude appears persistently if subtly throughout *Ikiru*. In the screenplay, for example, Watanabe's absence from the office as brought about by his cancer is described by the term *mujin* (無人), meaning "unmanned" or "uninhabited" in reference to his work desk.[9] More literally, however, this word aptly conveys the nothingness (無) that resides within Watanabe in the form of his impending death. If this term alludes to an absence, then its deeper significance in Kurosawa's film appears in the fact that Watanabe's own presence in his life is gradually being negated from within. A similar perspective is offered by the writer, who acts as Watanabe's guide through the red-light district in a vain attempt to seek diversion from his suffering. Upon hearing Watanabe's confession that he is dying, the writer proclaims: "Misfortune teaches people the truth. Your stomach cancer has opened your eyes to your own life. People are so frivolous. Only when they confront death do

they realize how beautiful life is. But there aren't many people like that.
The worst kind die without knowing what life is."[10] As illustrated by his
language, the "truth" disclosed by the writer consists in the inextricability
of life and death. Their connection is not to be sought in the manner
with which death finally commences upon the completion of life, for
such standpoint perceives the bridge between these points as appearing
only once. On the contrary, the strange beauty glimpsed by the writer
lies in the fact that each moment of life is potentially followed by its
destruction. Rather than life monovalently passing into death, the writer
realizes that it is the constant presence of death within life that provides
existence with its vast richness and unpredictability.

Perhaps the most poignant manifestation of finitude, however, can
be detected in the famed "Gondora no uta" (Gondola song) as sung by
Watanabe first during his evening of debauchery with the writer and then
again in the final death scene in the park. Critics have long pointed to
the pivotal role played by this song within the film,[11] but rarely does this
analysis explore the philosophical implications of the music as discerned
by Kurosawa. The lyrics of the song appear as follows:

Inochi mijikashi, koi seyo otome	Life is brief, so fall in love, young lady
akaki kuchibiru asenu ma ni	Before the crimson fades from your lips
atsuki chishio hienu ma ni	Before the heat of your passion cools
asu toiu hi no nai mono wo	For there is no tomorrow.
Inochi mijikashi, koi seyo otome	Life is brief, so fall in love, young lady
kurokami no iro asenu ma ni	Before the black fades from your hair
kokoro no honoo kienu ma ni	Before the flame in your heart disappears
kyō ha futatabi konu mono wo	For today will not come again.[12]

What is so crucial in these two stanzas is the allusion to time. The
brevity of human life, we come to see, derives most essentially from

the negativity that is intrinsic to temporal succession. In order for one moment to pass into the next, in other words, it must first disappear. In the particular context of the song, such negation emerges in the negative form of the verb: *nai*, or "to not be," in the final line of the first stanza, and *konu*, or "to not come," in the concluding line of the second. The destruction that allows time to proceed threatens all temporal life. This movement of time brings about aging, withering the bloom of youth and annihilating desire as part of the inevitable advance toward death. Yet it is of course this same movement, departing from the immediacy of birth, that first permits youth to develop and desire to flourish. Here the "Gondola Song" implicitly points to the underlying productivity of temporal destruction, without which nothing at all could ever arise.

It must be noted, however, that these two stanzas end with a markedly different emphasis. Despite the apparent resemblance between these lines, to say that "there is no tomorrow" is not identical to the claim that "today will not come again." Whereas the former refers most directly to the experience of time, the latter can be said to describe a general feature of time itself. Rigorously speaking, there must be—or indeed, there must *have been*—a "tomorrow" or some type of futurity in order for this first line, whether sung or written, to be received and thus arrive at its meaning. Hence the sentiment appears to be rather that no futurity can be guaranteed to finite life, that such life is, on the contrary, at each moment potentially vulnerable to its destruction. Death announces its presence in the mode of possibility, a possibility that was also signaled in Kimura's fateful words, "But any one of us could drop dead at any time!" In the second line, however, the point is that it is the element of difference or nonrepeatability that acts as the very condition of existence for time. Here the term "today" functions more broadly to designate any present instant whatsoever. "Today will not come again" because its return would indicate the ability of a temporal moment to survive its own demise, but this capacity would be tantamount to the yielding of time to presence in the form of God or atemporality. If this is in fact impossible, it is because each coming of the present is necessarily distinct from all others. It is this constant difference, in which the birth of each new moment is inseparable from its death, that allows time to live and develop. In the specific context of the "Gondola Song," the extreme risk involved in the coming of "tomorrow"—when the possibility exists that hair will turn gray, passion grow cold, and life lost to death—can be seen in the impossibility of any recurrence of "today."

THE MEANINGFUL LIFE OF THE DEAD

One of the most fascinating aspects of *Ikiru* lies in its decisive shift from the question of finitude to that of socially determined meaning. For the originary violence that appears in the complex relation between time and life is perceived as an evil that must be overcome, and the wounds that it has inflicted must in some way be healed. This is the work of the community, which assumes a variety of forms in Kurosawa's film and yet remains united in its goal of successfully mourning the dead Watanabe. *Ikiru* reminds the audience that those who have perished never truly die alone. The remarkable series of six cuts introduced by Kurosawa in response to Kimura's indignant message about mortality shows the bureaucrats singly framed, as if the director were emphasizing that death is something that one must confront as an individual.[13] Yet if death is irreducibly singular, it is no less true that *all* people alike must die. Viewed together, these individual framings form something like a community of the dying, and this establishes a certain identity between the dead Watanabe and his living colleagues. However, these petty officials are only part of the larger group of people who have gathered at the wake to commemorate his life. Led by Watanabe's immediate family, the community in its diversity comes to claim the dead as integral to its own evolving life.

 Ikiru shows how Watanabe is introduced to his own death, but such death has already announced its presence throughout his entire family. If Watanabe's demise specifically appears divided between the modes of possibility (the first half of the film, as he attempts to reckon with his cancer) and actuality (the second half, as he is commemorated during the wake), then this partition corresponds to the several brushes with mortality experienced by his son Mitsuo and the instance of real death represented by his late wife. Kurosawa brilliantly links these three instances of possible and actual death to call attention to the intimate relation between death and the institution of the family. For it is the family that typically functions as the first line of defense, as it were, when death attacks the individual. Of course the family is powerless to protect its members from the event of physical destruction. However, it responds to this crisis by introducing a vital distinction between the physical and spiritual: although the departed may no longer exist in flesh and blood, his life will now be raised to the level of spiritual meaning as preserved by his surviving family members. At issue here is the unique manner in which the family overcomes the natural immediacy of death in order to incorporate it within the totality of its own spiritual life. Or as Hegel writes in *Phenomenology of Spirit*, "The Family keeps away from the dead this dishonouring of him by unconscious appetites [i.e., the forces of decomposition] . . . and puts its own action in their place . . . thereby mak[ing] him a member of a community."[14]

The elevation of the dead Watanabe from mere physical corpse to honored communal member commences with the work of Mitsuo together with his wife Kazue. Yet this labor of mourning is not one that gives itself oppositionally as an aiding of the deceased on the part of the living. As I have mentioned, Kurosawa represents Watanabe's immediate family as already touched by death. *Ikiru* uses the particular technique of flashback in order to show that the strength of the familial bond derives chiefly from the shared experience of death. This is revealed relatively early in the film when Watanabe, devastated by the realization that he has only several months left to live, returns to his bedroom to gaze at the photograph of his late wife. This action sets in motion the first of a series of flashbacks that bring together in the form of recollection the living Watanabe of the present (the subject of memory), his living wife of the past pictorially reproduced in the present (the memorative trigger),[15] the dead wife of the past (object of memory), and finally Mitsuo at various moments of the past (object of memory). Significantly, the flashbacks of Mitsuo focus primarily on those instances in which his life is perceived to be endangered—either literally or figuratively—as, for example, the hospital scene where he must undergo an appendectomy, the train scene where he is being sent off together with other soldiers to fight in the Pacific War, but also the baseball scene where he is thrown out while attempting to steal a base.

These three scenes of Mitsuo are notable not simply because the risk of life that they suggest functions to consolidate his place, together with his deceased mother and dying father, as a member of a family that has been uniformly marked by death. Kurosawa here can also be seen as attempting to broaden the meaning of death beyond its strict biological determination. Crucial to these instances is Mitsuo's terror at being abandoned by his father, whose disapproval he fears after being tagged out (in Japanese, the baseball term "out" is translated as 死, or "death"), who rejects his plea to be present during the surgery, and who finally must remain on the platform while the military train slowly departs. This powerful association of death with the notion of absence

recalls the very first flashback when the grieving Watanabe and Mitsuo
are shown riding behind the deceased wife's hearse in the funeral procession. As the hearse turns a corner, briefly disappearing from view, the
child Mitsuo screams in desperation: "Hurry, hurry! Mother is leaving!"[16]
From Mitsuo's perspective, death does not truly take place if the dead
remain visually present. Insofar as one is able to continue accessing the
dead through the senses, life has not been fully extinguished. Although
there is a considerable difference in age between the Mitsuo who attends
his mother's funeral, the Mitsuo who participates in the sporting event,
the Mitsuo who must undergo surgery alone, and finally the Mitsuo
who reluctantly goes off to combat, the disappearance of the parent is
nevertheless perceived as in some sense equivalent to death.[17]

This traditional determination of death as absence and life as presence is deeply ironic. For, as we have seen, one of Kurosawa's central
insights in *Ikiru* is that life and death can never be purely identical to
themselves. Watanabe's stomach cancer does nothing more than hasten
the approach of death that must come to everyone regardless. In this
sense, the very title of the film can be understood to mean "to die" as
much as "to live," for these two acts cannot occur in abstraction from
one another. Moreover, Watanabe's mummified form of existence, as
the narrator explicitly remarks, appears as a form of death. This view is
supported by the fact that Watanabe is revealed to be most fully alive
in the second half of the film when he is, of course, already dead. More
specifically, it must be borne in mind that these thoughts on absence
and presence are framed within the context of the flashback. That is
to say, Watanabe realizes that it is through the faculty of memory that
the past, which is otherwise dead and gone, is capable of somehow
resurrecting itself so as to create forceful effects in the present.[18] Yet
if the absent past can thus be shown to return to the present, then it
becomes difficult to conceive of these notions of absence and presence
as in any way contrary.

Watanabe's immediate family—his wife and son Mitsuo (and, more
broadly, his daughter-in-law Kazue as well as his older brother and sister-
in-law)—plays a formative role in his existence. But this community must
yield to the even larger and more complex community found within
the social space that Watanabe as citizen is forced to negotiate in his
everyday life. This latter community is ultimately that of the nation-
state Japan. Kurosawa names this national community twice in the film:
first by Kazue as she complains about the inferior quality of Watanabe's

house in which she and Mitsuo live ("Oh, it's so cold! It's just as cold inside the house as outside. That's why I hate Japanese homes!") and then again, considerably later in the film, when Toyo, having quit her position under Watanabe at the Citizens Section to work in a small toy factory, tells him of her great pleasure in making these objects ("Even if it's not much, it's fun to make things like this. Ever since I began making them, I feel like I've become close to all the babies in Japan").[19] Significantly, this community is internally mediated in such a way as to be primarily divided along the lines of gender. Its constituent parts are introduced from the very beginning of *Ikiru* when a group of women visits the municipal office to lodge a complaint about an unsanitary ditch in the neighborhood. By ignoring their grievance, the bureaucrats, who are overwhelmingly men, initiate the central conflict in the film that actively pits these two factions against one another. The resolution of this conflict, and thus the return to what is perceived to be the normative state of communal unity and wholeness, is accomplished strictly through Watanabe's death.

Ikiru begins by exposing the fallen state of community. From Kurosawa's critical standpoint, this loss of proper communality must be traced back to the abject failure of government to protect the interests of the people that it claims to represent. Here we glimpse the main criterion that determines the difference between just and unjust political rule. Whereas the former is implicitly defined in the film as a type of governance in which popular support corresponds to the state's capacity to ensure the general welfare of its citizens, the latter appears when this correspondence between people and state suffers the violence of rupture. The notion of "the people" that grounds both types of rule is merely assumed as opposed to actively explored. Kurosawa introduces the ideal of just governance in the opening of the film by means of a poster that hangs prominently in the reception area of the Citizens Section: "This is the counter where all citizens are directly connected to City Hall."[20] A division is thus acknowledged to exist between the represented people and their official representatives, but this split is of course necessary for any form of political representation at all. Everything depends, however, on the precise status of the bond or "connection" between ruler and ruled. If the connection is "direct" or "immediate" (*chokusetsu*), then governance is justified. In *Ikiru*, however, Kurosawa depicts a government apparatus in which such immediacy has been lost, resulting in a debased political environment marked by apathy and petty territoriality. His primary task in the film consists in showing how the painful damage done to political representation can be healed and the community restored to its original unity.

One of the foremost achievements of Kurosawa's work lies in showing how the tragic event of the individual's death comes to reveal some of the general features of modern society. As citizens section chief, Watanabe is responsible for acting as the bridge between the populace and its elected officials. This relation is enormously complex, but Kurosawa, with characteristic economy, distills it to its essence by focusing specifically on children, whom he regards as the most vulnerable segment of society. The women who come to petition the municipal office are chiefly concerned about the health of their offspring, who have been forced to endure the stench and mosquito infestation caused by the leaking sewerage, leading in some cases to skin problems. It is through the grievances voiced by this group of mothers that the inertia of the larger bureaucratic system is first uncovered. In this manner, the abstract political question of the link between ruler and ruled comes to be concretized, so to speak, as an issue of childcare, i.e., the government's capacity to protect and nurture the progeny of the citizens whose interests they represent.

Watanabe begins the film as leader of the Citizens Section, which, as I have noted, occupies a position directly opposed to that of the group of women. During the course of *Ikiru*, however, he gradually departs from this faction and becomes affiliated with the women whose complaints he originally ignored. Here we touch upon a point persuasively made by Mitsuhiro Yoshimoto, who argues that "[t]hroughout *Ikiru*, Watanabe is consistently feminized."[21] Ample evidence can certainly be found to support this contention, as for example Watanabe's unusual attachment to Toyo, whom he ardently wishes to emulate. Indeed, the force of this identification is explicitly underlined by Toyo, who at one point feels compelled to remind Watanabe of the fact of their physical difference. When he notices her torn stockings and insists on presenting her with a new pair, she protests, "But it's not that the hole in my stockings means that *your* feet are cold."[22] Moreover, it is revealing that the relative power enjoyed by the bureaucrats over the local residents can be seen to at least symbolically recede in Watanabe's association with women. While ice skating with Toyo, he suffers a fall,[23] and this accident is significantly repeated later in the film when Watanabe dangerously stumbles while visiting the site of the new playground, which is still under construction and filled with heavy machinery. Two neighborhood women rush to his aid, suggesting that Watanabe's frailty has as much to do with his isolation from the other male bureaucrats as it does with the debilitating effects brought about by his advancing cancer.

However, the proximity shared between Watanabe and the group of women rather than his colleagues at the municipal office is alluded to most forcefully in the wake scene. There the bureaucrats drink and pontificate, regarding the dead Watanabe with the same attitude of casual neglect that they displayed while he was still alive. Suddenly their conversation is interrupted by the entrance of the women, who have come to light incense and pay their respects to the deceased. Gazing collectively at the altar photograph of Watanabe, they begin sobbing loudly, emotionally devastated by his death in a manner that contrasts sharply with the reserve and stiff formality exhibited by the petty officials. This scene of public catharsis reveals Watanabe's initiation as part of the citizenry, a membership that is granted only posthumously. Upon his death, Watanabe is recognized as having successfully reconciled the otherwise conflictual realms of state and citizen, a relation that Kurosawa marks in the gendered terms of male and female. It should thus be clear that Watanabe's identification with women in *Ikiru* functions less as a statement about gender in and of itself than as the eventual incorporation of that part of the community that is initially ostracized by the state. The gender politics at issue illustrate that the fallen community that appears at the beginning of the film is finally restored to its status of wholeness, its painful divisions healed, through the sacrifice of that individual whose actions were required to bring about the synthesis between state and citizen, representative and represented, and man and woman.

In *Ikiru*, the community is found to be in crisis because the political contract between ruler and ruled has been violated. The conspicuous poster in the Citizens Section that describes the relation between state and citizen as one of "direct connection" indicates the hypocrisy of the present situation, for this bond has since fallen into abstraction. The communal unity that originally existed was putatively achieved on the basis of such directness or immediacy, as both government representative and represented citizen were oriented to the same goal of consolidating the community in its overall identity. Yet this mediation between the government and its people developed into a harmful rift between these parts, resulting in a merely formal type of political representation in which the latter's concerns were increasingly ignored. *Ikiru* begins by showing us this lapsed state of affairs. Restoration of the community must commence with a return to the kind of immediacy displayed by the grieving women at Watanabe's wake. Indeed, Toyo has already provided a crucial hint of this immediacy when she confides to Watanabe that making children's toys allows her to feel "close to all the babies in Japan." These words motivate him to undertake a similar project in the hope of finally overcoming the alienation of social relations, thereby allowing the community to regain what it has lost.

As is true of all his works, the Kurosawa of *Ikiru* reveals himself to be a keen observer of the internal dynamics of community. These dynamics primarily take two forms: the relation between individual parts and the relation between individual part and whole. This focus is announced from the very opening of the film when the viewer is shown a close-up of an unusual X-ray image of a stomach. The organ belongs to the film's protagonist, as we are informed by the narrative voice-over, and moreover contains traces of cancer within it. The presence of the cancer within the stomach that exists, in turn, within the character Watanabe effectively introduces the question of the whole-part relation, which is central to the movie's treatment of politics. As I have discussed, the bureaucratic faction openly sets itself in opposition to the faction of women, and yet both groups firmly identify themselves as part of the larger national community. In *Ikiru*, this community is rife with internal dissent, but such negativity comes ultimately to be utilized as a means to enhance the overall force of collective unity. It is this underlying complexity of the whole-part relation, I believe, that has frequently misled commentators to consider the film as a work of political protest. As, for example, the celebrated film critic and theorist Satō Tadao writes:

> With defeat in World War II, many Japanese, who had made the objectives of the nation their objectives in life, were dumbfounded to find that the government had lied to them and was neither just nor dependable. During this uncertain time Akira Kurosawa, in a series of first-rate films, sustained the people by his consistent assertion that the meaning of life is not dictated by the nation but something each individual should discover for himself through suffering. *Ikiru* is the clearest expression of not only this assertion but also of the essence of Kurosawa.[24]

As one of the most foremost scholars on Kurosawa, Satō's statement deserves serious consideration. My disagreement, however, stems less from his knowledge of the filmmaker's oeuvre than from his political belief that the existence of "the people" and the individual must be seen as inherently opposed to the government and the nation. To be sure, it is always possible to adopt such a standpoint of resistance, but one must remain sensitive to the manner in which these former entities may at any time be appropriated by the latter of which they are structurally part. One glimpses Kurosawa's attention to this whole-part relation in Watanabe's wake scene when he lists the various officers in attendance: the deputy mayor, director of general affairs, director of public works, public works section chief, parks section chief, Ōno, Saitō, Ohara, Noguchi, and Kimura of the Citizens Section, as well as various representatives from the Public Works Section, Park Section, and Sewerage Section.[25] These individual parts retain a certain degree of autonomy from one another, and yet all must work together in order to serve the interests of the community as a whole.

This articulation of the total community into discrete parts is foregrounded in Watanabe's decision to sacrifice his own individual life for the improved welfare of Japanese children. With Toyo's parting suggestion still ringing in his ears that he, too, make something for others, Watanabe finally returns to the Citizens Section to begin work constructing the park. This activity, significantly, centers on coordinating the various government departments so that all are oriented to achieving the same goal. As Watanabe tells Ōno, "The Citizens Section must be the core. It's a matter of coordination. That is, it is not an issue for the Public Works Section alone. The Parks Section and Sewerage Section must also help."[26] What is foremost at stake in this remark can be seen in Watanabe's use of the word "core," or *shutai*, which is also the philosophical term for "subject." A dangerous gap has opened up between the people and their government, and this division is reflected within the government itself in the abstract separation of parts that do not work toward a common objective. It is in order to ensure that these individual differences remain tied together that the core or subject becomes necessary. In this view, the disintegration of community can be attributed to the fact that the parts have lost sight of the overarching presence of the whole. In assuming the position of subject, Watanabe sets out to realign the various departments by emphasizing that parts only come into their identity by virtue of the whole to which they belong. It is strictly through this act of mobilization that the national community may now come to be restored.[27]

SUCCESSORS AND GHOSTS

A community can never be reduced to its synchronic existence, which remains rooted to the present. Diachronically, the community reveals itself to possess a shared history, and it is at this level that one must speak of the interrelated questions of succession and death. Here let us recall that the first character of the surname Watanabe, 渡, means "to cross" or "to pass" in the sense of a movement that occurs between distinct points. *Ikiru* depicts a man who, in dying, yet passes on to future generations an essential part of himself in the form of a park. The fact that Watanabe dies in the park that came into being chiefly through his own efforts reveals Kurosawa's insight that the border between life and death is essentially porous. In death, Watanabe has now crossed over into something that survives him. The film's final scene shows Kimura traversing an overpass while gazing down at the children playing in the park that Watanabe has left behind. Here the act of crossing is both literal and figurative, spatial and temporal, for Kimura realizes that traces of Watanabe continue to live on into the future despite the fact that his physical existence has now been finally delivered over to the past.

It is noteworthy that those who are expected to succeed Watanabe are seen as patiently awaiting his disappearance. Kurosawa appeals to individual psychology to portray these potential successors unsympathetically: Mitsuo is selfish and ungrateful, refusing to listen when his father attempts to explain his unfortunate circumstances, while Ōno, who is perceptively nicknamed "sea slug" by Toyo, is a mere sycophant. What must not be overlooked in these relationships, however, is an awareness that death forms an essential part in ensuring that the distinction between institutional position and individual occupant remains preserved. That is to say, the survival of the former is predicated upon the departure of the latter, a departure whose extreme form is death. This relation must be understood as analogous to that of the line and point. If a line can be said to first appear only upon the emergence of a point, then its extension depends upon that point being transcended. The formation of the line requires both the establishment of an initial point and its subsequent negation. In precisely the same manner, the protagonist's status as head of the Watanabe family as well as chief of the Citizens Section is originally presented in *Ikiru* only to finally be annulled by the film's end. In dying, however, Watanabe provides the necessary opening for these lines of succession to continue.

With regard to this relation between line and point in the particular context of *Ikiru*, I wish to make two claims. First, because the negativity intrinsic to the line is already at work within the point from its very beginning, the point never fully exists in a state of self-presence. The point, in other words, cannot be understood as immediately identical to itself. The nature of the link between two contiguous points is such that they are neither purely different nor purely the same as one another. Kurosawa illustrates this message by means of the parent-child relation between Watanabe and Mitsuo. The individual difference that separates these two men is transcended by the fact that both come to occupy the position of head of the Watanabe household. In order for Mitsuo's potential as leader of this family to be actualized, his father must die. Kurosawa subtly indicates the shared identity between them at the wake when Mitsuo, in his role as "chief mourner" (*moshu*),[28] repeats Watanabe's similar function earlier in the film upon suffering the untimely loss of his wife. Moreover, just as Watanabe's death allows control of the family to now pass to Mitsuo, the fact that Mitsuo, too, must eventually die means that the Watanabe line must be further extended. This, I would like to suggest, is the reason why Kurosawa includes the scene where Mitsuo and Kazue appear to have sex. When Kazue demands that Mitsuo make love to her ("*Daite!*" she urges, chastely rendered by the subtitles as "Hold me"), it seems clear that Watanabe's survival beyond his death might possibly take the form of future descendants in addition to that of the park itself.

A similar logic of succession can be seen in Watanabe's office at City Hall. From early in the film, Kurosawa carefully draws attention to the issue of *atogama*, or the "successor" of Watanabe, who will come to replace him should his absence from work portend something more serious. The institution of the workplace of course differs from that of the family in that Watanabe does not need to first die in order for succession to take place. Nevertheless, Toyo, with characteristic acuity, explicitly refers to this link between succession and death in her conversation with Sakai and Noguchi regarding Watanabe's absence. When Sakai raises the question of Watanabe's successor, Toyo caustically replies that "Quite a few people would need to die first before you two get a turn!"[29] Death, then, as the event that consolidates the line between one citizens section chief and another.

My second claim concerns the movement from an earlier point to a later point in the ongoing line of succession. Despite appearances,

this succeeding point can never be determined in advance, for an irreducible element of contingency pervades this operation. Evidence of
this can be seen in the two main institutions with which Watanabe is
affiliated: that of the family and workplace. Here Kurosawa reveals his
mastery of parallel narrative. Mitsuo is regarded as the obvious heir of
the Watanabe family, just as Ōno is considered the leading candidate to
replace Watanabe as citizens section chief. Nevertheless, both potential
successors find themselves confronted with unexpected competition as
the true claimant of Watanabe's legacy. In the context of the family,
Mitsuo is extremely disturbed by the possibility that his father may be
romantically involved with Toyo, for such an affair would carry certain
financial repercussions. The issue of professional succession in the Citizens
Section presents no such direct rivalry, but Kurosawa actively intervenes
in this process to pose the question of whether Kimura might not be
Watanabe's most faithful beneficiary in understanding how best to serve
his fellow citizens.

Mitsuo's fear is that his position as Watanabe's rightful heir will
suffer usurpation. From his perspective, society must uphold the tradition that inheritance be determined by the blood ties between father
and son. Contingency is in this instance trumped by nature, which is
seen as the truest guide to establishing continuity. Once succession is
thus fixed, the property that once belonged to Watanabe will now be
transferred to Mitsuo, for the passage from a preceding to a succeeding
point has been rendered impervious to risk or accident. Mitsuo is thus
shocked to discover that the line of succession might exceed the limits
of formalization, and promptly takes action to ensure that the money
that he believes to be his not be frivolously spent on Toyo.

In contrast to Mitsuo, Ōno appears to experience no anxiety when
contemplating the transfer of power from Watanabe to himself. Here
Kurosawa depicts the struggle for succession as one that is known only to
the spectator, who comes to realize that Watanabe's work as intermediary
between government and citizen is continued not by Ōno but by Kimura.
Kimura's role as the real inheritor of Watanabe's legacy is revealed at
the end of the film when the camera slowly pans down from him to the
swing on which Watanabe died before then cutting to a ground shot
of the swing with Kimura framed prominently in the background. The
visual message is clear enough, but Kurosawa emphasizes the point by
focusing on two children playing on the swing who are suddenly called
away for dinner by their mother. The camera lingers meaningfully on

the empty swing before finally panning back up to Kimura on the bridge. Just as Watanabe's creation of the park clears a space for any number of future recipients of his action, so too does his death open a path for others such as Kimura to continue his work. Although Watanabe's desk at the Citizens Section may now be officially occupied by Ōno, Kurosawa's long gaze at the vacant swing appears to suggest that the line initially formed by the dead man's labor remains unfinished, his future successors yet unknown.[30]

In considering the issue of succession, it should be clear that the presence of ghosts is not merely incidental to this notion. On the contrary, ghosts are an intrinsic feature of all relations between predecessor and successor. As soon as the former disappears in order to make way for the latter, haunting is already underway. For in disappearing, the predecessor may nevertheless always remain in some form to disturb the successor and remind him or her—or even it—that their present existence can never be entirely insulated from the past. Yet this phenomenon of haunting, in the sense of a retracing of a past element beyond itself into the future, cannot be restricted to succession as it is traditionally understood. Even in relations that are not discernibly marked by succession, ghosts from the past can appear at any time. At issue here is a need to think the act of succession more generally beyond its typical social determinations to include all phenomena that involve a before and an after.

In *Ikiru*, Watanabe's death is the occasion for succession in both his family and workplace. When viewed from an even broader perspective, however, the film reveals other instances of succession that are not often regarded in the same manner as the father-son and chief-subordinate relationships. The line formed by the continuation of a before into an after can be seen, for example, in the ability of Watanabe's late wife to survive genetically within her son as well as commemoratively within her husband. But she also lives on within Kazue, who occupies the same home where the wife once lived and repeats her act of marrying into the Watanabe family, as well as within Toyo, whose easy familiarity shown toward Watanabe when she helps remove his coat when they are alone together in his room unexpectedly reminds him of his deceased wife.[31] When the notion of succession is grasped in its most fundamental sense, it becomes apparent that the ghostly presence of Watanabe's deceased wife informs many unrecognized aspects of *Ikiru*.

In this regard, Akira Mizuta Lippit is surely correct to claim that cinema "is where the ghosts are and is itself ghost."[32] In the particular context of Kurosawa's film, one notes that ghosts come to be released the moment that present identity begins to falter. The most succinct statement of such identity in *Ikiru* is voiced by Kazue, who in attempting to reinforce the intimacy of her relations with Mitsuo declares, "Father is father . . . and we are we."[33] According to this formulation, no difference may come to intervene in an entity's presentation as itself. Insofar as all confirmation or repetition of identity ($X = X$) must take place in time, however, the presence desired is now irremediably stretched between a before and an after, generating a plurality of entities that cannot be immediately equated to one another. As Kurosawa suggests, Mitsuo can never be entirely present to himself because his identity derives in part from a father who precedes him while concurrently being carried over into the future by his son's own survival. Succession, that is to say, requires the presence of a before and after, but the complexity of time is such that this order may at any time be reversed and distorted.

This insight is most powerfully revealed in the figure of the parent-child relation as it informs Watanabe's ties to both Toyo and the park. In the café scene that marks Watanabe's transition from death to life,[34] his seniority and status as father as well as Toyo's earlier remarks about her own parents indicate that the bond between them is metaphorically that of father and daughter. Yet it is the child Toyo who introduces the inchoate idea of the park that the parent Watanabe will then go on to inherit. When he begs her to divulge her secret of living life with such vitality, moreover, he is described as "like a child whose heartfelt question to an adult has been dodged."[35] This unusual fungibility between parent and child, or predecessor and successor, reappears later in the film when Watanabe is already dead, and his colleagues debate his role in the creation of the park. Kimura insists that Watanabe be acknowledged as father of this space: "For Watanabe was the parent who raised that park." Shortly thereafter, however, Watanabe is shown in flashback staring wondrously at the beauty of a sunset, "the expression in his eyes exactly like the innocent gaze of a young child."[36] At moments such as these, Watanabe appears as both haunting and haunted, occupant of points both before and after. Although it may be true that ghosts come from the past to haunt those in the future, the problem is that it is not always possible to distinguish past and future. *Ikiru* illustrates the disturbance to identity unleashed by the presence of ghosts, who are capable of haunting both people and places. Yet this disturbance occurs most originally at the level of time itself, jeopardizing our most basic understanding of what comes earlier and what comes later.

CONCLUSION

In *Ikiru*, Kurosawa reminds us that the notions of life and death must not be taken at face value. Although it may seem that these terms exist in a relation of strict oppositionality, the truth is that dying inevitably commences upon the introduction of life. Kurosawa reveals his sensitivity to this strange interweaving by showing how the protagonist of his film, Watanabe Kanji, only first comes to life after he is dead. The initial part of *Ikiru* shows Watanabe directly, as it were, as he goes about his mummified existence. Paradoxically, this immediacy of his life is characterized as wan and bloodless. Watanabe's death three-quarters into the film opens the way for his resurrection in the remaining final part. This rebirth takes place over the course of his wake through the technique of flashback in the form of the various memories shared by his colleagues. It is when Watanabe reappears through this double mediation of the past and the recollection of others that he seems most fully alive.

One of the great merits of Kurosawa's work is that death is revealed to be an event that includes within its tragic scope both the deceased and the survivors. These victims of death are typically distinguished from one another by the criterion of death's actuality, such that the former is considered the primary sufferer and the latter the secondary. Certainly this manner of organizing death can brook no argument. From a slightly different perspective, however, an understanding of death in the mode of possibility reminds us of its generality, and this generality serves as a valuable corrective to any thinking that seeks to remove death from the realm of the living. Kurosawa presents this notion of death in the form of finitude, emphasizing the anxiety that comes with the realization that death is to be located not beyond but rather centrally within life. Yet he also illustrates how death possesses the capacity to transcend itself in the instance of survival. When Watanabe recalls his late wife as he stares longingly at her photograph,[37] his desire for her presence in no way mitigates the fact of her loss. That loss is not absolute, however, for part of her remains within him to be commemoratively revived. It is this reanimation of his deceased wife early in the film that paves the way for his own resurrection by his colleagues thereafter. In both cases, Kurosawa shows how a before that had been completely extinguished may yet be retraced as an after, sufficiently present to remind us of the continuing power of its loss.

CHAPTER 2

TSAI MING-LIANG
AND THE TIME OF SURVIVAL

Because Miao Tien's character dies in *What Time Is It There?*, I had
been thinking about how to use him again in my films.

—Tsai Ming-liang[1]

INTRODUCTION

In this second chapter, I turn my focus to the works of the Malaysian-
Taiwanese director Tsai Ming-liang (b. 1957). At first glance, Tsai's
cinematic oeuvre, with its unsettlingly long takes, motionless camera,
and paucity of dialogue, appears to have little in common with the far
more active filmmaking style of Kurosawa Akira. Both directors, however, reveal an acute understanding of death. While Kurosawa's *Ikiru*
presents a view of mortality that is relatively unique in his work, Tsai's
thinking of the fragile link between life and death can be seen as an
abiding feature throughout all of his films. In its stark minimalism—a
starkness that is, however, not straightforward, offering moments of the
most flamboyant excess—Tsai's cinema regularly insists on the importance
of the mundane, often overlooked activities of existence. Characters are
constantly engaged in the acts of eating, drinking, sleeping, urinating, and
defecating. Yet if such behavior forms an indispensable part of "everyday
life," as one says, this life remains at all times exposed to the threat of
death. As seen through the patient, searching gaze of his camera, Tsai
directs attention less to these activities in and of themselves than to

the manner in which they are all forced to participate in a more general movement of transience and loss.

Tsai's meditation on death takes a variety of forms, but certainly one of the most striking can be found in his practice of intratextuality. As a filmmaker committed to the task of revisiting instances already introduced in his own previous work, Tsai can easily be mistaken as gratuitously narcissistic or self-absorbed. It is vital to grasp, however, that this technique of self-referentiality is conceived in a rigorously temporal sense, one in which the return to the past from the vantage of the present involves an essential acknowledgment that the past is now dead. A sequence from Tsai's 2009 film *Lian* (*Visage; Face*) will serve to illustrate this point. The protagonist, a Taiwanese filmmaker played by Lee Kang-sheng (aka Hsiao Kang, Tsai's principal actor and collaborator), has suspended shooting of his current film in Paris and returned home to tend to his dying mother. There his routine turning of a kitchen faucet releases a violent stream of water that proceeds to flood the entire apartment. For those familiar with Tsai's oeuvre, Hsiao Kang's vain attempts to stanch the flow invariably recall a scene from Tsai's 1992 *Qingshaonian Nezha* (*Rebels of the Neon God*) in which a young hoodlum, played by Chen Chao-jung, tries to stem a similar tide of water. His efforts largely unsuccessful, Hsiao Kang finally attempts to plug the fixture with the use of a mop. Here, too, one is reminded of the actress Yang Kuei-mei's identical gesture of filling the hole that has suddenly opened up between her apartment and that of Hsiao Kang in Tsai's 1998 *Dong* (*The Hole*). Hsiao Kang then leaves the flooded kitchen to care for his bedridden mother in the next room. He applies ointment to her belly, whereupon she abruptly forces his hand downward toward her genitals. This action functions as an inverse repetition of Tsai's 2006 *Heiyanquan* (*I Don't Want to Sleep Alone*), in which the mother forces the housemaid, played by Chen Shiang-chyi, to masturbate her comatose son when she applies cream to his stomach. Without further explanation, Tsai then directly cuts from Taipei back to Paris, the site of Hsiao Kang's new film, and this change of location reflects the alternating focus on these two cities that formed the parallel plotlines of the 2001 work *Ni nabian jidian* (*What Time Is It There?*).

What is implied by this action that so skillfully condenses references to a number of different pasts within the span of a bare several minutes of cinematic time? Entirely unobtrusively, Tsai reveals how a brief sequence that unfolds in a work from 2009 surreptitiously communicates with previous instances from the years 1992, 1998, 2006, and 2001. One might perhaps be forgiven for seeing in this technique nothing more than a glib, needlessly solipsistic variation of intertextuality. When considered against the backdrop of Tsai's cinematic project, however—a backdrop informed by death, illness, and multiple forms of privation and suffering—it gradually becomes clear that such self-referentiality must be regarded as an attempt to give life to a past that is now dead. Here death demands to be understood beyond its everyday meaning of organic or biological expiration to signify the very passing away of time into an unrecoverable past. In this view, Tsai's practice of intratextuality is to be grasped at its most fundamental level as an attempt to engage with time and death. In creating *Visage*, Tsai occupies a moment that has already witnessed the disappearance of all his films that preceded it. From the present perspective of *Visage*, those works now belong to a dead past, a past that gives itself strictly in the form of loss. Through the act of intratextually returning to these disparate pasts, however, instances that are otherwise lost may now be resurrected and take their place in the present. To be sure, Tsai's revival of his own cinematic past never succeeds in fully recovering that lost time as such. In *Visage*, the apartment's flooding is a problem that must now be confronted by Hsiao Kang rather than by Chen Chao-jung; the mop used to plug the hole is now wielded by Hsiao Kang rather than by Yang Kuei-mei; the suggestion of mother-son incest (which in turn refers, of course, to the notorious scene of father-son incest in the 1997 film *Heliu* [*The River*]) now involves the actress Lu Yi-ching rather than Pearlly Chua; and finally the transition from Taipei to Paris now takes place alongside an association of Hsiao Kang with Paris and Chen Shiang-chyi with Taipei rather than the reverse. The past is regained, Tsai tells us, but only at the cost of sacrificing its original form and being more or less violently replaced by something else.

My aim in the following pages will be to trace out this strange relationship between keeping and loss, survival and death, that I believe to exist at the very core of Tsai's project. If Tsai's works are replete with instances of people and things passing away, in the broadest sense of this expression, then they must also be recognized as populated by ghosts. The incessant passing of existence into the past means that it is forever lost to us, but this death is to be grieved less by resignation or paralysis than by its most artful reproduction in the form of memory. In Tsai, the figure of the ghost reveals that the return of the dead takes place only by way of an injunction that forbids any recovery from rising above the level of loss. The ghost puts pressure, in other words, on the re- that allows for all forms of return, recovery, revival, recuperation, restoration, and rebirth. On the one hand, it is undeniable that people and things constantly come back from the past into the present in ways that enable us to identify them as themselves. In this manner, the reappearance of these entities appears to fully negate their previous disappearance, which is now seen to have been merely provisional. On the other hand, however, the journey back from the past into present reappearance never occurs without loss, and this loss effectively "ghosts" the entity, so to speak. That is, the process of return renders that entity less wholly itself than a mere ghost of its former self. Tsai's insight, I propose, consists in recognizing that the appearance of ghosts is not to be considered an anomaly, one that takes place following a typically tragic event at this or that particular time and place. On the contrary, ghosts must now be reconceived in their most general aspect. For Tsai, existence should not be understood as divided between ghosts and nonghosts, for everything that appears does so as a kind of self-resurrection,[2] and it is precisely this return to present life that reveals the ghostliness of all things. Haunting, then, would now appear as another name for survival. In the cinematic world created by Tsai, the haunting presence of ghosts functions as a synthesis between life and death, forming a general milieu in which all acting takes place.

DEATH ANNOUNCEMENTS

Among Tsai Ming-liang's feature films, it is *The River* in which Hsiao Kang first appears as dead. This death is actually no more than an appearance, however, since Hsiao Kang has agreed to play the role of a corpse floating in the polluted Tamshui River. Tsai meticulously sets the stage for this mock death in a number of ways. His protagonist is dressed in white—the traditional color of death and mourning—and these clothes, particularly the white T-shirt, seem virtually identical to those worn by the mannequin that is initially deployed in the role of the drowned man. Furthermore, Hsiao Kang's very presence on the film set results from an earlier chance encounter with an old friend (Chen Shiang-chyi), who, upon exchanging greetings, abruptly pulls his right arm toward her so as to check the time on his wristwatch. Time, as I have already suggested, bears an essential relation to death for Tsai, and the filmmaker rarely passes up the opportunity to foreground this link by focusing on a variety of devices (calendars, watches, clocks, etc.) used to record time.

Chen's apparently casual act of reading time follows directly upon a brief dialogue with the laconic Hsiao Kang:

CHEN: What are you doing here?

HSIAO KANG: Nothing. (沒有啊)

. . . .

CHEN: What are you doing now?

HSIAO KANG: I'm doing nothing. (沒做什麼)[3]

It is this repetition of the word "nothing" that invites attention. This is especially the case because Tsai's films famously contain only a modicum of dialogue, and so the few words that do appear must be regarded with vigilance. Just as the choice of white for Hsiao Kang as well as Chen's explicit noting of time anticipate the former's death, so too does the particular language used in this context. Hsiao Kang's replies are undeniably colloquial, but the term that he utters twice contains the sense not only of negativity but also of death, disappearance, and—unsurprisingly, given the "water" radical—sinking. When, for example, this word appears in compound form together with the character signifying a person's crown or uppermost part of the head—沒頂—the meaning formed is "to drown." Tsai carefully embeds this term in an otherwise innocuous conversation, one hardly worth dwelling upon, and yet this allusion to sinking and death clearly presages the fate that now draws increasingly closer to Hsiao Kang.

At one and the same time, the simulated death that Hsiao Kang will suffer in *The River* refers both to the past and instances of death or near-death that have already taken place and to the future in which associations of death will once again come to the fore.[4] Chen's glance at Hsiao Kang's watch serves very practically to remind her of the day's shooting schedule—she works as an assistant on the film set—but it functions no less as a device directed to the audience to link time together with death. For the fact is that Hsiao Kang's demise has already been announced in Tsai's previous films. In the opening of *Rebels of the*

Neon God, for instance, Hsiao Kang is shown attempting to remove a cockroach that clings to the outside of his bedroom window. He accidentally shatters the glass, thereby cutting his hand, and Tsai's camera lingers for several moments on the drops of blood that spatter over his school textbook. The wound is superficial, barely life-threatening, and yet Tsai's intent seems to be to underscore the fact of Hsiao Kang's mortality. Indeed, Tsai proceeds to reinforce this sense of his protagonist's mortality in his subsequent film, the 1994 *Aiqing wansui* (*Vive l'Amour*). There a despondent Hsiao Kang attempts suicide by slitting his wrist with a pocketknife, and the camera remains fixed on the drops of blood that fall to the floor in a way that unmistakably recalls his previous work. It must be borne in mind, moreover, that this act of self-mutilation immediately follows a scene in which the character appears to contemplate ending his life by means of drowning. He lays in a bathtub, sinking beneath the surface of the water in a manner that anticipates the mock death scene in *The River*. Thus we see Tsai repeatedly emphasizing the fact that Hsiao Kang will die, but the precise time, place, and cause of that death vary considerably depending upon a host of contingent circumstances.

The simulated death in *The River* forms a line with scenes from *Rebels of the Neon God* and *Vive l'Amour* that extend back into the past, but this same line can be seen to continue into the future in a way that further develops its meaning. Here the character 沒, signifying negation and death, reappears in a form that intensifies the link between death and time. The following dialogue occurs toward the end of the 2003 *Bu san* (*Goodbye, Dragon Inn*):

> MIAO TIEN: I haven't seen a movie in a long time. (好久都
> 沒看電影了)
>
> SHIH JUN: No one goes to the movies anymore. (都沒人看
> 電影了)
>
> SHIH JUN: And no one remembers us anymore. (也沒人記得
> 我們了)[5]

The lines spoken by Tsai's actors in this film are especially scant, and this again serves to call attention to the repetition of the term 沒. In *The River*, as we observed, Hsiao Kang repeats this word immediately before the question of time arises in a scene that anticipates his simulated drowning.

The ideogram's explicit connection to water was thus foregrounded, and this formed part of a larger semantic chain that included the elements of death, negativity, and time. When this double repetition of 沒 comes to reappear sixteen years later as a triple repetition in *Goodbye, Dragon Inn*, however, the reference to water, and particularly to the acts of sinking and drowning, is diminished (if, indeed, it is possible to ever describe the association with water in Tsai's films as diminished), but in its place there now appears a significant link to the perfective particle 了.

When these two characters appear together, the meaning formed is equivalent to the English expression "no longer." The sense, in other words, is of a transition from presence to absence: that which once existed in the past has come to cease to be in the present. And this devolution represents, of course, the most central insight of *Goodbye, Dragon Inn*.[6] Here a vital change must be recognized in Tsai's use of the term 沒. When Hsiao Kang repeats this word in *The River*, his own biological death is at issue in a way that recalls both his attempted suicide and physical wounds suffered in the two earlier films, *Rebels of the Neon God* and *Vive l'Amour*. When this same term now reappears in *Goodbye, Dragon Inn*, however, the meaning of death shifts from the specifically organic or biological to the general domain of the temporal.

Unlike *The River*, where it is Hsiao Kang alone who repeats the character 沒, its usage in *Goodbye, Dragon Inn* now comes to be shared or divided between Miao Tien and Shih Jun. Yet it is remarkable how these two distinct individuals appear to speak the same language, despite the extreme brevity of their exchange. For both men are similarly forced to confront the devastation wreaked by time. Their world seems now to have dwindled to an irreparable state of "no longer." Tsai points to the various forms of loss incurred by this world: the decline of what is seen as a golden age of Chinese cinema, above all, with its stately theaters, flourishing box office, and rapt audiences. Undoubtedly, the tears shed by Shih Jun together with the overall sense of wistfulness and melancholy that pervades the film are provoked by the realization that that world is presently dead. The now derelict, nearly empty Fuhe Grand Theatre is shown in the middle of its final screening before being forced to permanently shut its gates. However, Shih Jun cries not only for the loss of this world, in which, as one of the leading actors of that generation, he himself played a decisive role. He is also mourning the disappearance of his own former self. Tsai carefully shoots Shih Jun watching himself onscreen, but this former is of course no longer the same young, physically powerful actor that appears in the martial arts film being shown. As with the older film world that he represented, that younger self is now dead. Certainly Shih Jun remains alive in a biological sense when he watches these distant scenes in *Goodbye, Dragon Inn*, but the life that he previously possessed, and of which he is now both pleasurably and painfully reminded, has since been destroyed by the violence of time.

In concluding this section, I would like to insist on the essential (as opposed to merely accidental or contingent) nature of this link between time, death, and negativity. In *The River*, Tsai introduces this connection in the brief, otherwise unremarkable dialogue between Hsiao Kang and Chen Shiang-chyi. That conversation can be viewed as a kind of gift exchange par excellence in Tsai's cinema, for Hsiao Kang's offering of 沒 is met with equal generosity by Chen's return present of time. It is only in this pairing, I believe, that both negativity (death) and time achieve their proper status. Tsai effectively repeats this message many years later in *Goodbye, Dragon Inn*, but there the relation has now aged, displaying an even greater degree of nuance and complexity. No longer does Tsai remain content to depict death, or the threat of death, as merely happening *in* time; on the contrary, it is now time itself that reveals itself as death. In this enhanced meaning, the death that is time claims as its own not only physical corpses, but indeed all things in the world that are given a chance to survive.

TIME AND ITS POSSIBLE PRESERVATION

In the course of an interview conducted in 1999 with the filmmaker and editor Danièle Rivière, Tsai Ming-liang is prompted to reply to Rivière's observation about his work: "It feels almost as if you're filming not space, but time." As Tsai responds:

> For me, the notion of time is tightly bound up with the notion of space . . . they are always linked . . . I'm starting to become interested in this notion of time. . . . It's clear that our notion of time has changed with our ways of life. When I write a letter to someone which says: 'How are you? Today is Friday . . . I'm writing to you . . . etc.,' I don't think about the day and the time when he or she will get my letter. I

don't wonder what time it is where they live, or when the letter will arrive.[7]

Tsai continues this train of thought several lines further:

> I don't think real time is something that you can control. You can't dictate that one thing or another will last a particular time. It isn't controllable and, for me, that's the interesting thing. . . . What I find very interesting in cinema is that you can preserve states of the world. You can even preserve time. For instance, in 1992 I made *The Rebels* and already many of the things I filmed then are no longer there or have changed. It's the same with actors. They change as their life, their self-development, progresses. The very interesting thing about cinema is that it isn't just photos, you see it in real time. So it's a way of preserving time.[8]

Before directly commenting on these lines, I would first like to note that Tsai's remarks provide an invaluable tool in understanding the multiple layers of complexity embedded in *Goodbye, Dragon Inn*. If this film, as I argue, represents a more expansive way to conceive of the relation between death and time in comparison with the depiction in his early works, then we must also recognize that the death that is temporal destruction exists in tension with the possibility of spatial or material preservation. In *Goodbye, Dragon Inn*, one witnesses a world that is no longer. Time has taken its toll upon both the human and nonhuman: signs of physical degeneration can be seen on both the actor Shih Jun (and also Miao Tien, who will in fact die not long after the film is released) and the Fuhe Grand Theatre alike, and even the more abstract notion of a cinematic golden age is now shown to be in unmistakable decline. Nevertheless, Tsai's point is not simply to document the brutal effects of time. As he declares, cinema allows one the chance to "preserve states of the world. You can even preserve time." In his role as a spectator viewing King Hu's celebrated 1967 film *Dragon Gate Inn*, in which he starred, Shih Jun is forced to confront the fact that that past time together with the intervening years are now irretrievably lost. In that very loss, however, Shih is nonetheless able to revisit a moment when youth and physical vigor were still preserved within him. In *Goodbye,*

Dragon Inn, Tsai places his audience in a structurally similar position. While we may be unable to glimpse our past selves in this work, we are nevertheless given a chance to experience a past that has survived the ravages of time, presenting us with a vision of that world that remains cinematically preserved. From Tsai's perspective, the audience can only truly understand the force of temporal destruction by witnessing the preserved remains of what is no longer.

Tsai is not a philosopher, of course, and yet his thinking clearly touches upon problematics of great import throughout the history of ideas. In considering the relation between time and space, Tsai openly contradicts Rivière in insisting on the inseparability of these terms. Time and space cannot be seen as oppositional, Tsai suggests, because the appearance of one is necessarily conditional upon the other.[9] How are we to understand the meaning of this formidable claim?

Let us confirm that for anything to be at all, it must exist temporally. It is insufficient for a thing to merely be present since that presence is constantly negated by the movement of time. Tsai's *Goodbye, Dragon Inn*, for example, confirms this point in its focus on the ineluctable aging of both people and things. It is the passage of time that introduces change into entities, ensuring that their mode of existence is one of radical difference as opposed to stable identity. Yet the dynamic force that is time must confront some form of resistance, or counterforce, if it is to be properly recognizable as time. And this counterforce to time is space. Here space must be grasped as that which has the capacity to remain or survive despite the ongoing movement of temporal flux. *Goodbye, Dragon Inn*, significantly, is less a film about time as such than it is about the palpable effects of time—and these effects can only be understood spatially. Such visual elements as the wrinkles on Shih Jun's face or the leaks and overall decrepit state of the Fuhe Grand Theatre testify to the punishing effects that time bears upon space. These elements are unambiguously spatial or material, but they have been brought about and indeed can only appear to us now through the medium of time. The audience necessarily perceives these spatial marks of degeneration in time: the traces of age refer to a past that precedes the creation of Tsai's film, but their very ability to appear and be identified as such (facial wrinkles qua facial wrinkles, structural leaks qua structural leaks, etc.) is conditioned by the future.

It is this question of the future, I would like to suggest, that remains somewhat unresolved in Tsai's response to Rivière. There can be no doubt that one of the great virtues of cinema is its ability to "preserve" or record time. In this sense, it must not be overlooked that Tsai's enduring fascination with such devices as clocks, watches, and calendars stems from precisely this same virtue, for their unique ability to archive time is shared by the camera as well. Nonetheless, any act of preserving time remains by definition precarious.[10] Here let us point to Tsai's valuable reminder that time is essentially uncontrollable. "I don't think real time is something that you can control," as he states. "You can't dictate that one thing or another will last a particular time." This insight, however, appears to slightly put pressure on the filmmaker's earlier remark about the evolving forms of communication: "It's clear that our notion of time has changed with our ways of life. When I write a letter to someone which says: 'How are you? Today is Friday . . . I'm writing to you . . . etc.,' I don't think about the day and the time when he or she will get my letter. I don't wonder what time it is where they live, or when the letter will arrive."

If time is indeed uncontrollable, then this example of the temporal effects upon communication appears insufficient to take such uncontrollability into account. In the practice of letter writing, as in all forms of communication, the general presence of time does not simply introduce a temporal lag or difference between the various parties in contact. On the contrary, time in its uncontrollability opens the possibility for a number of infelicities that pose a far greater risk to the intersubjectivity established by communication. When a letter is sent, for example, the most fundamental question is not merely "*when* the letter will arrive," but rather *if* it will arrive at all.[11] Yet even this infelicity is dwarfed by other possibilities that in principle cannot be excluded from such communication. The letter's intended recipient might die while the letter is in transit, for instance, or conversely the sender might have already perished by the time the missive is successfully received and read.

I raise this objection because Tsai's statement on the relation between time and time's cinematic preservation appears inadequate to the radical negativity of time. As Tsai rightly asserts, cinema possesses the ability to preserve both time and "states of the world." However, what is the precise status of this preservation? The relation between time and its inscription by film is such as to involve not only the spatialization of time, about which Tsai speaks profoundly, but also the temporalization of space. Here the question of the future reappears in a manner that is analogous to the various dangers exposed by the example of communication. Time is inscribed in the letter, as Tsai reminds us: " 'How are you? Today is Friday.' " This inscription is necessarily spatial or material, but it is impossible for such spatiality to ever give itself as such, in its original identity. In order for this spatiality to appear, it must proceed to negotiate time in a way that reverses its initial capturing of time by inscription (or "preservation"). It is this journey from time to space and then again to time (and thereafter to space ad infinitum) that is implied in this otherwise simple act of writing a letter, sending it, and then finally having it read by its intended recipient. The same logic holds in the case of cinematic preservation. Time does not merely allow itself to be captured by film, since the sound and images thus preserved must appear in order for that past time to be recognized at all. This transition from preservation to appearance is necessarily temporal. As such, it contains the possibility that this past time and states of the world, despite being so painstakingly preserved, may always be destroyed. Preservation, in other words, remains essentially exposed to the threat of death.

Nevertheless, it would be a mistake to think that Tsai, undoubtedly one of the greatest filmmakers of time and death, is not in fact familiar with this danger. Here one perceives a certain wavering or inconsistency between Tsai's remarks, at least those quoted above, and Tsai's works. Two scenes from *Visage* can be said to demonstrate his acute sensitivity to the problematic of the temporalization of space. The first appears midway through the film and involves the appearance of several of the most celebrated actresses of the French New Wave (all commonly associated with the works of Truffaut): Jeanne Moreau, Nathalie Baye, and Fanny Ardant. These women are shot in a sumptuous dining room where they engage in light conversation over a glass of wine. Tsai then cuts to a shot of the younger actress Laetitia Casta mysteriously applying strips of black tape to her dressing room mirror. Thereupon the scene changes to one of Hsiao Kang sitting together with Jean-Pierre Léaud (known in the film as "Antoine"), the actor most closely linked to Truffaut beginning with his leading role as Antoine Doinel in the latter's widely acclaimed 1959 film *The 400 Blows*.[12] Hsiao Kang and Léaud share what appear to be some trivial pleasantries before Tsai suddenly cuts back to the now empty chairs of the three actresses. A variety of sounds can be heard offscreen, but visually the camera merely holds this shot of an unexplained vacancy for a full thirty seconds before finally taking its leave.

In characteristic fashion, Tsai offers no overt clues with which to interpret this sequence. Nevertheless, it is significant that the song Léaud sings to Hsiao Kang in their scene together is taken from Jean Renoir's 1932 film *Boudu sauvé des eaux*. This title, literally translated as "Boudu saved from the waters" (referred to more commonly as *Boudu Saved from Drowning*), appears as an oblique reference not only to the constant presence of water throughout Tsai's work but also more specifically to *The River*, in which, as we have seen, Hsiao Kang plays the role of a drowned man on a film set. Yet Tsai chooses this song for an even more important reason, I believe, one that reveals itself by closely following its lyrics:

Les fleurs du jardin	Flowers from the garden
Chaque soir ont du chagrin.	Grieve each night
Oui, mais dès l'aurore	Yes, but from the dawn
Tous leurs chagrins s'évaporent	All their grief evaporates

The song continues with an encomium to the sun: "What is the enchanter/Who heals so much pain?/What is this magician?/It is the sun." However, Tsai decides to cut both the lyrics and the scene itself at the word "s'évaporent." This verb serves to reinforce the link to water that appears in the title of Renoir's film, for the apparent reference is to the dew that moistens the flowers in the evening before vanishing the next morning when the plant is exposed to the heat of the sun. From the song's perspective, the disappearance of the dew is seen in strictly positive terms as necessary for the restoration of intimacy between the flower and the sun. In poetic imagery, the flower grieves for itself because it senses that its life is somehow threatened by the addition of the dew, and desires only for that grief and dew to vaporize and cease to be.

Tsai subtly but drastically reverses this meaning in such a way that the protection of life must now be reconceived along the lines of death. Here he is aided by the fact that the verb "s'évaporent," in its meaning of disappearance, can by extension also be understood as "to die." And indeed this is how the song's final lyric comes to be translated in the English subtitles of *Visage*: "but as the day rises/their gloominess dies." As Hsiao Kang nods in agreement, Léaud meaningfully stretches out the syllables of this closing word before Tsai shockingly cuts to a shot of the empty chairs. The women are "no longer," and their disappearance suggests not only that they are presently absent from the camera's frame but that the very presence of their lives is steadily approaching its evaporation in death. In point of fact, Tsai has already prepared the spectator for the ambiguity of this dual absence when Léaud, playfully naming a variety of directors together with Hsiao Kang (Pasolini, Welles, Mizoguchi, Truffaut, etc.), suddenly gestures at their immediate surroundings: "Tout le monde est parti," he exclaims, "Everyone is gone." Certainly the set now appears to be empty apart from the presence of these two actors. But Léaud's words extend beyond this physical immediacy to include not only every filmmaker they have listed, but indeed all people in general. Everyone is gone because, in our status as mortal beings, everyone from birth is condemned to die.

The temporalization of space can be seen in Tsai's depiction of the aging actresses of the New Wave. Tsai preserves their presence in the dining room by the invariably spatial and material act of cinematic inscription. As Tsai demonstrates, however, this preservation is an exceedingly fragile one. For when the camera returns from its encounter with Léaud and Hsiao Kang, the women have all vanished. Just as Léaud's song testifies to the power of time to transform the threat of death into life, so too does Tsai reveal how the interval of time that separates the initial scene of the actresses from the next (and in fact final scene, for they are never shown together again) opens the possibility for their lives to change to death. The lingering emphasis on the word "s'évaporent" immediately followed by the visual representation of their absence can mean nothing less. As their offscreen voices attest, Tsai is not of course suggesting that these women have died in the interim between their scenes. Recognizing the strange interweaving of necessity and contingency, Tsai alludes only to the fact that their deaths will come, but that the precise time of that demise cannot be determined in advance. There can be little doubt that Tsai wished to include these well-known actresses in his film in order to preserve the "states of the world" that was both the New Wave of the past and their present lives many years later. Yet this spatialization of time made possible by cinematic reproduction is helpless to shield itself from the possible loss that attends each temporal moment. The audience may audibly recognize the women's presence offscreen, but visually Tsai reminds us that that presence is essentially mortal and so constantly exposed to the threat of its own destruction.

Tsai's insight can be seen to extend even beyond this point, however. For it is crucial to realize that the alternating movement by which time is spatialized and space temporalized is properly endless. Here we must return to the otherwise perplexing scene in which Laetitia Casta gradually covers her mirror with black tape. This scene, in fact, replicates an earlier scene where she is shown taping over a window, a gesture that she will again later repeat in what appears to be a different room together with her lover, played by Norman Atun. The significance of this act is revealed only by reference to Tsai's previous film *What Time is it There?*, which in its travels between Taipei and Paris clearly forms a pair with *Visage*. Whereas the former work is dedicated to Tsai and Hsiao Kang's fathers (who died in 1992 and 1997, respectively), however, the latter appears as an homage to Tsai's own mother, who passed away in 2008 during the preproduction stage. *What Time is it There?* shows Hsiao Kang's fictional mother (Lu Yi-ching), who later dies in *Visage*, mourning the death of her husband (Miao Tien), who nevertheless returns to life at the end of the film. Utterly distraught over the loss of her spouse, the mother performs various tasks and rituals in the hope of his return. Perhaps most striking among these is her act of taping over all the windows in the apartment, thereby creating an environment of complete darkness.[13] "He's afraid of the light," she explains to her son. "Too much light and he won't come back."

Visage now stages the death of the mother rather than the father, but the practice of mourning remains unchanged. Here mourning is not simply a psychological act by which the bereaved remembers the past life of the dead. On the contrary, the aim is the overcoming of death through the restoration of the departed's actual presence. It makes little difference that such bereavement is experienced by the character played by Casta, who appears to have no direct connection to Hsiao Kang's mother. Rather, the point is that Tsai himself has just suffered the loss of his own mother, and this event comes to suffuse the entire film with an unrelieved sense of mourning. Tsai boldly shoots the absence of the three actresses of the New Wave, thereby announcing their future death. He thus points to the manner in which time will erase their physical presence, a presence that he recognizes in advance will be lost in the future and so must be cinematically inscribed or preserved now. This temporalization of space that opens up the possibility of their absence, however, comes to be complemented in *Visage* by introducing the question of the mother's resurrection. In *What Time is it There?*, the mother's act of eliminating all external light succeeds in bringing about the return of her husband. She enjoys sexual relations with what seems to be his ghostly presence before he finally reappears—now in Paris rather than Taipei—in more substantial, physical form. In the same fashion, Casta attempts to effectuate the mother's return from death to life. Tsai reveals that spatial preservation must constantly reckon with the essential contingency that is time, but he also shows that absence and death are at all times susceptible to the capture of spatial representation. In *Visage*, time comes to deprive the mother of life, yet this loss may be spatialized in some form that nevertheless allows her to remain.

The second instance in which Tsai can be seen to cinematically represent the temporalization of space appears in the very opening of *Visage*. There we glimpse the interior of a café as shot from the outside of one of its windows. A single coffee cup sits on a table, but the drinker of this coffee remains nowhere in sight. Audibly, a dialogue is taking place, but both the location and identity of the speakers remain obscure. It seems that a man is looking for someone named "Antoine," who has unfortunately just left. The respondent, whom the audience gradually deduces to be perhaps a waiter or manager of the café, promises to call Antoine while confirming that the coffee cup is indeed his. As numerous cars and passersby appear and then disappear in the reflected window glass, a telephone conversation commences in which the missing Antoine is addressed by a man who identifies himself as "the production manager on [Hsiao] Kang's film." He reminds Antoine of their original plans to meet at the café, but it seems that Antoine has mistaken the precise time of the gathering as nine o'clock rather than ten. In the course of this discussion, entirely held offscreen, a man dressed in gray suddenly appears from the left and slowly approaches the vacated table. His head is initially severed by the top part of the frame—a not inconsequential detail in a film titled "face"—but, upon seating himself in the chair previously occupied by Antoine, he is now revealed to be Hsiao Kang.

Tsai offers a subtle clue to understanding the dynamics of this scene when Hsiao Kang, apparently noticing something on the floor, bends over and picks up a feather, which he studies for a moment before placing down on the table next to Antoine's cup. This inconspicuous act that occurs inside the café seems to somehow trigger the upward flight of a group of pigeons outside, their startled activity visible in the reflected glass. Hsiao Kang appears deep in thought, unaware of the birds' movement. Tsai then cuts away to a length of wire tufted with feathers, and this protracted shot of the pigeons' perch clearly marks the fact of their absence. No explanation is given regarding the nature of the relation between Hsiao Kang's discovery of a feather within the café and the flight of the pigeons without.

The reflective surface of the window produces a sense of disorientation on the part of the spectator, for the visual illusion created by this technique makes it unclear exactly where the boundary between the café and its exterior is to be drawn. At certain moments, Hsiao Kang seems perhaps to be seated outside together with the pigeons; at other moments, however, the sudden ascension of the birds appears to take place within the internal confines of the café. The separation between this inside and outside is moreover disturbed by the presence of the feather, which provokes confusion in both Hsiao Kang and the audience. The feather naturally elicits an association with the pigeons—an association that Tsai proceeds to reinforce in the subsequent shot of the wire perch—and so one is forced to conclude that this object that should be outside has somehow managed to gain entry to the space of the inside.

Tsai directly takes up this question of the distinction between inside and outside in the latter part of his interview with Danièle Rivière:

> RIVIÈRE: But when we watch your films, what are we supposed to think when we see external or internal water?

> TSAI: I can't make the distinction you make between exterior and interior.[14]

Let us briefly linger over this response before returning to *Visage*, since Tsai here touches upon a point of considerable importance. Whereas Tsai previously took issue with Rivière's view of time and space as oppositional, as we observed, he now signals his disagreement with the basic division between interiority and exteriority. Once again, Tsai is not a philosopher, and he makes no attempt to defend his position by developing an argument that might expose the false reasoning behind thinking of things as fundamentally distinct from one another. A refusal to accept this distinction is equivalent to rejecting the notion of identity itself, for philosophy has traditionally claimed that for anything to be, it must first of all be indivisibly itself. This demand for self-unity entails that the opposition between interiority and exteriority must be present in order for anything to be identical to itself (in its interiority) and so different from other things (in their relative exteriority).

On the table in front of Hsiao Kang rest two objects: a coffee cup and feather. Both these things are present in a way that indicates that a fuller presence once existed in the past, but that such presence has now suffered eclipse and given way to a present absence. The cup points to Léaud, who has already departed, while the feather gestures to the pigeons that have since flown away. In this film dedicated to his recently deceased mother, Tsai begins by focusing on people and things whose current absence has nevertheless left behind some remainder of their previous selves. These remains of the past possess a spatial or material existence, and Hsiao Kang stares hard at them in a manner that underscores both their present concreteness and their quality of abstraction in referring to a past that is no longer. By making use of the window's reflection, however, the camera shoots this interior space and its physical objects in a way that directly puts them in relation to an outside. Tsai's point, I would like to suggest, is that the immediacy of spatial identity must be considered unknowable. The interiority of things is the site of their proper identity, but this identity can only give itself in the movement to an outside. And this act of exteriorization is precisely the thing's opening to time.

For Tsai, the glass window functions as the ideal tool with which to represent this seeming paradox. The surface of the glass is both transparent and reflective: it allows visual access to an interiority whose boarder it guards, but it nevertheless projects that interiority beyond itself to an uncontrollable outside. In other words, the glass simultaneously discloses these things as they are (transparency) and threatens such identity by connecting it to the contingency that is the world of time (reflectivity). Yet if a thing can only be itself by reference to an outside that exceeds it, then that thing can never truly be itself at all. Thus we see the cof-fee cup, whose spatial muteness is overcome strictly by its relation to a future that comes and retroactively determines what it will have been. In this future glance back to the past in order to establish its identity in the present, the cup points first of all to the vanished Antoine. Yet this Antoine himself ceased to exist many years ago when Léaud stopped playing the role of Antoine Doinel, and there can be no guarantee that the actor's youthful "Antoine Doinel" under Truffaut is identical to the much older "Antoine" now played under Tsai. The same point can be made with regard to the feather, which Tsai seems to introduce in order to reinforce his message that present things will in time disappear, but in disappearing possibly leave behind a spatial vestige of themselves. This logic applies no less to Hsiao Kang, who now occupies the same chair as the departed Léaud. Not coincidentally, Léaud is chosen to play the role of a king in *Visage*, but for Tsai even kings must die in their status as mortal beings. The very beginning of the film announces Léaud's disap-pearance, and yet this gap is immediately filled by people and things that come to take his place. In this regard, Hsiao Kang's presence is formally analogous to that of the coffee cup insofar as both serve to replace the absent Léaud. Just as the window's reflection suggests that the essential unity and interiority of identity is already divided and external to itself, so too is Léaud forced to cede his place to those people and things that follow him in his name. Beyond question, Léaud's position in cinematic history is unique and irreplaceable. Yet part of that uniqueness stems from the actor's long and fruitful association with Truffaut in his various roles as a maturing Antoine Doinel. Tsai broadly replicates the dynamics of this relation in his association with Hsiao Kang, but this repetition in no way replaces the collaboration between Truffaut (who is now dead) and Léaud (whose future death Tsai cinematically announces).[15] In the vanishing of that earlier relation, rather, future spatiotemporal opportunities arise in which to pay homage to that past by reiterating it otherwise.

SUCCESSION, CIRCLE, REBIRTH

This question of the relation of succession between a past instance and its future iteration features prominently throughout the works of Tsai Ming-liang. From Tsai's perspective, this relation must chiefly be understood in the context of the family. The family cannot be viewed as a purely synchronous unit because it constantly seeks to reproduce itself over time, and in this way protect itself from the eventuality of death. Here Tsai is especially interested in the bond between father and son. As he explains with regard to his principal actors Miao Tien and Hsiao Kang:

> There is something mysterious about him [i.e., Miao Tien]. On one level, he resembles my father; then again, there are times when I feel that even more than Miao Tien, it is Hsiao Kang who truly reminds me of my father.[16]

To viewers familiar with Tsai's oeuvre, this statement gives pause for several reasons. First of all, in an autobiographical vein, the director acknowledges the considerable force wielded by his father over himself personally. This force is such as to provoke identification with others who are perceived to be similar. Because similitude is strictly a relative term, however, the projection does not find satisfaction in any single individual and so comes to yield a plurality. Person X may be like the father, in other words, but person Y is now seen to be *more* like the father. Secondly, in conceptual terms the figure of the father is paradoxically revealed to be both powerful and powerless. He is powerful because his presence generates a desire in the son to reproduce him in others, thus triggering the mechanism of psychic identification. By the very success of this reproduction, however, the father shows himself to be essentially vulnerable to replacement or substitution. At any time, others may come to usurp his position and claim for themselves what was originally his. And thirdly, when considered from the viewpoint of Tsai's actual professional or artistic decisions, the relation between Miao Tien and Hsiao Kang has consistently been portrayed as one of father and son.[17] Hsiao Kang's identity as son is so firmly determined by Tsai that, at least in *What Time is it There?*, Miao Tien's status as biological father soon comes to be supplemented by Jean-Pierre Léaud's role as spiritual father. (And *Visage* clearly continues this specific line of paternity.) Nevertheless, Tsai now declares that it is Hsiao Kang who must be seen to occupy the place of the father even more so than Miao Tien. Certainly Tsai appears in these lines to be rethinking the relation of succession, but how are we to make sense of such reversal?

It is important to recognize that the dynamics of this relation remain essentially unchanged regardless of whether the father is living or dead. In *Vive l'Amour*, Hsiao Kang plays the role of a columbarium salesman whose company pamphlets are designed to solicit potential clients with the reassuring words, "Together with your Ancestors" (與祖先同在). It is this notion of "togetherness" (同在), Tsai suggests, that maintains the familial line between living individuals in the present and the now absent dead of the past. In the beginning of *What Time is it There?*, the marked site of the columbarium returns when Hsiao Kang is shown transporting his father's funerary urn there. The very first words the actor speaks in the film are addressed to the deceased, whose ashes he carries in his hands: "Dad, we're going through the tunnel. You have to follow us, ok?" The final verb Hsiao Kang uses here is 跟來: as with *Vive l'Amour*, the possibility that death might somehow nullify the bond between father and son is foreclosed by the promise of "togetherness," but now this attachment is given a more definite spatiotemporal shape. It is no longer sufficient that father and son remain joined or bonded, for the question of the precise nature of that jointure must be resolved. This relation is of course one in which the father precedes the son, and even death is unable to disturb such fixed order or priority. In this early scene, however, Tsai quite clearly suggests that it is now the father who occupies the secondary or derivative position of the son. He must follow the son who comes before him, a position of priority otherwise reserved exclusively for the father.

I would like to contend that Tsai's careful redrawing of the line of succession must be understood in terms of the notion of time presented in *What Time is it There?* In this film, time appears most insistently in the figure of the circle. Tsai boldly links this thinking of time with the interrelated themes of death and rebirth that structure the work. For one of his most penetrating insights is that death can only take place in a world of time. Rather than signifying a state of pure or absolute bliss, timelessness must be conceived strictly as a realm of presence in which nothing occurs, and would thus eliminate death at the very cost of life itself. In order for events to occur, there must be a minimal interval between a prior and succeeding instant, and this opening of time introduces the general possibility of death or disappearance in the ceaseless passing away of the present into the past. In this regard, it is hardly coincidental that Tsai chooses to focus on the father-son relation in this complex meditation on time. For what is most centrally at issue is the nature of the bond between an earlier instance that disappears and a later instance that remains to take its place. While this particular familial link can be approached from a number of different perspectives—cultural, historical, anthropological, etc.—Tsai's project in this film consists in grasping its most fundamental rootedness in time.

Circular time permeates the world of *What Time is it There?* from beginning to end. Hsiao Kang's father Miao Tien dies at the start of the film only to return—now resurrected, handsomely dressed, and living in Paris—at its closing. The many clocks that appear are invariably circular in form, and this focus on the physical shape of the timepieces serves to reinforce the work's overall circular structure. This structure both contains and is exceeded by certain thematic elements marked by a similar circularity. The mother's profound sense of loss at the death of her husband, for example, comes finally to be assuaged when he reappears to offer her the companionship she craves. Even before this scene, however, the mother seems convinced that her husband has in fact already returned in the guise of the large fish that swims in their aquarium. This notion of circular return that allows the mother to at least temporarily regain her husband can be seen to inform the developing romance between Hsiao Kang and Chen Shiang-chyi as well. *What Time is it There?* records the initial moment of their attraction (although they have in truth already physically consummated their relationship a few years earlier in *The River*, although the characters now appear to be different), which then survives the loss produced by absence and misrecognition in the 2002 *Tianqiao bu jian le* (*The Skywalk Is Gone*), and is only recovered in fully realized form several years later in the 2005 *Tianbian yi duo yun* (*The Wayward Cloud*).

Yet it must be recalled that this attention to circularity in its relation to rebirth that is so decisive for *What Time is it There?* appears in Tsai's very first feature-length work, *Rebels of the Neon God*, and moreover does so from the first scene involving Hsiao Kang. There we witness the teenager, at home studying for his college entrance exams, apparently killing a cockroach with the use of his compass. He tosses the dying insect out his window only to discover, with some amazement, that it has now returned and settled on the window glass. The figure of the compass thus suggests that death is not final but that, on the contrary, it is a necessary stage in the completion of circularity that is the act of rebirth.[18] However, even this notion of rebirth yields to a broader interpretation when we consider Tsai's unique practice of casting. Here it is not simply that the same actors so frequently reappear in film after film; it is that they do so with often the same names and the same relations of identity. The routine practice in filmmaking is for the individual character to disappear upon the work's completion. For Tsai, however, each new film represents a chance for these characters to return to life and continue what in retrospect will have been but a mere interruption of their overall trajectory.

Two additional points must be included here in order to gain a sense of the depth of Tsai's commitment to this link between circularity and rebirth. The first concerns the astonishing presence of water in Tsai's films. Certainly water sustains life and thus postpones the moment of death (although, as *The River* reminds us, water just as easily destroys life), but it is important to note Tsai's persistent focus on the various ways in which this liquid passes through the human. Time and again, characters are shown drinking water. Yet this water soon leaves these characters, returning to the world in such multiple forms as urine, feces, vomit, and semen. It is this circular reappearance of water that seems to determine the human not as the nominative subject *of* the world, but rather in its verbal sense as helplessly subject *to* the world—ultimately a mere agent or (leaking) vessel for the world's general movement of self-relation. And two, the meticulous chronicling of Hsiao Kang's life as he develops from teenager into adulthood (and, professionally, from student to columbarium salesman to film extra to food store owner to watch vendor to porn actor to foreign vagrant to film director to sign holder, etc.) brings this grand cinematic experiment close to the circularity inherent in the notion of formation. Here the triadic passage whereby an original simple unity suffers negation only to finally arrive at the stage of self-reconciliation can be seen in the process of the individual's maturation. The various qualities he possesses initially exist only latently, and he is thus forced through his interactions with the world to actualize them over time. In this way, the act of aging and gaining distance from his younger self paradoxically brings him closer to that self, although now in actualized form. Here we see that circularity and rebirth can also be found entirely within the individual. As Hsiao Kang moves increasingly away from youth and toward the realm of death, his self-realization as an individual can be seen to carry him full circle.

Nevertheless, the question of the circular figuration of time remains unanswered. The most problematic aspect of this view of time is that it artificially spatializes time in a way that fails to do justice to time's negativity. Indeed, it is possible to argue that the figure of the circle is antithetical to the basic movement of time. And this for the interrelated reasons of closure and return. In terms of the former, the circle is by definition closed. It therefore contains both an inside and outside. Yet the critique of this duality has been articulated by none other than Tsai himself. "I can't make the distinction you make between exterior and interior," as he tells Rivière. In order for something to be closed, it must continue to remain closed over time. It must constitute a presence so pristine that neither past nor future would be able to substantially alter it. Given that this enclosed presence is forced to repeat itself in order to sustain its identity, however, it constantly exposes itself to a noncircular time that may at any moment undo its circularity. A similar problem arises with the notion of return. In its negativity, the movement of time must ceaselessly destroy each instant in order for the succeeding instant to occur. As soon as one instant follows another, the latter disappears without possibility of recurrence. Yet a circle presupposes that its starting point coincide with its endpoint, and this would involve the entire movement of circularity taking place without loss. However, any passage from one point to another takes time, such that even return journeys reveal that the original site of departure no longer remains purely itself.

Nevertheless, Tsai also seems fully aware of these difficulties. All of the clocks may be round in *What Time is it There?*, yet the circular relations depicted are not in fact circular at all. For example, the father returns at least thrice in the film, but each of these returns is different. He returns as a fish rather than as human; posthumous sexual relations with his wife are conducted ethereally or spiritually rather than physically; and the geographical site of his return is Paris rather than Taipei. This differential return can also be seen in the resumption and development of Hsiao Kang's relationship with Chen Shiang-chyi. In the four-year interval between their initial encounter in *What Time is it There?* and the consolidation of their romance in *The Wayward Cloud*, they are forced to suffer a fundamental loss. *The Skywalk is Gone* represents this loss in purely physical terms in the disappearance of the site of their incipient bonding, but it is clear that what is "gone" (不見了, an expression that repeats what we earlier examined as 没了) far exceeds any architectural structure and touches upon the disappearance of time that they can now never regain. The restoration of their bond does not allow the circle to finally return to itself from its period of self-exile, for the intervening loss prohibits any thinking of their past as now blissfully doubled in the present. Yet if Tsai underscores the fact of this loss with the most vigilant attention,[19] why does he nevertheless insist on this problematic figure of the circle?

In order to answer this question, let us first consider another view of time that appears in *What Time is it There?* To be sure, this alternate conception does not feature prominently in the film. Compared to the stunning final scene where Miao Tien has returned from the dead and stands directly in front of the rotating *Grande Roue*,[20] the enormous Ferris wheel in Paris, this reference to time might seem nothing more than an afterthought. In the scene that interests me here, Tsai's camera shows Chen Shiang-chyi riding the metro home to her hotel when suddenly there occurs an interruption in service. An announcement is heard in which it is explained that a serious accident has taken place, and this unforeseen event now requires all passengers to exit the train. This brief message concludes with the formal expression of regret typically issued in such public settings: "We apologize for any inconvenience." The final term used here is *contretemps*, a word that produces no impression on Chen, who does not speak French. Upon conclusion of this announcement, the passengers all proceed to disembark. Chen, visibly confused by this sudden turn of events, follows anxiously behind them.

In addition to "inconvenience," the noun *contretemps* is typically translated by such words as "setback," "mishap," or "difficulties." In broad terms, it signifies that a countercurrent has unexpectedly emerged in the otherwise normal flow of time, resulting in a sense of disruption.

By extension, it has come to be used in a more specialized sense in the diverse fields of music, dance, and fencing to refer to moments that are somehow offbeat and so resistant to anticipation. The adverbial phrase *à contretemps* means "untimely," and this denotes not something that happens outside of time but rather a temporal occurrence that is somehow wrong or inopportune. In Chinese, one might be tempted to render this term as 反時 if not for the fact that such translation is meaningless since the word does not exist. Nonetheless, this otherwise senseless translation carries the advantage of showing how time is capable of suddenly pitting itself against itself, opening up a space for interruption to occur.

Unlike Tsai's presentation of circular time, this notion of untimeliness receives no explicit development in *What Time is it There?* The term is heard only once and, to the best of my knowledge, appears nowhere else in Tsai's oeuvre. Yet a thinking of time as radically interruptive, as at any moment capable of disturbing what is otherwise perceived to be time's proper flow, is one that cannot be contained by circular time. When viewed as circular, time can be predicted to ultimately return to its point of origin. Its departure from that origin unleashes all manner of negativity, yet that negativity comes eventually to be reconciled at the end of its journey, since endpoint and origin must coincide. Nevertheless, it is Tsai himself who shows that the return to origin takes place strictly by way of irrecuperable difference. The resurrected Miao Tien now finds himself elsewhere, in another land with other languages, for example, just as the restoration of relations between Hsiao Kang and Chen Shiang-chyi must now be defined by the loss ("gone," 不見了) of their former world. From the perspective of this restituted presence, such difference and loss might appear as nothing more than an untimely inconvenience, a hitch that unavoidably takes place from time to time. Yet the question arises as to whether such *contretemps* is to be seen as anomalous or, in fact, a general feature that reveals time to be essentially at odds with itself. The latter exposes the difficulty of conceiving of the relation between one moment and the next as governed by order or priority, for it is always possible for distortions to arise that upset what seems to be the overall arc of time and those systems built upon it. When Miao Tien appears at the end of *What Time is it There?* framed entirely within the circular structure behind him, is his rebirth merely a repetition of the same? Has his return to life left everything fundamentally intact? No doubt one can perceive here certain *effects* of circularity, but perhaps the most disquieting aspect of this closing scene lies precisely in its resistance to closure.

CONCLUSION

The cycle of death and rebirth that appears throughout *What Time is it There?* and *Visage*—the two films that Tsai Ming-liang dedicates to his deceased parents—includes reflection on the director's own relationship in cinematic history to François Truffaut and Jean-Pierre Léaud. It is striking how the fictional staging of parental death in these works takes place alongside focus on the figure of Léaud, particularly in his early role as Antoine Doinel in Truffaut's *The 400 Blows*. The lasting importance of this film for Tsai is well known. In *What Time is it There?*, Hsiao Kang turns to Truffaut's work precisely at the moment when he seems most grief stricken over the death of his father. He lies in bed sobbing, unable to sleep, before suddenly sitting up and playing the DVD he had purchased earlier. Hsiao Kang watches the famous scene of Doinel stealing and then hurriedly drinking a bottle of milk, a choice that is hardly surprising given Tsai's own fascination with the act of drinking. For our purposes, however, it is the protagonist's gesture of turning to Léaud for solace in his time of mourning that demands attention. The passage from death to rebirth is not experienced by Hsiao Kang's father alone, for Tsai clearly suggests that Hsiao Kang himself must be seen as a contemporary repetition of the young Léaud. We thus observe how the dead father has been replaced by Léaud, who himself has now come to be replaced by Hsiao Kang.

It is important to recognize the full complexity of this relation between death and rebirth. Tsai already alludes to this relation when Hsiao Kang first watches *The 400 Blows*, for the camera positions the protagonist as physically adjacent to the onscreen Léaud while the latter spins in circles on the rotor in the celebrated funfair scene. Truffaut himself appears in cameo as one of the other passengers on the ride, such that he, Léaud, and Hsiao Kang are now miraculously seen to occupy the same visual space despite the fact that Truffaut is long dead and Léaud, as we soon discover in Paris, aged virtually beyond recognition.[21] The circularity of the rotor is vital here, for Tsai reconceives this amusement ride in a manner that departs radically from Truffaut's original vision of the scene. From Tsai's perspective, the rotor now appears as a wheel of rebirth that points to both Léaud's repetition of Truffaut and Hsiao Kang's repetition of Léaud. Yet Tsai, too, must be included in this circularity, for Truffaut's direction of Léaud can now be seen to be replicated by Tsai's own direction of Hsiao Kang. When we consider that these various relations appear in *What Time is it There?* partly as a response to the death of Hsiao Kang's fictional father, Miao Tien, which itself represents a staging of the death of Tsai's and Hsiao Kang's own actual fathers, then the highly convoluted nature of this chain of sons, fathers, death, and rebirth can begin to be appreciated.

Here I would like to suggest that the strange dynamics of rebirth lead to a situation in which the son reveals himself to be in truth father of the father, a reversal that itself comes to be immediately reversed in the latter's reclamation of a paternity once removed. In this movement without end, Tsai may be said to precede Truffaut in casting or recasting the rotor scene as a grand site of reincarnation where Truffaut and Léaud are not merely fellow riders but indeed linked participants in the larger cycle of death and afterlife. As father, Truffaut will in principle predecease his son Léaud, but the latter will by his very presence continue to animate the director's legacy in his absence. For Tsai, the original meaning of this scene, regardless of Truffaut's actual intentions, is that the father circularly lives on after death in the guise of the son that he has produced. The scene seems designed to emphasize both the terror and thrill, the loss of control that literally sweeps one off one's feet, that Antoine Doinel will go on to experience in the unpredictable course of his life. For Tsai, however, this interpretation, while certainly true and entirely consistent with Doinel's character, must yield to the necessarily prior fact that Doinel exists purely by virtue of his creator Truffaut. The issue of character psychology, then, is judged to be derivative with regard to the properly original status of the relation itself. This unusual reversal in order whereby Tsai now appears as the true author of the 1959 work can be represented as an act by which he turns to the departed Truffaut, whom he in a sense carries in his hands, and addresses him with the same words spoken by Hsiao Kang to his dead father: "You have to follow."

Yet if Tsai must be regarded as the original creator of the rotor scene in the full depth of its circularity, it is nevertheless also true that Truffaut returns this gift by revealing to Tsai the secret intimacy between death and rebirth. Here it is necessary to examine *The 400 Blows* from a standpoint that is typically associated far less with Truffaut than with Tsai, but which Truffaut can now retrospectively be seen to have pioneered. Two scenes in particular call for this reading, both of which concern the question of death. In the first, Antoine Doinel is sarcastically asked by his schoolteacher to provide an excuse for his previous day's absence. "It's my mother, sir," lies Doinel. "She's dead!" The second scene, which follows not long after the first, involves Doinel composing an essay titled

"My Grandfather's Death" in which he plagiarizes a famous passage from Balzac. Despite the widely disparate circumstances of these episodes, the common thread that runs between them can be found in the fact that death is curiously linked to deception. Although this link appears nowhere else in Truffaut's film, and is generally not considered characteristic of his oeuvre as a whole, it can nevertheless be said to anticipate Tsai's own nuanced reflections on the question of rebirth. For Tsai time and again underscores the paradoxical duality of death. On the one hand, death is absolutely final, a point from which no return is ever possible. On the other hand, however, death can at any moment be cheated, its sense of finality betrayed, in the acts of memory that allow the dead to reappear and stand before us. Certainly Tsai conceives of this issue of death's duplicity in a manner that drastically raises its level from the individual to the general. It is no longer a matter of this or that person speaking untruths about death; on the contrary, death itself is shown to be internally divided, both uniquely irrecuperable and multiply recuperable. *What Time is it There?* is a film about ghosts who seem to appear in both spiritual and physical form. But what is a ghost if not a figure who has somehow deceived death in its repetition of life?

As should be clear, Tsai's relation to Truffaut is not to be reduced to the simple question of influence. Rather, what now reveals itself is Tsai's keen understanding of the unsettling ways in which time relates to itself. In the present time of his films, Tsai constantly returns to the past so as to better grasp its formidable ability to shape what follows it. Yet he also acknowledges that the past is now dead and gone, and can only be accessed on the basis of those present remains that have somehow survived the passage of time. While openly recognizing the importance of Truffaut as a model for his own works, Tsai nevertheless insists on thinking of his relation with the great filmmaker in the essential terms of death and rebirth. Truffaut is dead, but he has left behind him the inimitable character of Antoine Doinel, which continues to survive in the person of Jean-Pierre Léaud. For Tsai, these dynamics of death and memory—and thus the synthesis that is mnemonic resurrection—provoke reflection on various other fathers who have died and yet continue to live on in their works. Here the notion of works, Tsai realizes, refers not only to tangible accomplishments that have been produced but also, as it were, to the numerous "children" spawned by this paternal labor.[22] These children, who represent the vestiges of an earlier instance now vanished but to which they continue to give life, will eventually themselves disappear. It is this awareness of the essential transience of existence, I believe, that underlies all of Tsai's films. Rather than producing a sense of resignation in the face of past and future loss, however, such awareness instills in Tsai a firm commitment to the task of creating cinematic records that may possibly be preserved.

CHAPTER 3

FROM CULTURE TO FINITUDE

THE QUESTION OF DEATH IN
TAKEUCHI YOSHIMI'S READING OF LU XUN

If you want a true friend, you will find few better than him.

—Lu Xun, referring to the
spirit Wuchang, or "Transience"[1]

INTRODUCTION

Among scholars of Asian studies, the social critic and China scholar
Takeuchi Yoshimi (1910–1977) is perhaps most widely known today for
his probing insights into the nature of modernity. Coming of age at a
time when Japan had deeply absorbed the lessons of Western imperialism,
Takeuchi grasped that the nation's domestic vitality and international
prestige were inseparable from its recent history of military aggression
throughout Asia. This violence contributed to the ongoing process of
global homogenization, one that could be glimpsed in the widespread per-
ception that modernization and Westernization signified one and the same
thing. The most powerful nation-states were those that formed empires,
and Japan sought to emulate the various successes of the leading Western
nations by creating its own empire in Asia. As Takeuchi realized, this
identification between modernity and the West was utilized by the latter
as a way to legitimize conquest, for it was strictly through colonization
that the defeated areas could begin to experience the overcoming of what

were seen as its feudal, benighted traditions and undergo the reforms essential to modernization. Yet this same identification also exposed the fact that the West and non-West could no longer be understood in the fixed terms of geography. If Japan hoped to resist the imperial expansion of the West, then its only viable course of action would be to Westernize and modernize itself to such a degree that it could effectively compete with the West on the West's own terms. In this way, Takeuchi recognized that one of the great quandaries of modernity lay in the fact that the West could only be resisted by becoming part of it, thereby furthering its overall expansion and development. Throughout his work, Takeuchi sought to call attention to the unsettling force of this paradox while exploring ways in which it might possibly be resolved.

This insight into the complex movement of modernization both reaffirmed Western identity and jeopardized it from within. On the one hand, the global expansion of the West in the modern era pointed to the increasing subsumption, and hence potential disappearance, of the non-West as an external force whose borders marked the limits of Western encroachment. On the other hand, however—and Takeuchi was particularly sensitive to this point—the disappearance of the non-West threatened to produce in turn the loss of the West itself insofar as this latter identity was in some sense grounded upon the presence of its opposite.[2] For Takeuchi, reflection on the questions posed by modernity demanded that one interrogate not only the imbricated identity of the geopolitical entities "West" and "non-West," but indeed the very process of identity formation itself. Here he recognized that historical and social inquiry could not fully make its home in the regional disciplines of historiography and sociology. On the contrary, the answers provided by such forms of knowledge were themselves based upon certain philosophical presuppositions that remained as yet unexamined, and thus silently endorsed and repeated. Although Takeuchi was not formally trained in philosophy, his diverse writings testify to a sustained engagement with concepts that directly challenged much of the received wisdom and established norms of the empirical sciences. Nowhere is this truer than in his thinking of the general notion of identity.

What I wish to demonstrate in this chapter is that Takeuchi's interpretation of modernity reveals, beyond its valuable focus on a wide range of historical, social, and literary phenomena, an underlying commitment to exposing a core of instability to be found within all entities as such. In the history of thought, this tension between how something appears in its identity and how it disturbs that identity in its multiple manifestations has traditionally been conceived in terms of the opposition between the notions of being and becoming. In Takeuchi's analysis of modernity, for example, the selfsameness of the West must first be granted if one is to then speak about Westernization, or the spread of Western-style modernity, and yet the very movement of Western expansion in its subsumption of the non-West serves to endanger that identity by revealing its essential mutability. Here the distinction between being (identity) and becoming begins to waver in that no absolutely fixed instance of the former can be identified prior to the movement of the latter. In the discourse of philosophy as much as in the empirical sciences, this tension has typically been resolved by conceiving of being or identity as original, and it is only from this initial point of stability that the flux of becoming is then seen to depart. Yet Takeuchi gestures toward another thinking of this relation by identifying a vein of negativity that runs throughout everything that appears. My contention is that this understanding of negativity must be closely examined in order to comprehend Takeuchi's contribution to our thinking of modernity. By broadening the scope of inquiry beyond the regional sciences toward a more general form of questioning, Takeuchi was able to give fresh insight into the way we regard the modern world. In order to properly take account of the force of his ideas, however, it is imperative that we follow and carefully reconstruct their logic.

In point of fact, Takeuchi's thinking of modernity must be traced back to his wartime reflections on the great Chinese writer Lu Xun (1881–1936). Much of the richness and originality that can be seen in his postwar writings had already begun to emerge prior to that time, and provide ample evidence of a thinking consistently drawn to the strange lacuna inherent in present identity. No doubt the most noteworthy instance of this thinking appears in his 1944 study *Ro Jin* [Lu Xun], which Takeuchi had completed the previous year while anxiously waiting to be called up for military service. In his "Afterword" to the 1952 Sōgensha paperback edition of this text, Takeuchi offers an intriguing glimpse of the ideas and concerns then taking shape in his mind: "For me, this *Lu Xun* book is a nostalgic one. I wrote it with a sense of being urged on, wanting desperately to leave behind this one thing in an environment that provided no guarantee that I would still be alive the next day. Although the text was not something so grand as a 'testament' [or "posthumous writing": *isho*], that is nevertheless close to how I felt about it."[3] He concludes these retroactive remarks by pointing to a certain vulnerability that his work allowed him to perceive: "By writing *Lu Xun*, I came to acquire my own particular awareness of life."[4]

This "life" (*sei*, 生) that Takeuchi names is certainly not to be understood in the everyday, platitudinous sense of the term. On the contrary, the context of this statement leaves little doubt that Takeuchi is referring to a life that remains disconcertingly close to death. Still in his mid-thirties, he composes *Lu Xun* as he would a text that one intentionally leaves behind in the anticipation that it might be one's last, for historical events are such that *ashita no seimei ga hoshigatai*, as he writes, literally "it is difficult to guarantee that there will be life tomorrow." And yet if the overall meaning of these lines seems more or less clear, how is it possible for us to grasp the uncanny type of "awareness" that Takeuchi wishes to describe? In recalling that life appeared imminently threatened by its extinction, Takeuchi might be seen to suggest that it was primarily biographical or historical factors that lay behind his awakened sense of vulnerability. That is to say, the central reference in these remarks would be to his own life, a life uniquely lived as an individual who now finds himself faced with the prospect of dying on an overseas battlefield alongside other Japanese soldiers. The possibility of Takeuchi's death could then be attributed to a tragic convergence of the personal and historical, and would have to include reflection on how a human being born at a certain time and in a certain place becomes subsequently enmeshed in an entire network of larger geopolitical forces that decisively shapes his existence and determines his fate. Understood in this manner, the question of his anxiety would appear to be settled. If, however, Takeuchi's awareness of life in its exposure to death can be adequately explained neither by the biographical facts of an individual existence nor by the historical facts of extensive global developments, this is perhaps because such awareness is ultimately irreducible to factual knowledge.

How might Takeuchi's reflections on life in its relation to death bear upon his notion of identity? As we observed in his interpretation of modernity, the very unity or integrity of the West is implicitly called into question by the presence of a non-West that both provokes its expansion and threatens its internal cohesion. Self-identity, as Takeuchi discovers, is strangely enabled as well as endangered by elements that exist beyond its borders. Here it is important to recognize the full breadth of this insight, for Takeuchi's point exceeds restriction to any specific historical era and instead encompasses all forms of identity formation as such. Regardless of whether an instance of identity appears as geo-political region or individual human being, for example, its emergence immediately exposes it to forces greater than itself and over which it ultimately has no control. This is because emergence invariably takes place in a world marked by temporal difference, and it is precisely this quality that brings about the phenomenon of death. Here we begin to grasp why Takeuchi in attending to the question of the rupture of iden-tity feels compelled to turn to the problematic of death, and particularly death in its disquieting proximity to life.

In what follows, I shall examine Takeuchi's complex engagement with Lu Xun in order to trace out the development of his conception of identity. The reason why present identity proves insufficient is due to the general medium of negativity that affects entities from both within and without. In his dialogue with Lu Xun, Takeuchi recognizes that this negativity must be understood in terms of death, but a death that no longer allows itself to be conceived along the reassuring lines of tradition. According to the established view, death is that which marks the mere endpoint of life, such that life is seen to give itself in all fullness and presence up until the moment of its expiration. Takeuchi's dissatisfaction with this interpretation stems from his recognition of a certain generality possessed by death: if death befalls an entity, then attention must be shifted away from the instant and circumstances of its actual demise to a kind of negative possibility—the possibility of its own destruction—that inheres within the entity from its very incep-tion and accompanies it throughout the course of its existence. This generalization of death is simultaneously a generalization of negativity insofar as death is understood to be the entity's complete and utter negation. The major consequence of this reconception of death is that life and death can now no longer be conceived as fundamentally distinct from one another. Directly to the contrary, the negativity that is death makes itself felt at every instant of life, thereby forcefully confuting the widespread view that determines life as identical to presence. Grasped in its proper generality, as Takeuchi reads Lu Xun, the negativity that is death moreover vastly exceeds the scope of biological death and must now be rethought along the lines of essential disappearance or loss, that which affects any type of functioning of entities in a way that constantly foregrounds their vulnerability. Only by engaging with Takeuchi's text at this more elemental conceptual level, I believe, can we begin to assess the full effects of his thinking of identity.

FUNERAL SCENES

From the opening pages of Lu Xun, Takeuchi signals his intent to approach the famed Chinese writer from a perspective that departs notably from the accepted conventions of Sinology at the time. Whereas the titles of the various chapters of his work appear more or less standard—"Questions Relating to Biography," "Intellectual Formation," "On the Individual Works," etc.—the "Preface" is unusually entitled "On Death and Life." What motivates Takeuchi's decision to place death in its relation to life at the very beginning of his discussion of Lu Xun? It seems inarguable that this decision was largely influenced by the death several years earlier of Lu Xun himself. Takeuchi recalls the particular circumstances of that death to his readers: it took place in Shanghai during the early dawn of October 19 in the twenty-fifth year of Minguo, Lu Xun was then fifty-six years old, and he was at work preparing a translation, appropriately enough, of Gogol's novel *Dead Souls*.[5] And yet if Takeuchi now finds himself contemplating the recent death of his object Lu Xun, he is also, as I have mentioned, confronting the possible erasure of his own subjectivity as he awaits the arrival of his military draft notice. Before commencing my reading of Lu Xun, I would like to first draw attention to this curious identification that Takeuchi displays toward the celebrated writer. This identification, upon which many scholars have remarked,[6] is a curious one in this context precisely because it centers on death, for death is of course that which strips away all individuality or particularity in the universal fact that every human being must die. To identify with a fellow mortal over the shared fate of one's mortality would seem to impair the operation of identification by hyperbolizing it beyond measure. This law of mortality is issued at the very origin of life, and Takeuchi seems to underscore the unique status of death as primary by situating this matter at the very outset of his work. In this way, everything that will subsequently be written about Lu Xun must in some sense be drawn back to this initial point of finitude.

It is noteworthy that Takeuchi singles out for commentary the event of Lu Xun's funeral. As he suggests, the purpose of the memorial service may have been to acclaim Lu Xun as an individual, but its effects immediately surpassed that level and came to bear upon the collective. As Takeuchi describes:

> Even at the instant of his death, he [Lu Xun] was part of
> the minority of the literary world. . . . His opposition to the

majority faction was rendered meaningless by that death; or more accurately, his death rescued that meaningless opposition. It was through his death that the unification of the literary world subsequently came to be realized, a unification that during his life he desired above all in his status as an enlightenment thinker, but that no doubt ran counter to his character as a writer. With thousands in attendance, the procession on October 22nd unexpectedly took the form of China's first "people's funeral" (Ba Jin). Wrapped in a white sheet upon which the words "soul of the nation" were written, his coffin was interred in the faint dusk of Wangguo Cemetery by a group of young writers. There were not a few leading writers who embraced the coffin and wailed, although their cries were perhaps accompanied by the noise of the throngs of people. All the literary journals issued memorial editions the following month. This represented the first time that the literary world experienced no controversy since the "Literary Revolution."[7]

Biological death is not to be regarded as similar to other events in human life, Takeuchi observes in relation to Lu Xun. Death possesses a momentous quality that has the capacity to shape external circumstances more powerfully than other actions performed by humans. Here Takeuchi notes the bitter history of antagonism or opposition (*tairitsu*) that divided the Chinese literary world from itself, one in which Lu Xun occupied the position of minority that sought to voice its claims and safeguard its interests vis-à-vis those writers from the majoritarian camp. This opposition is now vanquished and overcome by a single death. However, if death is justly recognized for the force it subsequently exerts upon the living, Takeuchi identifies in Lu Xun's demise an oddly redemptive feature that comes to aid the Chinese literary world and, by extension, the Chinese people as a whole. As he writes, "His opposition to the majority faction was rendered meaningless by that death; or more accurately, his death rescued that meaningless opposition. It was through his death that the unification of the literary world subsequently came to be realized." In other words, Lu Xun's death served to repair the rift among writers that his own actions paradoxically helped exacerbate. Through his death, the opposition he had spent his life cultivating and from which he in turn suffered was now strikingly transformed into a unity that would now survive him.

A significant historical nexus motivates Takeuchi's view of Lu Xun's death in its ability to alter the course of modern Chinese society. Lu Xun dies in 1936, and the war of resistance against Japan effectively commenced the following year after the creation of a united front between the Kuomintang and the Chinese Communist Party. Takeuchi explains this quite clearly in his 1946 essay, "Ro Jin no shi ni tsuite" (On the death of Lu Xun): "It was through Lu Xun's death that the path was opened for the Anti-Japanese Popular Front to unite at that time and in that manner. The literary world had experienced disputes up until his death, but that death marked the turning point for the literary world to unite under one banner. This brilliant unity would have been impossible had Lu Xun not died then."[8]

It is important to recognize a decisive shift in emphasis in these two passages, for the positive early postwar reference to the Anti-Japanese Popular Front would have been unimaginable in the wartime text on Lu Xun. Takeuchi remains committed to surveying the concrete historical effects wrought by Lu Xun's death, but we must not fail to note the presence of a strong conceptual bias or desire that underlies his interpretation of Chinese history. What binds the later essay on Lu Xun's death to the book *Lu Xun* is the core notion of unity, or *tōitsu*. The transition effectuated by that death is one from opposition to unity, and this transition runs parallel to the movement from meaninglessness to meaning. According to this narrative, Lu Xun strove during his life to oppose the positions staked out by the majoritarian camp, but his death then rendered that struggle meaningless. Yet Takeuchi discernably hesitates in this judgment, as can be seen in the phrase *to iu yori mo mushiro*, meaning "or rather," "or more accurately." Something in this initial statement is found unsatisfactory and so must be revised: it is therefore not so much that death makes the opposition meaningless than, more precisely, it is that death *rescues* (*sukui*) that meaningless opposition. And this meaningless opposition, once saved or rescued or redeemed, finds itself transformed into the unity experienced by the Chinese literary world, a unity that for historical and political reasons is to be determined as meaningful. In this way, the rescue operation performed by Lu Xun's death is that which specifically emancipates unity from meaninglessness.

Previously I identified Takeuchi's thinking of death as that which haunts life from its inception in the essential indivisibility between these two realms. Yet this understanding of finitude is now replaced by another view of death, one that could properly be described as dialectical.[9] It is evident that Takeuchi sees Chinese unification as necessary in order for China to defend itself from the dangers posed by Japanese imperialism, which itself emerged as a response to the Western project of modernization. The problem, however, is that national unity is here achieved strictly through the mediation of death. Takeuchi's view is dialectical because he determines the site of political conflict on the basis of an opposition between two forces that initially appear to be irreconcilable. But this very irreconcilability generates a dynamic tension between the two that works to overcome their mutual negation and create a pathway toward resolution. This sublation of opposites takes the form of unity, Takeuchi concludes. Here unity names the synthesis arrived at by simultaneously annulling and elevating the negative interaction of oppositional forces through the act of death.

However, it must be asked whether death truly allows itself to be conceived in this manner. In Takeuchi's account, death comes to be incorporated within the general edifice of dialectical logic. Lu Xun's death functions as the bridge leading from the concept of "opposition" to that of "unity," but nowhere does he show how the radical negativity that lies at the heart of death resists appropriation by the dialectic. Death is effectively asked to submit to the organizing principles of opposition and unity, for it is through the mediation of Lu Xun's demise that the painful division or disparity of a two can now be healed in the coalescence of a one. In this way, death loses its quality of utter senselessness and is redetermined along the lines of sacrifice. If Lu Xun's struggles with the Chinese literary world during his lifetime are described as "meaningless" (*muimi*), then his death must be invested with meaning since it directly makes possible the restoration of wholeness in China. That death will not have been in vain, it will not resound with emptiness, for social unity will now be reborn phoenixlike from his ashes. Here Takeuchi's thinking can be seen to take its place within a long tradition that insists upon viewing death as the necessary if unfortunate price to be paid for communal formation.

Having explored some of the complexity that informs Takeuchi's notion of death, I would like now to return to the scene of Lu Xun's funeral. As Takeuchi recounts: "With thousands in attendance, the procession on October 22nd unexpectedly took the form of China's first 'people's funeral' (Ba Jin). Wrapped in a white sheet upon which the words 'soul of the nation' were written, his coffin was interred in the faint dusk of Wangguo Cemetery by a group of young writers. There were not a few leading writers who embraced the coffin and wailed, although their cries were perhaps accompanied by the noise of the throngs of people." In this description, Lu Xun's individual corpse appears surrounded by a collectivity that bestows upon him the status of synecdoche whose part uniquely distills the essence of the whole. The dead body is thus transformed into a vessel of signification—he is less cadaver than the exalted "soul of the nation" (*minzu hun*)—and this impression is reinforced by the writer Ba Jin's grandiose designation of the event as the "people's funeral" (*minzhong zang*).

Attention must also be directed to the white sheet that envelops the coffin that in turn envelops the body. What is the purpose of this double concealment? Is it to protect the corpse, which has in any case already begun its inevitable process of decay and putrefaction, or is it rather to protect the mourners from witnessing this discomfiting sight and hence being reminded of their own mortality? Significantly, however, the sheet is inscribed, and the message it conveys to all assembled is that death has now fully released the spirit or "soul" from its long confinement in the physical body. Certainly Lu Xun occupies a privileged position in this context, for his soul belongs less to his own individual self than to the national whole that he represents. And yet all funerals must memorialize the dead in some way as to introduce the possibility of relation between themselves and the living, and this relation is fundamentally a spiritual one.[10] Lu Xun's presence at the funeral must in other words be purified of its physicality in order for the living to continue communicating with him. Indeed, just as Takeuchi sought to interpret Lu Xun's death as a form of "rescue," so too does this act of spiritualization function to save the dead from the finality of death.[11] Above all, death is something that must be rescued, saved from itself so that it can signify in ways that provide consolation to the living. A merely physical death offers no such hope that the deceased can transcend its state of loss or disappearance and remain together with those who still have life and who desperately long for its return.

For readers of Lu Xun, it will come as no surprise that Takeuchi's account of the great writer's funeral is echoed in several works by Lu Xun himself. Any discussion of funerals in the oeuvre of Lu Xun must at some point include reference to the written instructions that he famously prepared for his own memorial. These directives appear in an essay entitled "Si" (Death) that Lu Xun composed a few short weeks before he finally succumbed to tuberculosis, and contain the following items: "Just quickly put the body in the coffin and bury it at once"; "Do not hold any commemorative activities"; and "Forget me and mind your own lives. If you don't, you're just fools."[12] What figures so prominently in this message is Lu Xun's concern that death be recognized in its absolute finality. Focus should thus not be on his life as he lived it but rather on the unmitigable termination of that life, and any activity of keeping such as temporarily preserving the corpse or honoring his memory either publicly or privately must be prohibited. These forms of memorialization are governed by a logic that aims to deprive death of its character of loss and irreducible absence by artificially extending the presence of the deceased. In a strange way, immediate burial and forgetting appear as the concrete responses that most fully do justice to the power of death in their acknowledgment that the painful vacuum now left by the deceased can never be filled.

Is one thus forced to conclude that Takeuchi's decision to linger over and mourn Lu Xun's death represents in fact a betrayal of the Chinese writer? Lu Xun had specifically requested of the living immediate concealment and oblivion, and Takeuchi ignores this plea by linguistically resurrecting him in a way that serves only to expand Lu Xun's scope of readership and extend his memory to future generations. And yet it is not difficult to see that Lu Xun himself bears responsibility for his own reanimation in leaving behind a body of works to be read. Here an essential contradiction can be detected in Lu Xun's wish that his memory be buried in all haste together with his body. For this desire can signify nothing more than the particular content of his message. In order for these words to be understood, however, they must transcend their original point of creation in time and space and travel into a future over which they have no control. It is this infinitely more general form of meaning's occurrence that allows Lu Xun's own words to be read. Already in setting forth these instructions, Lu Xun grasped that their meaning would only go into effect at some future time when he was no longer alive. Precisely by surviving him, however, this language would act to call forth his memory after his own physical body had grown cold and lifeless. Once inscribed, in other words, the posthumous demand that one be immediately forgotten can only fall into self-contradiction insofar as this writing continues to be read after one's death. In this sense, Takeuchi's desire to keep the memory of the dead Lu Xun alive must be seen as entirely consistent with the logic displayed by these writings themselves.

There is another way that Takeuchi's apparent disregard for Lu Xun's demand that he be forgotten in truth reveals a deeper level of fidelity to the iconic writer. In Lu Xun's works, one finds an abiding commitment, at once historical and political, that the dead not be allowed to die completely. If the living must suffer the absolute loss of the deceased, as Lu Xun suggests, then they must also ensure that the dead receive the gift of reanimation in memory. For how else can one explain Lu Xun's repeated attempts to commemorate in writing those whose lives have now been lost? Here one could cite any number of texts, as for example the 1926 essay "Wu hua de qiangwei zhi er" (Roses without blooms, Part II), where Lu Xun recalls the lives of "the hundreds of young men and women whose intent was to lend their support in China's diplomatic dealings with foreign powers," but whose early promise was abruptly destroyed when "Duan Qirui's government ordered guards with guns and bayonets to surround and slaughter the unarmed protesters in front of the gates of the State Council."[13] One might also examine the short but powerful pieces in which Lu Xun memorializes his friend Wei Suyuan and the actress Ruan Lingyu.[14] As made clear by the very titles of such similar works as "Jinian Liu Hezhen jun" (In memory of Liu Hezhen) and "Weile wangque de jinian" (Remembrance for the sake of forgetting), the concept or task of *jinian* (紀念), "commemoration," occupies a central place in Lu Xun's thought.[15] This term is of course the same one used in the essay "Death" when he demands of his survivors, "Do not hold any commemorative activities" (*bu yao zuo renhe guanyu jinian de shiqing*). Do as I say, Lu Xun seems to advise, and not as I do. But of course the sentiment goes far deeper than this. Regardless of his own personal humility, Lu Xun sought to call attention to the complex twofold quality of death in its effect upon life: on the one hand, no act of commemoration can ever help return the dead to the living; and on the other, the absolute loss of presence that is death can only be recognized in the repetition or return that is commemoration.

Commemoration must fail because what it presents to the living is not the dead themselves. Paradoxically, however, it is out of this very impossibility that commemoration becomes possible insofar as memory is drawn *of* or *from* the dead. Not the dead themselves, then, but rather something like a spectral remnant of their lives that comes to be sent beyond the grave to the living. This spectrality must not be confused with the traditional notion of "soul" or spirit that Takeuchi describes in the context of Lu Xun's funeral. Nevertheless, it would be equally incorrect to determine spectrality along the lines of the materiality of the decaying corpse itself. Neither spirit nor matter is able to grasp the haunting presence that emerges from the dead because the specter testifies to the ability of the deceased to differentially repeat itself in the form of memory. Yet this apparent spiritualization of the material corpse reveals itself to be less than spirit since what comes to be remembered is not a higher or purer form of the deceased but rather its mere simulacrum. Whereas a materialist conception of death would insist upon regarding the spectral memory of the deceased as nothing more than a derivative representation whose real ground is the physical presence of the body itself, a spiritualist view would seek to rob the event of death of any importance beyond its finally making possible the full release of the soul, whose functioning was handicapped and rendered merely partial by its entrapment within the body. In this way, the materialist account shows itself unable to explain the duplicative sending of the dead in memory, while the discourse of spirit refuses to acknowledge how this sending is forced to constantly differ from itself over changes in time and space. In marked contrast to both these positions, the notion of spectrality recognizes that memory of the dead is something that is sent from the dead themselves *without*, however, thereby equating the dead with its memorialized double.

In this regard, Takeuchi's stress on the importance of Lu Xun's funeral can already be seen to be anticipated by the significance that Lu Xun himself places on these commemorative events. A striking example of this can be found in Lu Xun's 1925 short story, "Gudu-zhe" (The loner). This work focuses on the narrator's friendship with Wei Lianshu, a bond rendered highly unusual by the fact that it was "bracketed at its beginning and end by funerals," as we are told in the text's opening line.[16] The first funeral is that of Lianshu's grandmother and the last that of Lianshu himself. This dyad formed by the dead Lianshu and his dead grandmother is set off against the larger division between the two responses to death that appear in Lu Xun's description of what might be called authentic grief, as exemplified by Lianshu for his grandmother and then the narrator for Lianshu, and the socially prescribed type of mourning that is codified in traditional funerary rites. Returning from town (where he teaches history at a high school) to his mountain hamlet, Lianshu is immediately pressured by the villagers to conduct his grandmother's funeral in the fixed manner sanctioned by tradition. As Lu Xun writes:

Every relative that could be rustled up—together with a number of idle spectators—now assembled. When Lianshu arrived, they calculated, it would be time to place the deceased in her coffin. Everything was ready—the objects to accompany her on her journey to the afterlife, her burial clothes; no further preparation was required. The principal obstacle to be anticipated was this chief mourner of hers: everyone was convinced he would insist on 'modernizing' the funeral in some way. By the end of the conference, everyone had fixed upon three conditions. One, that he should wear white, the conventional colour of mourning; two, that he should kneel; and three, that Daoist and Buddhist monks should be called in to perform the proper ceremonies. In sum: that all should be done in absolute accordance with tradition.[17]

Much to the surprise of the assembled villagers, Lianshu immediately consents to these conditions. Only upon the conclusion of the memorial service does he begin to mourn his grandmother's death in a more personalized manner: the tears that he withheld during the performance of the numerous rituals now suddenly burst forth from him, and his inconsolable sobbing continues until he leaves to return to his grandmother's home, where he falls asleep on her bed. The intensity of Lianshu's grief is conveyed by Lu Xun through use of an arresting phrase, as his cries are "like the nocturnal howls of a wounded wolf in the wilderness, rasping with an agonized grief."[18] And yet the death that claims his elderly grandmother eventually comes full circle to take Lianshu himself. The narrator attends this second funeral, noting the various details that accompany the honoring and final parting with the deceased, when he abruptly finds himself walking outside into the night. Away from the mourners the narrator remembers his friend and, overcome with emotion, begins to weep loudly, "like the nocturnal howls of a wounded wolf in the wilderness, rasping with an agonized grief."[19]

How is the reader to understand this repetition that appears so skillfully crafted by Lu Xun? To be sure, the distinction proposed by the author between an artificial or inauthentic type of mourning as represented by the traditional funerary rites and the authenticity of individual grief as displayed by Wei Lianshu and the narrator is not without problems. But if the act of mourning proves irreducible to such formal oppositionality, the duplication of death that frames the narrative at its beginning and end indicates a far more disturbing truth. In commemorating the grandmother that he has so dolefully lost, Lianshu enables her to continue living within the parameters of his own life. Although her death marks a severing of presence, that presence was necessarily already severed during her lifetime in her status as a finite being. For finitude, as I have suggested, represents the emergence of death at the very inception of life, such that each instant of life is haunted by the original possibility of death. It is strictly because of this element of negativity that life can never be identified in terms of the plenitude of presence. At no time can the grandmother ever fully coincide with her own existence, and the moment of her physical death shines a strange light on this incapacity insofar as she will henceforth primarily reside within the memory of her grandson.

Lu Xun signals, however, that this sending of the grandmother in death to her grandson in life provokes a grief so profound that the fact of his own mortality now comes visibly to the fore. Of course Lianshu always bore the mark of that mortality, but the text's verbatim repetition of the description of grief from the scene of the grandmother's death to that of the deceased grandson serves to underscore how death travels from one family member to the next. Indeed, it is tempting to regard this transmission of death from an older generation to a younger as a kind of inheritance, as if the grandmother in predeceasing her grandson leaves behind for him a gift in the form of a reminder or even command that he must eventually follow her. In this sense, it is important to recall that the character *lian* (連) in the name Lianshu carries the meaning of "connection" or "joining" but also, relatedly, "succession." At first glance, Lu Xun's short story may appear to be divided between the death of Lianshu's grandmother at its beginning and the death of Lianshu himself at its closing. Yet the thread that joins these two events together is that of a spectral presence that survives death on the strict condition that its commemorative reanimation irretrievably divide that presence from itself. These two deaths, two funerals, and two instances of living memory do not admit of any oppositionality, however. Here the two are connected by a more general spectrality that itself refuses any neat division between life and death, thereby ensuring that life be continually interlaced with death in the form of finitude and that death, in turn, be complexly interwoven with life in the form of memory.[20]

Takeuchi Yoshimi offers some highly provocative if elusive remarks on "The Loner" in his book *Lu Xun*. These comments appear in the context of a general evaluation of Lu Xun's literary oeuvre, and Takeuchi finds himself forced to appeal to a notion of "non-existence" (*hisonzai*), which he then specifies through use of the term *mu*, or "nothing." As he writes:

> As for what that point [of non-existence] is, it cannot be spoken in language. If I were forced to describe it, it could only be called something like 'nothing.' But in any case, something like this is certainly present in Lu Xun. For if such 'nothing' were lacking, various appearances (*araware*) would potentially cease to exist. For Lu Xun *qua* appearance would have to vanish. Conversely, then, this hypothesis is a fixed one insofar as Lu Xun exists. We must recognize that something fundamental must exist . . . As for what is elucidated there, I imagine that if, figuratively speaking, it were to be shaped into a person's image, it would approximately express the personality of the 'loner' that Lu Xun tried unsuccessfully to create. Or, conversely, what is found there is the matrix of the 'loner.' Yet this is above all figurative language, for in truth this thing cannot be expressed, however approximately. If I were forced to express it, it could only be described not as life but rather as the mere phantom of life.[21]

This is unquestionably a difficult passage, but Takeuchi's meaning seems to be that an essential aspect of Lu Xun's work cannot be understood without consideration of the concept of negativity. This negativity, he suggests, acts as something like the ground that enables that which appears or manifests itself to come into being. Insofar as appearances spring forth from this site of negativity, however, they cannot be said to present themselves in all fullness—that is, they are never simply there in the form of a self-sufficient reality. Takeuchi expresses this attenuated form of being as a kind of lifeless life, a life that has been stripped of content or substance such as to become a mere shell of itself: not *seimei* (生命), he points out, but rather *seimei no keigai* (生命の形骸). And this existence that is neither purely alive nor purely dead comes to be compared to the figure of Wei Lianshu, who appears as the unfortunate "loner" of Lu Xun's tale.

Takeuchi returns to this short story several years later in his *Introduction to Lu Xun*. It is in this later account that he presents a more elaborate description of Lianshu's forlorn character. His commentary takes as its point of departure what he refers to as Lianshu's "principle of life," which consists of the message "Live for those you hate!"[22] These words appear in Lu Xun's text as part of a letter written by Lianshu to the narrator, but Takeuchi reads them more broadly as providing a key to understanding the psychological pain and sense of bleakness afflicting not only Lianshu but indeed Lu Xun himself. In the following passage, both these figures occupy the position of grammatical subject:

> He "failed" at criticizing evil with his capacity for good. He "failed" at opposing the old (which for him is evil) with his capacity for the new (which for him is good). As a result, he tries to destroy the old and evil with the old and thus evil. He tries to overcome despair with despair. There exists in Lu Xun a kind of consciousness of original sin (although this phrase is inappropriate). Yet he absolutely refuses to seek out God. He altogether 'failed' at seeking salvation from the outside. . . . There is no salvation. Do not seek light outside of the darkness. Just fight that darkness. Destroy the entirety of evil with evil. "Live on for those you hate!"[23]

It would be unfair to overlook the several problems that attend Takeuchi's interpretation of Lu Xun's work. First of all, the hasty iden- tification between author and protagonist reveals a certain naiveté in Takeuchi's comprehension of literature, one that shines a harsh but not inaccurate light on his limitations as a literary critic.[24] Secondly, and despite the contextual difference between these two discussions of "The Loner," Takeuchi displays a tendency to conflate general ontological claims with far narrower analyses drawn from ethics and individual psychology. Surely these otherwise distinct fields of knowledge can be fruitfully placed in relation with one another in the service of develop- ing a fuller, less parochial mode of textual understanding. Yet such task must be conducted with a patience and exactitude that pays heed to the multiple levels of mediation required to achieve this synthesis, and Takeuchi at times unfortunately collapses these differences in his desire to pursue what he regards as the essential in Lu Xun.

Nevertheless, it would be a far greater mistake to neglect the con- siderable riches that Takeuchi is able to mine from "The Loner." Precisely because Takeuchi avoids treading the well-worn paths of conventional literary criticism in his effort to identify more obscure conceptual elements in Lu Xun's work, his singular manner of reading comes to yield valuable insights into the way the literary text finds itself disturbed in its interior by discourses that are typically seen to exist outside of it. This is especially true in the case of philosophy. It is in this sense that Takeuchi's sustained focus on the notion of life must be understood, for a fictional text that concerns itself from beginning to end with the matter of funerals would appear to encourage an interpretation that treats instead the topic of death. Yet Takeuchi's gaze remains steadily fixed on the question of life, whether in the form of Lianshu's "principle of life," which involves living on for the sake of those one despises, or that of his own conception of life so bereft of plenitude that it can only be regarded as a "mere phantom of life," one that remains persistently haunted by negativity and is associated with the desolate figure of Lianshu.

Takeuchi realizes that the honoring of the dead at funerals is of no concern for the dead, whose loss of life naturally makes them unable to accept the tribute. The elaborate staging of the deceased that forms the center of these events is performed by the living and for the living. Yet this community of the living now finds itself in some way touched by the dead, for indeed the true purpose of the funeral consists in initiating the dead into the realm of the living, and this involves a certain spiritual or rather spectral resurrection. In this way, the concept of life must be broadened so as to accommodate the dead within it. It is this commemorative carrying of the dead within the living that demands, following Takeuchi, that "life" paradoxically be more capaciously reconceived as a "mere phantom of life." Life can no longer be determined as full presence because it contains death at its core. But such purity of presence would in fact render impossible the act of mourning insofar as this commemoration proceeds by investing life with death, thereby diminishing its plenitude. In what shows itself to be only an apparent contradiction, the lack of fullness denoted by the figure of shell or phantom is precisely that which allows for the possibility of openness to the world in all its diversity, a diversity that must now be reconceptualized to include the dead.

Here Takeuchi reveals his great proximity to Lu Xun. In an important scene in "The Loner," the narrator attempts to rescue Lianshu from his isolation. "You've spun a cocoon of loneliness around yourself," he warns his friend. Lianshu's reply indicates that he is still in profound mourning for his grandmother: "Maybe you're right. But where did I get the thread for my cocoon in the first place? And there are plenty of people like me in the world; my grandmother for one. . . . [M]aybe I inherited her fate."²⁵ What is at stake in this exchange are the interrelated notions of "thread" (*si*, 絲) and "inheritance" (*jicheng*, 繼承). Even prior to bequeathing to Lianshu her particular trait of loneliness, the grandmother has already passed down to him her infinitely more general fate of mortality. Just as Lu Xun's story depicts the occurrence of their two funerals in succession, so too does the act of inheritance establish a temporal line or "thread" that ties these two relatives together. Following Takeuchi's terminology, this thread that puts into relation the dead with the living can be conceived on the basis of a nullity or negativity (*hisonzai*, *mu*) that comes to penetrate what otherwise gives itself as the plenitude of "appearance" (*araware*). To say that the grandson must follow his grandmother in death is to recognize that, for essential reasons, life can only ever be a "mere phantom of life." For the presence of anything that appears or becomes manifest in the world rests on a ground of negativity, and it is this negativity that originally introduces within things finitude and thus death.

In the above passage from *Introduction to Lu Xun*, it seems evident that Takeuchi wishes to think this negativity in its association with such things as hatred, evil, despair, and darkness. For Takeuchi, life must be recognized as imbued with these various forms of negativity, and it is nothing more than self-deception to claim otherwise. This explains the otherwise unusual use of religious imagery in these lines. In their recognition of negativity as original—or "something fundamental" (*kongenteki na mono*), as Takeuchi puts it several years earlier in *Lu Xun*—both Lianshu and Lu Xun stand firm in disbelieving the existence of an external force that would somehow transcend and thus relativize that negativity. "There exists in Lu Xun a kind of consciousness of original sin (although this phrase is inappropriate)," as Takeuchi declares. "Yet he absolutely refuses to seek out God. He altogether 'failed' at seeking salvation from the outside." The infinite presence traditionally associated with God must yield to something that Takeuchi conceives, however uncomfortably or hesitatingly, along the lines of "original sin" (*genzai*). It is not difficult to surmise why Takeuchi takes pains to qualify this notion: Lu Xun must not be understood to possess a consciousness of original sin itself but rather merely something that resembles it, only "a kind of" such consciousness; moreover, this theological notion is introduced only to then be immediately rejected, for the expression is deemed inapt.

Original sin, it should be recalled, is in Christianity not truly orig-inal at all. For this state is famously preceded by what is held to be the perfection and full presence of Eden, which suffers corruption only upon the disobedience shown by Adam and Eve in partaking of the forbidden fruit. This narrative of the fall effectively installs within the postlapsarian world of negativity a hope or desire that such condition will eventually be overcome through mankind's achievement of a return to presence. From Takeuchi's perspective, the chief fault of this influential narrative lies in its unwillingness to think negativity as sufficiently radical. If negativity is to be conceived in all rigor as "original," then it cannot be preceded by a higher state in which such negativity is yet absent.[26] This is why there can be no recourse to a form of salvation that exists beyond the current world, where by contrast the presentation of what appears takes place strictly within the general medium of negativity. Takeuchi's point is that Lu Xun's text boldly foregrounds this irreducible presence of neg-ativity within life. The desirable exclusion of such negativity sets forth a static opposition between what is to be treasured as good (presence, life, love, hope, light) and what must be scorned as evil (negativity, death, hatred, despair, darkness). Such conception illegitimately strips life of its inherent complexity by promoting the fantasy that the contingency that is time can ultimately be vanquished by appealing to the binarity offered us by logic.

Here one must make a rigorous distinction between two different forms of negativity. Takeuchi warns against viewing negativity in spatial terms such that a realm of pure positivity or presence may be seen to exist outside of it. If negativity is to be conceived as truly original, he asks, why must it yield to the spatial division between interiority and exteriority? Once negativity is seen to be governed by this division, it undergoes a transformation into mere negation. Given its exemption from the restless force of negativity, the difference between inside and outside appears as a result of mutual negation. Interiority, that is to say, gives itself strictly as the negated opposite of exteriority, and vice versa. It is this limited form of negativity that Takeuchi criticizes as utopian insofar as it holds out the promise of an absolute outside of death and evil. The uniqueness of Lu Xun, he insists, lies in his resistance to this utopian narrative as enabled by his recognition of the primordiality of negativity. Once extended beyond the reach of logical opposition, negativity refuses to respect the difference between exteriority and inte-riority as one of mutual negation. Even prior to negating its putative opposite, exteriority and interiority alike already find themselves forced by negativity to submit to the movement of *self*-negation. By calling attention to the merely derivative status of exteriority and interiority, the inability of this opposition to withstand the more original force of negativity, Takeuchi shows that pure life and good are nothing more than illusions to be rejected.

I would now like to conclude this section with a brief glance at another funeral. In his autobiographical account, "Wo de diyi ge shifu" (My first teacher), written in his final year of life, Lu Xun recalls a peculiar funerary rite that he witnessed as a youth:

> When rich folk in our district had a funeral they held a mass every seven days, and on one of these days the ceremony of "undoing the knots" was performed. For since the deceased must have made enemies during his lifetime and some of their enmity towards him must remain, after his death all knots of enmity had to be untied. . . . The monks sat round a table chanting sutras as they undid these knots; and when the knots were undone, the coppers found their way into the pockets of the monks while all the dead man's knots of enmity were untied.[27]

What type of logic or desire can be seen to inform this practice? Enmity incurred during a person's lifetime is regarded as unfortunate but inevitable. In contrast to an individual's biological life that finds its end at the moment of death, the quality of enmity is believed to possess the capacity to transcend this division between life and death. Enmity can *remain*, Lu Xun emphasizes, and this is significant in light of the fact that the object of that enmity is now deceased. Yet these remnants function to deprive death of its precision, since the antagonism that others bore for the deceased threatens to continually pursue him, thereby robbing him of the prize of death's tranquility after a life filled with tension and strife. The posthumous ritual of untying the knots serves to restore the strict opposition between life and death, purifying the deceased of the world's hostility and ensuring that the misfortunes of life do not trail after him now that he is gone.

This insistence on spiritually purifying the dead openly acknowledges the negativity that forms part of life so as to better negate that negativity in creating the conditions for a more restful death. In his essay "Death,"

Lu Xun refers to a broadly similar practice that takes place in Europe: "I remember also that during a fever I recalled that when a European is dying there is usually some sort of ceremony in which he asks pardon of others and pardons them."[28] Despite certain difference between these two rituals, they are bound together by a common belief in the power of exculpation. Just as the untying of the knots is said to dissolve any residual hatred for the dead, so too does the deathbed rite of pardon function to remove the dying from the sphere of offenses committed both by him and against him during his lifetime. In this way, the dying may be granted the peace of mind that he is going to his death unsullied by the various animosities that attend life.

In a manner entirely consistent with Takeuchi's reading of negativity, Lu Xun expresses his disdain for these attempts at purification as follows:

> Now I have a great many enemies, and what should my answer be if some modernized person asked me my views on this? After some thought I decided: Let them go on hating me. I shall not forgive a single one of them either.[29]

It is perhaps a mere detail that this passage so impresses Takeuchi that he quotes it not only in his book *Lu Xun* but then again two years later in the final lines of his essay "On the Death of Lu Xun."[30] No doubt this response owed much to the fact that Lu Xun wrote these words in full awareness of his own imminent demise. However, the question of Lu Xun's personal fortitude, commendable as it certainly was, must not divert us from the far more urgent task of determining how these divergent views on forgiveness and reconciliation form part of the overall conception of death in its relation to life as found in the thought of Lu Xun and Takeuchi.

For both these thinkers—and Takeuchi shows no hesitation whatsoever in designating Lu Xun in this manner[31]—the most pressing question is whether negativity admits of resolution. In this regard, Lu Xun's decision to abstain from forgiveness and continue hating his enemies must not be reduced to a simple matter of personal will. On the contrary, one finds here a staunch refusal to conceive of life and death as diametrically opposed in order to recognize negativity in its proper generality. The difference between life and death does not give itself in the logical terms of mutual negation. Nor does the negativity that one freely acknowledges in existence (in its particular forms of hatred, evil, despair, and darkness, as Takeuchi reminds us) allow itself to be partitioned in such a way as to suffer exhaustion merely at the end of life, thereby permitting death to claim its traditional privilege of stillness and quietude. If the energy that is negativity must be characterized as restless,[32] then it does not find rest even from the position of the grave. From Lu Xun's perspective, the act of forgiveness represents an artificial cessation of negativity. And with the completion of this energy comes peace, according to the belief system expressed in the rituals of pardon and undoing knots. The rejection of such attitude stems from an awareness that negativity is never halted at the boundary between life and death. In this sense, Lu Xun's appeal to the notion of hatred is nothing other than an assertion of the truth of continuity or transgression or remaining, one that runs directly counter to a belief in the possibility of absolute stoppage that he identifies with the purifying effect of forgiveness.

Takeuchi grasped that the dying Lu Xun's endorsement of hatred and dismissal of forgiveness demands from us a reconceptualization of these acts beyond the level of individual psychology. Hatred is, in this case, not simply an emotion, nor is forgiveness ultimately governed by subjective agency. On the contrary, the determination of these elements on the basis of negativity serves to draw attention to their primarily temporal character. Time, in this regard, must be understood above all as a question of *remaining*. Lu Xun's disagreement with the ideas that underlie the rituals of pardon and undoing knots is grounded in his awareness that negativity does not reach its conclusion in the place where organic life yields to death. "The Loner" illustrates how the energy that continues after the termination of the life of Lianshu's grandmother retains such potency as to persistently haunt Lianshu in his mourning for her, and that indeed this negativity comes eventually to claim his own life. Funeral practices that seek to provide peace for the dead are implicitly shaped by the desire that the end of organic life coincide with the end of negativity. In this way, a hope is expressed that existence in its totality be bifurcated between a realm of negativity and that of nonnegativity, or presence. Exculpation finally delivers the dead from the negativity of the world because it promises the achievement of a state of absolute rest. Yet such an end of negativity can only be accomplished by arresting the movement of time, for the future appears strictly on the condition that there be a remaining or continuation of the present moment beyond itself. By rejecting the false promise of forgiveness in favor of the force of animosity to prolong itself in its negativity, Lu Xun shows why all gestures of purification and absolution must necessarily leave behind a residue of themselves.

"THE CALLS OF THE DEAD":
SOME DEBATES ON DEATH

In *Lu Xun*, Takeuchi explores the complicated question of life in the work of the Chinese writer with reference to the critic Li Changzhi. Here Takeuchi makes use of Li's *Lu Xun pipan* (A critique of Lu Xun), which, originally published in 1935, was the first book-length study to appear on Lu Xun. From Li's perspective, Lu Xun must be viewed as a writer whose valuation of life was conceived in merely rudimentary fashion, one that remained chiefly grounded on the biological drive for survival. As Takeuchi writes:

> As part of his long critical commentary, *A Critique of Lu Xun*, Li Changzhi points out that there are many places where death is treated in Lu Xun's works. He uses these passages as supporting evidence to show that Lu Xun was not a thinker, that this focus on death did not leave the realm of the bio-logical notion that "man must live," which represents the foundation of Lu Xun's thinking. I believe that Li Changzhi's theory is a penetrating one. I agree with his opinion that Lu Xun's basis as a thinker is to be found in the simple conviction that "man must live."[33]

Takeuchi goes on to explain that Li attributes Lu Xun's conception of life to his educational background in the sciences, which were at the time largely influenced by the evolutionary theory of Darwin. Takeuchi readily agrees with Li's point that Lu Xun's thinking emphatically circles around the question of life, but he finds this understanding of life to be far more intimately connected to the notion of death than Li's inter-pretation would conceivably allow. Takeuchi expresses this divergence of opinion with Li in three separate works: *Lu Xun*, *Introduction to Lu Xun*, and the 1947 essay "'Kyōjin nikki' ni tsuite" (On "Diary of a Madman"]. The relevant passages appear as follows:

> Lu Xun was not a thinker in the typical sense of this term. His fundamental thought was that people must live. Li Changzhi immediately identifies this thought as evolutionary theory, but I perceive in the depths of Lu Xun's philosophy of biolog-

ical naturalism something instinctive, which is simpler and rougher. People must live. He did not perceive these words as a concept. Rather he lived them in martyr-like fashion as a writer. I imagine that Lu Xun believed that there is a certain time in this process of life when people must die precisely because they must live. This idea represents the literary form of pure enlightenment (*shōgaku*), as it were.[34]

Li Changzhi points out that Lu Xun's fundamental idea was that "man must live." I believe that this observation is an astute one. However, I cannot agree with Li's opinion that this idea must be identified as a philosophy of biological naturalism. There is here an even deeper "wisdom." And I think that it appears in the place where blood was shed by the victims of the Xinhai Revolution and functions as an inducement to conversion (*kaishin*). I believe that the words "man must live" signify an elevated life, a life of atonement. It is a life that should have been extinguished but wasn't; it is a life that had merely been relegated to him. I suspect that Lu Xun had the sense that "I should not be alive."[35]

The critic Li Changzhi astutely points out that there are many places where death is treated in Lu Xun's works. He explains this by appealing to Lu Xun's philosophy of biological naturalism. While I deeply agree with Li's theory, I would nevertheless like to point out that Lu Xun also felt a kind of responsibility toward those pioneers of the revolution who died untimely deaths. I think that he felt a sense of guilt that he had "outlived" these pioneers. Lu Xun possessed both an abnormal psychology and a susceptibility to hallucinations. These hallucinations took various forms (cf. the volume *Yecao* [Wild Grass]), but one of these was auditory hallucination in which voices were constantly calling out to him. Whenever he tried to rest, those voices ordered him to keep walking. He had no choice but to go on walking. Even if he got lost, he could not stop walking. Even in the darkness, he had to set off walking by groping his way about. I suspect that those voices were likely the calls of the dead.[36]

These lines reveal the unusual significance that Takeuchi attaches to this issue of life and death, for he returns over and again to Li Chang-zhi's theory only to immediately signal his dissatisfaction with it. The same argument is rehearsed over the course of these three texts, but it is important to observe that Takeuchi develops his antithesis each time with slightly different emphases and the incorporation of new information. These serve to cast a more probing light on his reading of Lu Xun's notion of life. Both Li and Takeuchi recognize the centrality of this notion for Lu Xun, just as both seek to understand life in relation to its counterpart or opposite that is death. In this regard, Li's attention to the persistent appearance of death in Lu Xun's works can be regarded as a vital influence in Takeuchi's own approach to Lu Xun.

But if Li helps Takeuchi focus on this question, Takeuchi immediately announces that he will conduct his investigation in an entirely different manner. This difference is articulated as one of depth. Whereas Li aims to trace Lu Xun's thinking of life back to the scientific discourse of evolutionary theory,[37] Takeuchi will insist that this matter requires engagement at a more foundational level. "There is here an even deeper 'wisdom,'" he declares in response to Li. To be sure, Lu Xun's commitment to science is not to be contested, "but I perceive in the depths of Lu Xun's philosophy of biological naturalism something instinctive, which is simpler and rougher." In effect, Takeuchi's rebuttal consists in appealing to the need to change discursive terrain so as to arrive at truths that are more elemental or primary than those available to science. This gesture must be recognized as characteristic of Takeuchi, and goes far in illustrating the presence of philosophical components of his thinking. Indeed, his insistence upon seeking deeper levels of grounding clearly echoes his attempt in *Lu Xun* to draw the surface play of "appearances" back to their hidden basis in "nothing," as I quoted earlier. Certainly Takeuchi's debate with Li Changzhi takes place in a different context from his theorization of negativity, but what is noteworthy is the firm conviction that the relation between life and death contains elements whose fundamental nature renders them ungraspable from the more limited perspective of science.

The descent to this more primal level in Lu Xun involves the abandonment of abstraction, a point that appears to be lost from the scientific standpoint of Li Changzhi. "People must live. He did not perceive these words as a concept (*gainen*). Rather he lived them in martyr-like fashion as a writer," as Takeuchi claims. For Takeuchi, a thinking of this essential relation between life and death can no longer allow itself to be guided by conceptuality, which tends to view the particular things in the world in reductive fashion as mere matter to be extracted in the creation of universals.[38] Prior to the operation of abstraction there appears the concrete truth that life is finite. Takeuchi approaches this insight by oddly repeating the same verb attributed to Lu Xun: "People must live (*ikineba naranu*)," as Takeuchi writes, and it this very message that Lu Xun "lived" (*ikita*). In other words, an authentic understanding of life must depart not from conceptual thought but rather from life itself, as it were, from the preconceptual immediacy in which one lives. This is why Takeuchi rejects intellection in favor of something "simpler and rougher," as he puts it. And the secret that is revealed in this preconceptual examination of life from within life is that living, in fact, is dying: "I imagine that Lu Xun believed that there is a certain time in this process of life when people must die precisely because they must live."

If, as Li Changzhi argues, Lu Xun's foremost notion is that "man must live," then Takeuchi rejoins that this living is necessarily also a dying. Here the concept of life appears to give itself doubly: first, following tradition, as the symmetrical opposite of death; and secondly, as the more general or totalistic "process" that contains within itself both life and death. In order to truly make sense of this twofold quality of life, however, we must first scrutinize the understanding of death as it unfolds in these passages. For what remains unresolved is the question of Li's assertion that "Lu Xun was not a thinker, that this focus on death did not leave the realm of the biological notion that 'man must live,'" as Takeuchi presents it. This seems to suggest that a notion of death that stays within the framework of the biological drive for self-preservation is one that must be excluded from life. The frequent recurrence of death in Lu Xun's works would thus point to the failure of self-preservation without, however, jeopardizing the status of this biological principle itself. Lu Xun's conception would then appear as follows: man must live, every effort must be made to ensure his survival, both by himself and by others; but unfortunately external circumstances develop in such a way that man ultimately dies. Such a basic argument would seem to explain Li Changzhi's claim that Lu Xun's ideas were not sufficiently sophisticated to merit the term "thinker."

The insight that "man must live" must be coupled with that of "man must die" is to be found in the lines taken from *Lu Xun*, but this notion of death gains even more prominence in the two succeeding passages quoted above from *Introduction to Lu Xun* and "On 'Diary of a Madman.'" At first reading, it appears that Takeuchi seeks to explain Lu Xun's thinking of death in largely historical terms, terms that are then modified through appeal to individual psychology. According to this interpretation, Lu Xun's confrontation with death must be situated "in the place where blood was shed by the victims of the Xinhai Revolution." The trauma that Lu Xun suffered in the context of this 1911 political uprising, which ended the Qing dynasty and established the Republic of China, can be understood as a kind of survivor's guilt. Takeuchi describes this sense of guilt with great sensitivity. What lies behind the words "man must live," he suggests, was nothing other than death. Having witnessed the deaths of fellow revolutionaries, Lu Xun was now forced to live "a life that should have been extinguished but wasn't; it is a life that had merely been relegated to him. I suspect that Lu Xun had the sense that 'I should not be alive.'" For the next quarter-century, from the time of the Xinhai Revolution to his death in 1936, Lu Xun thus endured a life haunted by the memory of his fallen comrades and the lingering sense that he, too, should be among the dead.

Takeuchi describes the transformation that Lu Xun undergoes when confronted with death as a kind of "conversion," or *kaishin*. This term also carries the meaning of "repentance," thereby pointing to the emergence of what Takeuchi calls an "elevated life" whose privileged status derives from the awareness of its proximity to death. Whereas previously life was experienced without regard for the dead, without recognition that one is separated from their ranks by nothing more substantial than contingency, the dead are now seen to occupy an ineliminable place within one's own existence. The act of conversion thus marks an essential boundary between, on the one hand, life hitherto lived as presence in the immediacy of the present and, on the other, life lived henceforth in recognition of the absence or emptiness created by the fact that the dead are no longer. Accordingly, the present is redetermined as one that is painfully mediated by the past in which the dead now reside. From Takeuchi's perspective, Lu Xun "felt a kind of responsibility toward those pioneers of the revolution who died untimely deaths. I think that he felt a sense of guilt that he had 'outlived' these pioneers." Takeuchi's fascination with this peculiar psychology stems from his realization that it is *guilt* that bonds the survivor in the present to those he has survived from the past. In this regard, concepts such as "guilt" and "responsibility" gradually come to reveal their temporal character in situating the past strangely within the present.[39]

Penetrating as this reading of Takeuchi may seem, however, it remains excessively deferential to the borders staked out by the disciplines of history and psychology. Here I am not claiming that Takeuchi avoids framing his analysis of Lu Xun in these specific terms. The evidence is clear that he draws heavily from these fields in support of his interpretation. However, this appeal to history and psychology does not take place without the appearance of certain contradictions that, in fact, function to detract from the authority that Takeuchi otherwise wishes to invest these disciplines. At stake here is an issue of textuality that proceeds beyond what appears to be Takeuchi's own authorial intent. For it must be emphasized that the recourse to history and psychology represents an attempt to engage with problems that arise, respectively, *outside* and *inside* the subject. The truths sought by the historian are primarily objective insofar as they are grounded on external events that occur in the world,[40] whereas the secrets pursued by the psychologist are by contrast subjective in nature in the sense that they are determined to exist within the interiority of the soul or mind that is *psychē*. In Takeuchi's reading of Lu Xun, reference to the Xinhai Revolution takes its place alongside a discussion of guilt and atonement in order that the analysis become as comprehensive as possible. Here the criterion of comprehensiveness is measured according to both the quality of argument and quantity of information presented with regard to the historical outside and psychological inside of the object of analysis that is Lu Xun.

The difficulty appears, however, when the matter under investigation begins to implicitly question the possibility of such strict division between inside and outside. Here let us recall that the question being posed concerns the nature of Lu Xun's relations with the dead of the past:

> Lu Xun possessed both an abnormal psychology and a susceptibility to hallucinations. These hallucinations took various forms (cf. the volume *Yecao* [Wild Grass]), but one of these was auditory hallucination in which voices were constantly calling out to him. Whenever he tried to rest, those voices ordered him to keep walking. He had no choice but to go on walking. Even if he got lost, he could not stop walking. Even in the darkness, he had to set off walking by groping

his way about. I suspect that those voices were likely the
calls of the dead.

It is immediately apparent that Takeuchi attempts to resolve this
problem by, in effect, pathologizing Lu Xun. This pathologization focuses
on the internal or subjective issue of his psychological condition. Hence
the "calls of the dead" that he hears are traced back by Takeuchi to
the fact that Lu Xun "possessed both an abnormal psychology and a
susceptibility to hallucinations," as he reports. Ironically, the biological
reductionism for which Takeuchi criticized Li Changzhi now seems to
be replaced by Takeuchi's own psychological reductionism of Lu Xun.
For the underlying question posed by the calling of the dead is whether
such phenomenon allows itself to be treated purely in the restricted
terms of psychology. As has been widely documented, the methodological
trap of psychologism consists in determining all things, particularly the
problems and concepts of philosophy, as deriving from an individual's
psychic contents. Takeuchi attempts to avoid this snare by referring to
the concrete historical reality in which Lu Xun lived. Hence the dead
are not mere figments of Lu Xun's imagination; on the contrary, they are
the "pioneers of the revolution who died untimely deaths," as Takeuchi
recalls. The conundrum faced by Takeuchi centers on the question of
origin. If the presence of the dead can ultimately be drawn back to Lu
Xun's own mind, then the gains made by his gift of literary imagination
are at once nullified by his lack of historical responsibility. Takeuchi
wants to perform a precarious balancing act between locating the dead in
the external or objective reality of the historical past, on the one hand,
and situating their calls in the internal or subjective reality that is Lu
Xun's mind, on the other. From this perspective, it becomes evident that
Takeuchi seeks to resolve this tension between exteriority and interiority
by making a subtle distinction between, to follow his terminology, the
shisha (dead) and their yobigoe (calls).

For Takeuchi, the calls of the dead heard by Lu Xun represent a
unique synthesis between history and psychology. This synthesis carries a
marked temporal difference: the dead met their deaths during the Xinhai
Revolution, but their calls only come to present themselves to Lu Xun
thereafter. And this delay between the dead and their calls yields, in
fact, an entire series of additional delays, for these calls do not simply
take place once but instead "constantly" (or "continually": taezu), as
Takeuchi notes. A vaster timeline now comes into view in which these

calls are registered at numerous points throughout Lu Xun's life, but that have their proper source in the Revolution of 1911. Or, alternatively, this historical source might be seen as nothing more than the contingent trigger for this calling of the dead, which would then maintain its true origin in Lu Xun's "abnormal psychology." However, it is important to recognize that nothing substantially changes upon introducing this alternative interpretation, since the contradictory elements requiring synthesis remain that of external history and internal psychology. Far more urgent is the difficulty posed by the fact that the calling of the dead fails to be synthesized insofar as exteriority and interiority appear to be essentially allergic to one another.

In order to find a way out of this impasse, I would like to turn to Lu Xun's 1925 prose poem "Lilun" (On expressing an opinion). This short piece concerns a vivid dream seen by the narrator in which his teacher recounts to him a story:

> When a son is born to a family, the whole household is delighted. When he is one month old they carry him out to display him to the guests—usually expecting some compliments, of course.
>
> One says: "This child will be rich." Then he is heartily thanked.
>
> One says: "This child will be an official." Then some compliments are made him in return.
>
> One says: "This child will die." Then he is thoroughly beaten by the whole family.
>
> That the child will die is necessary, while to say that he will be rich or a high official may be a lie. Yet the lie is rewarded, whereas the statement of that which is necessary gains a beating.[41]

Significant differences exist between this tale and Takeuchi's attempt to explain the phenomenon whereby Lu Xun appears to hear the calls of the dead. Both of these instances dwell on the question of death, but the former thematizes the issue of mortality in the context of a single individual while the latter explores the manner in which an individual yet alive remains persistently haunted by other people who have now died. Another difference emerges around the question of necessity, or what Lu Xun calls here *biran*. The structure of "On Expressing an

Opinion" rests upon the fundamental distinction between necessity and contingency. Of the three guests invited to praise the child, only one speaks from the standpoint of necessity while the two others engage in flattery as based on what appears to be most desirable in the realm of contingency. In this regard, Takeuchi's reading of Lu Xun remains closer to the flatterers insofar as he identifies as merely contingent the great writer's haunting by the dead. The Xinhai Revolution may or may not have taken place, just as Lu Xun may or may not have suffered from hallucinations and an "abnormal psychology." These events are not truly necessary, for they could well have occurred otherwise.

Placing these two textual instances alongside one another in the context of a meditation on death, the following question arises: what is the difference between being confronted by the incontrovertible fact of one's own finitude and being pursued in life by others who are now dead? No consideration of this issue can truly avoid the claim famously made by Heidegger in *Being and Time* that death acts, in its irreducible singularity, to individualize man: "The unwavering precision with which Dasein is thus essentially individualized down to its ownmost potentiality-for-Being, discloses the anticipation of [zum] death as the possibility which is *non-relational*."[42] I raise this point for the sole purpose of asking whether death forms man as an individual, as Heidegger claims, or whether, on the contrary, death effectively disrupts the individual's capacity to identify himself as an individual in his difference from others. While Heidegger is certainly correct to argue that death is nonrelational in the sense that nobody can die in place of another, or that nobody can understand his or her own death on the basis of the death of another, I am far less convinced that death consolidates rather than unsettles the traditional notion of self-identity, no matter how defined.

In Takeuchi's analysis of Lu Xun, the latter is found to be pursued by the calls of others who are now dead. In Lu Xun's prose poem, meanwhile, a child will proceed to live his life while being pursued by the call of his own death. In this regard, just as Takeuchi used the term "constantly" to describe the nature of Lu Xun's haunting, so too will the child in "On Expressing an Opinion" be continually reminded of his own mortality, even if by nothing more substantial than the simple fact of aging. Here it gradually becomes clear that these two discussions of death are perhaps not as distant as they initially appeared. With implicit reference to Heidegger, it is worth considering how different the call of death appears when it is voiced by oneself, in one's own individuality, compared to when it is voiced by others. Is not this distinction between self and other already in some way undermined by the emergence of death? For Takeuchi, Lu Xun's experience of the calls of the dead have as their point of origin a time that precedes these calls. In similar fashion, Lu Xun's tale depicts a mortal being who is still in his infancy. From the very moment the child first appeared in the world, Lu Xun implies, death was already calling. And no doubt it is the very pathos of death coinciding with birth that Lu Xun sought to impress upon his readers.[43]

As Heidegger emphasized over and again, death cannot simply be conceived as a single event that occurs at the end of an individual's life. In the mode of possibility, death haunts man from his very inception. A remarkably similar thinking of death in this broader sense of finitude can be detected in these texts by Takeuchi and Lu Xun as well. If death announces itself at the beginning rather than at the end of life, thereby forcing us to recognize that the acts of living and dying are inextricably connected, then death can be said to accompany the individual at each moment of life. Even prior to the individual's own subjective reckoning with death, however, death has already begun its reckoning with the individual. Given the constancy of that reckoning, the fact that it stretches throughout the course of a person's life, one must understand this relation that death maintains with man as essentially multiple. In marking man as finite, death never calls on an individual in precisely the same way. With each new call, in response to the incessantly changing conditions of a mortal life, death finds that the individual it haunts never remains fully identical to himself. For the introduction of death within life acts as a kind of demand that difference be incorporated within the unfolding of individual identity. From the perspective of the individual, the call of death can only be heard as that which is primarily other to the sphere of self-identity. This is true not only because death represents the destruction of the self, but also because mortality operates by constantly resurrecting the self differentially, that is, as something nonidentical to what it previously was. Regardless of whether death appears in the form of oneself, as in Lu Xun's prose poem, or in the form of others, as in Takeuchi's reading of Lu Xun, the point is that death "as such" contains a more general scope of alterity that never leaves the self unchanged.

In concluding this section, I would like to circle back to the question that so troubled Takeuchi: should the calls of the dead be considered an external or objective phenomenon or rather an internal or subjective one? By considering the issue of individualization crucially raised by Heidegger in his treatment of death, I have argued that a reading of both Takeuchi and Lu Xun appears to indicate that the general alterity of death precedes its articulation in the more restricted terms of self versus other. Far from reinforcing the identity of the self, death on the contrary acts to disturb all attempts to conceive of difference merely at the individual level. This insight demands that we radically de-individualize death: even prior to being able to identify the calls of the dead as belonging to either ourselves (in our future state, one that has already been announced at birth) or others, we hear first and foremost the call of death. The calls of the dead, in other words, derive strictly from the call of death "itself."

By drawing the dead back to their ground in death, it immediately becomes clear that the calling of the dead exists neither fully outside nor inside the subject. Once death has been individualized in such a way as to allow for affiliation with either the self or others, then the debate between history and psychology can commence. To be sure, there is valuable knowledge to be gained in reflecting on the question of where the determinate border should be drawn in the context of the dead and their calls. And any comprehensive solution to this problem would conceivably aim for an equitable balance between the claims of exteriority and interiority, as sought by Takeuchi. However, insofar as these calls can be traced back to the dead, who must in turn take as their point of departure death "itself," then it is apparent that neither outside nor inside can be placed in the position of priority. Death inhabits the subject both from without and within. Indeed, this intertwining of exteriority and interiority can perhaps be seen to be hinted at by Lu Xun in his prose poem on mortality. As I showed, Lu Xun uses the device of the three guests to foreground the relation between necessity and contingency. In an analogous fashion, the fact that death exists internally in man is a necessity: man must die because he is essentially finite. In an external sense, however, the question of *when* that death will arrive is purely a matter of contingency.[44] When viewed from the perspective of death, such traditional distinctions as exteriority versus interiority and necessity versus contingency reveal themselves to be less oppositional than strangely interwoven.

CONCLUSION

In examining Takeuchi's analysis of modernity, it is remarkable how much he appeals to the notion of negativity in representing the relations between "East" and "West." In order to grasp the core meaning of this negativity, however, we must return to Takeuchi's wartime volume *Lu Xun*, for there a thinking begins to take shape that aims to trace all things back to their originary ground in nothing. In this book, together with his many other writings on Lu Xun, Takeuchi shows that the appearance of things in the world does not mark a decisive break with that nothing; on the contrary, negativity continues to haunt things throughout their existence. If the negativity of things is situated strictly prior to their emergence and after their disappearance, then an individual thing's existence can be determined purely on the basis of presence, such that it remains self-identical despite constant changes in time and space. It is this narrow conception that Takeuchi seeks to contest by thinking negativity in its proper generality.

It is no coincidence that Takeuchi begins contemplating the question of nothingness in its relation to being through a reading of Lu Xun. Here Lu Xun must not be seen as the mere object of Takeuchi's research, one to which is directly applied the methodological insights derived from the philosophical texts that he was studying at the time. As Takeuchi himself fully recognized, his debt to Lu Xun extended beyond the field of literature to include the realms of history, politics, psychology, and philosophy as well. In Lu Xun's works, the steady focus on death appears together with an uncompromising attachment to life. As I demonstrate through exploring the dialogue between Takeuchi and the critic Li Changzhi, this relation between life and death is a deceptively complex one. Lu Xun is committed to thinking life in its indivisibility from death. I represent this strange unity in two ways: finitude and memory. As Lu Xun disturbingly reveals in his 1925 prose poem "On Expressing an Opinion," mortality first appears at birth, and is indeed the very condition for anything to come into the world at all. Death, then, as the intrinsic shadow of life. Yet Lu Xun painstakingly shows that this relation is not a unilateral one. In his short story "The Loner," composed in the same year, death comes to effect a decisive transformation in individuals such that their biological destruction coincides with their spectral reanimation among those who have survived them. The dead are no longer, certainly, and yet they continue to live on in the form of memory. For Lu Xun, this life that is given to death in no way overcomes death, but it does yield a difference of the dead that testifies to the residual existence of the past within the present.

For both Takeuchi and Lu Xun, it is imperative to conceive of the relation between life and death beyond the fixed terms of oppositionality.

Once death is shown to inhabit life in the form of finitude and, conversely, life shown to reside within death in the form of memory, then
the stable presence required for such dichotomy is rendered impossible.
This radical eclipse of oppositionality opens up the space for what Takeuchi, in his reading of Lu Xun, referred to as a "phantom of life," one
that is populated by ghosts from different times and spaces that make
interminable demands upon the self. Yet this redetermination of life must
not be regarded as a deprivation or fall in comparison with life viewed
as presence. Precisely by revealing the negativity that inheres within
presence, the self now appears uniquely vulnerable in its exposure to
other times and spaces that come to claim that self as part of their own.
From the perspective of Lu Xun, this claiming appears most powerfully
in the phenomenon of commemoration, which Takeuchi later interprets
as a call from the dead. However, this hailing of the dead is not to be
understood exclusively as a relation between past and present. Because
of their commemorative ability to survive death, the dead continue to
make their effects felt each time anew in the future.

CHAPTER 4

INTERLACINGS OF NOTHING

THE QUESTION OF DEATH IN TAKEUCHI YOSHIMI'S READING OF LU XUN II

> You're the idiots! You know nothing about dying. Life is death, death is life; its slaves are its masters. I've traced life back to its very source.
>
> —Lu Xun[1]

INTRODUCTION

In the present chapter, I aim to build on the insights developed in chapter 3 and pursue some of the implications of conceiving of life and death in their essential intimacy. The thinking of life and death together opens up a general space in which many of the distinctions that govern our everyday understanding of these terms now come to be placed in question. Takeuchi's gesture of broadening the scope of negativity to include both the organic and inorganic can be seen to be anticipated in Lu Xun's discovery of the formidable ability of death to affect even those things that are typically held to be lifeless. A more expansive comprehension of death allows us to see that the traditional association of life with presence in fact conceals the manner in which negativity must be operative at each moment in order for any life to exist at all. In this regard, I suggest that a life that is fully present to itself in its imperviousness to death would be equivalent to death itself. Death is not a fixed state, I argue with regard to Lu Xun and Takeuchi, but instead a restless force that is productive of both regeneration and further annihilation.

Following Lu Xun, I attempt to conceive of death across the divide of the objective or external and the subjective or internal. In contrast to the view that death occurs exclusively as an empirical event that aligns with these former terms, I claim that the latter notions are equally mobilized by death in the unique form of forgetting. What Lu Xun invites us to think, in other words, is a strange concordance between the instance of biological death that takes place in the world and the instance of oblivion that comes to afflict the mind. In both cases, what is most directly at issue is the obliteration of a trace that had previously sustained life. If this transition from life to death and memory to forgetting is not rigorously examined, however, then it is easy to conclude that such change must appear as a fall from an original good to a subsequent evil. Hence the goal to be achieved from our own postlapsarian perspective would consist in restoring the site of that initial presence. In my reading of Lu Xun and Takeuchi, I show how both these figures vigilantly avoid this trap by appealing to a notion of haunting. Lu Xun and Takeuchi recognize that the connection between death and forgetting lies above all in temporal violence, in which something that appears at one moment is constantly exposed to the threat of disappearance at each succeeding moment. Just as Lu Xun seeks to commemoratively resurrect the dead, so too does Takeuchi acknowledge that his own efforts to sustain the posthumous "spirit" of Lu Xun's work stem from the fact that Lu Xun continues to possess him. Yet if finite life meets its end in death, then memory appears no less vulnerable to its own destruction in forgetting. It is precisely because of this fragility of life and memory vis-à-vis time that one finds oneself burdened with the task of remembering the dead.

An expanded thinking of death in its relation to the concepts of negativity, time, and forgetting comes finally to include the notion of darkness as well. Here I attempt to unfold the enormous implications of Takeuchi's insight that all light must be found to originate in shadow and darkness. Far from being merely a romantic reaction against the value of reason, I show that Takeuchi's claim represents a privileging of practical action in the context of the classical distinction between theory and praxis. In Takeuchi's reading of Lu Xun, a determination of being on the basis of negativity coexists with a stringent critique of the conception of man as sovereign subject. For Takeuchi, man's theoretical vision must ultimately be grasped as an action, because of which it is unable to entirely free itself from a kind of blindness. Such absorption of theory by action takes place alongside a bold attempt to historicize action, thereby demonstrating that practical being is at its core a complex interweaving of the past and future.

DEATH, GENERALIZED

As if summarizing the conclusions reached in my previous chapter, Takeuchi Yoshimi takes up the question of the relation between life and death in his book *Introduction to Lu Xun*. "In order for one to be born," he declares, "dying and death are necessary."[2] These are powerful words, surely, but what is their exact meaning? Is Takeuchi calling attention to the paradoxical way in which death is harbored within the most innermost region of life? Or is he instead setting forth a notion of negativity that ultimately yields to its own negation in the emergence of a space of pure presence and positivity? In order to answer this question, I would like to first turn to an essay that Takeuchi wrote in 1943 entitled " 'Chūgoku bungaku' no haikan to watakushi" (The discontinued publication of "Chinese Literature" and myself). In these lines Takeuchi attempts to explain why he has decided to dismantle the Chinese Literature Research Association and so cease issuance of the journal *Chinese Literature*:

> When the Chinese Literature Research Association was first formed, there was clearly inherent within it a fundamental contradiction needed for the Association to posit and gen-erate itself from out of the chaos . . . Society too came to properly recognize the Association as such, and it seems that we ourselves more or less complacently accepted that valu-ation. In this way, our basic contradiction disappeared and stability came. The days of sustaining things thus began. I am dissatisfied with such an Association. For me, the Asso-ciation must develop incessantly. It must eternally repeat its own self-negation. I find meaningless any notion of life that does not contain death, any thinking that does not issue from doubt, and any culture that does not carry out its own generation and development.[3]

Although there appears no explicit mention of Lu Xun in this passage, the logic formulated here is in fact directly pertinent to Takeuchi's analysis since Lu Xun represents for him the very embodiment of self-negation. For Takeuchi, significantly, the self that undergoes negation is not limited to individual humans. By including within the scope of negativity the Chinese Literature Research Association, Takeuchi indicates that the force of self-negation is to be understood in a properly general sense, affecting everything that appears. The energy contained within "fundamental contradictions" allows for things to first emerge as themselves from out of chaos. This emergence in the world, however, does not signal the end of negativity as culminating in the creation of life. Takeuchi is insistent that the self-negation that allows something to be born from nothing—and here we must recall his earlier remark that *mu* or "nothing" underlies all appearances—continues throughout the life of that thing. What he calls in these lines the activity of "generation and development" (*seisei hatten*) is really only another name for life itself, or rather dialectical life, as Takeuchi understands it. In his eyes, the Chinese Literature Research Association has unfortunately come to lose that initial energy in complacently accepting the recognition from society at large.[4]

The perceived debility of the Association can be understood in its most concentrated form in Takeuchi's statement that "I find meaningless any notion of life that does not contain death (*shi wo fukumanu sei*)." If life and death are held to be mutually exclusive, then the former easily falls prey to stasis or inertia. Moving somewhat hastily between the conceptual and empirical realms, Takeuchi diagnoses the problem of the Association in precisely this manner, for the deathless life that it gradually came to inhabit was brought about by the danger of excessive social acclaim. Viewed from this perspective, it is evident that Takeuchi does not conceive of death as a mere state from which all life has been extinguished, for this would be to render death as equally sterile as deathless life. On the contrary, death is regarded as a negative force or energy that paradoxically instills in life the capacity for change. A life that contains death is one in which this latter is determined not as a state in and of itself but rather as something that maintains a strictly parasitic relation with life. By feeding on life, as it were, draining it of what would otherwise be the fullness of its presence, death introduces the requisite negativity for life to generate and develop. In his demand for things to "develop incessantly," such that they "eternally repeat [their] own self-negation," Takeuchi is not merely conveying his personal dissatisfaction with the decline of the Chinese Literature Research Association. Far more broadly, he is attempting to pursue the implications of the insight that life involves death for its animation and that negativity doesn't destroy presence but, directly to the contrary, sets it in motion through the introduction of difference.

Based on this understanding, how are we to think the redetermination of death from a self-contained state of lifelessness to a productive force of negativity? Of course Takeuchi never develops this idea in any sustained manner, as his aims were primarily literary and historical rather than philosophical. Nevertheless, the priority that he grants to the concepts of death and negativity in his reading of Lu Xun cannot be so easily dismissed, for these form the foundation upon which much of his argument rests. Any consideration of death in a more generalized sense must take into account that the dead and dying include not only physical beings but indeed everything that can possibly appear. Here I would like to briefly refer to Heidegger and his vital claim that death not be reduced to an *actual* event that occurs once and for all at the end of an individual's life but rather that, in the mode of *possibility*, it be grasped as something that extends throughout a person's entire existence. As Heidegger argues in *Being and Time*: "Death is a possibility-of-Being which Dasein itself has to take over in every case. With death, Dasein stands before itself in its ownmost potentially-for-Being. This is a possibility in which the issue is nothing less than Dasein's Being-in-the-world. Its death is the possibility of no-longer-being-able-to-be-there."[5]

A thinking of finitude demands that the concept of death be generalized, Heidegger contends. Viewed merely as actuality, death allows itself to be identified in both quantity and temporal context: it happens only once and is situated at the far extreme of life. Determined as possibility, however, death comes to encompass every moment of an individual's life since its threat is by definition constant. Nevertheless, death still remains in this framework determined exclusively in terms of the individual human being. In its broadest possible scope, death must rather be seen to exceed the human and indeed even the organic, if one considers that anything that comes into being at one time must eventually disappear or suffer destruction at a later time. In order to fully comprehend the notion of negativity that shapes Takeuchi's reading of Lu Xun, then, it is necessary to speak of death in relation to time itself. Given that the appearance of all things in the world is conditioned by time, the question that now arises concerns the consequences of thinking of time as essentially marked by death and negativity.

In the following pages, I shall examine a series of texts by Takeuchi and Lu Xun in which this relation between time, death, and negativity comes explicitly to the fore. In order to clarify my conceptual approach, however, let me first provide a brief, formal account of what is most centrally at stake in the reading I pursue. My claim is that time can only proceed by the continual negation or destruction of itself. Each temporal moment that appears must immediately disappear so as to create an opening for the next moment to occur. In order for there to be movement in time, then, there must be temporal division. Far from giving itself as one, time must instead be recognized as irreducibly multiple in its activity of constantly differing from itself. Nevertheless, such difference cannot be restricted to the alteration between individual moments, for there would be no temporal movement whatsoever if time were composed merely of discrete, self-present points that remain otherwise unmediated.

The movement of time thus requires that each moment pass into the next in a succession that is based neither purely on identity (i.e., time as one) nor on difference traditionally conceived (i.e., the distinction between individual points). Each moment represents an individual now, but this now is structurally besieged by the invasion of the now immediately prior to it and the encroachment of the now that immediately succeeds it. Temporal succession can only take place according to this constant disfiguration of nows, which means that each present moment is inevitably contaminated by both the past and future. Each now moment meets its death as soon as it emerges, but is then instantly resurrected in the next now moment. For this succession to occur, however, the resurrection must proceed by way of a difference whose status is more originary than any points or unities that present themselves as such.[6]

This type of philosophical understanding is indispensable, I believe, in order to appreciate what is most urgently at issue in Takeuchi's reading of Lu Xun. As Takeuchi asserts in his prewar study *Lu Xun*, "The foundation of Lu Xun's literature lies in something that must be called nothing (*mu*). It was his achievement of this fundamental awareness that made him a writer."[7] In statements such as this, which indeed appear scattered throughout his writing on Lu Xun, the notion of negativity is determined on the basis of depth. Everyday reality seems to give itself as preconstituted, that is, as already existing in objective form prior to the subject's encounter with it. Yet this surface play of appearances, in which things present themselves as reified and static, in fact conceals an element that strips such positivity of its significance. This emptying force, Takeuchi indicates, is to be found at the "foundation" (*kongen*), thereby endowing Lu Xun's insight with a status that is properly "fundamental" (*konteiteki*). Despite the fact that Lu Xun is most commonly approached from the perspective of literature, Takeuchi claims that an investigation into the conceptual roots of his work will yield truths of major interpretive value.

In laying out a more philosophical interpretation of Lu Xun, I wish to recall Takeuchi's disagreement with the critic Li Changzhi that Lu Xun must not be regarded as a thinker. Already in 1944, then—upon the publication of Takeuchi's work, if not indeed as early as 1935 with the appearance of Li's book—a serious debate had emerged over the merits of Lu Xun's participation in the history of ideas. Yet a careful reading of Lu Xun's fiction and essays reveals a focus on death that is conceived in surprisingly general terms. As many scholars have noted, the theme of death is virtually omnipresent in Lu Xun. Death appears not only in the many descriptions of this actual event and circumstances surrounding it nor, as I demonstrated in chapter 3, in the minute attention paid to the funeral scenes. Significantly, death also appears in the scrupulous observations of mourning, and these reveal beyond doubt that Lu Xun understood how the dead come subsequently to be resurrected in the act of memory. But if death is thus shown to be given life in the minds of the survivors, then Lu Xun is equally committed to the task of depicting the anxious introduction of death within life in the form of finitude.

This generalization of death is such that its victims exceed even the domains of the human and animal.[8] Even cities die, as Lu Xun tells us in the 1924 short story "Xingfu de jiating" (A happy family). Portraying his protagonist writer at work on a new composition, Lu Xun writes, "He immediately stalled and stared up at the ceiling, considering where to place this happy family of his. 'Beijing?' he wondered. 'No. It's too dead—even the air smells dead.'"[9] In the 1925 prose poem "Xue" [Snow], Lu Xun crafts the final lines with great beauty and strangeness as a kind of eulogy for precipitation: "On this boundless plain, under heaven's chilly vault, this glittering, spiraling wraith is the ghost of rain. . . . Yes, it is lonely snow, dead rain, the ghost of rain."[10] Such images and figures of speech serve to exert pressure on the traditional distinction between the organic and inorganic, revealing how the interrelated notions of life and death remain fundamentally vulnerable to redetermination. In this regard, it is vital to recognize that an expansion in the way we typically conceive of death in no way comes at the cost of life. If such widely disparate things as cities and rain can be equally identified as dead, then this is simply because they have possessed life up until that time.

A related phenomenon can be seen in Lu Xun's masterful use of the character *si*, meaning "death," to foreshadow the tragic death that is to come, either potentially or actually. So we read his 1920 short story "Fengbo" (A passing storm). This particular tale creates a humorous, casual atmosphere, but one that is contrasted with the underlying reality of historical violence. A failed attempt to restore the Qing dynasty incites panic among some villagers as to whether they will now be executed for either keeping or removing their queues. Lu Xun hints at this threat of death by introducing the otherwise comic character Mrs. Nine-Pounds, who at seventy-nine years old immediately complains about a trivial matter, "I don't like watching everything going to the dogs—I'd rather die." After a brief spat with her great-granddaughter, the latter hisses, "Old Never-dying!"[11] Thus the duality that Lu Xun poses between the macrocosm of national politics and the microcosm of provincial life is shown to yield to an infinitely vaster power.

This same technique is deployed to quite different effect in "Mingtian" (Tomorrow), written in the same year as "A Passing Storm." In this story, Lu Xun examines the relation between life and death by focusing on a widow whose small child suffers from an unknown sickness from which he eventually perishes. For Takeuchi, the tale is structured by the stark contrast drawn between the reckoning with death experienced by the mother and son and the ongoing rituals of daily life that take place in the tavern next door.[12] Takeuchi is doubtless correct to note the presence of such contrast, but I believe that the difference revealed by the work is one in which the human tragedy appears strictly in relief against the larger, more encompassing representation of death as an intrinsic part of temporal existence. Hence not a duality in which life and death inhabit opposing sites, but instead a kind of nesting relation, as it were, in which man's confrontation with death occurs within a general medium in which time and death are necessarily synonymous.

Precisely as with "A Passing Storm," Lu Xun alerts us to the presence of death from the very outset, even prior to the first domestic scene where the mother is anxiously tending to her feverish son. In the adjoining tavern, one villager playfully strikes the other over a half-drunken conversation. Lu Xun describes the force of the blow as *yong sijin de*

(用死劲的), meaning "with all one's strength." The two standard English translations render the sentence more or less identically: "punched the other hard in the back" (Yang and Yang) and "punch him hard on the back" (Lovell).[13] These translations are of course perfectly accurate, but what is gained in precision is unfortunately lost in the disappearance of Lu Xun's resonant term *si*. Why is this significant? Although this character is used here strictly as an intensive rather than in its literal meaning, the fact is that it is only by noting the appearance of death in the beginning of the narrative that one can make sense of the ending. After the child's death and the portrayal of the mother's inconsolable grief, Lu Xun concludes, "Only the dark night, eager to change into tomorrow, was journeying on in the silence."[14] Here it becomes clear why Lu Xun chose for this particular story the title "Tomorrow." The focus is not simply on time, but even more urgently on the notion of temporal change. As I have explained, time in the sense of radical flux gives itself to be understood precisely as the death of an initial now moment that can only be resurrected in the succeeding now moment. Because such succession must take place by way of difference, however, *today*, to follow Lu Xun's language, must die if it is to be reborn nonidentically as *tomorrow*. At one and the same time, "tomorrow" indicates both the destruction of the present and past and the opening of a new future that will commence once tomorrow meets its own death.[15]

The real tragedy depicted in Lu Xun's short story goes beyond the unthinkable agony suffered by the child in death and the mother in mourning. By pointing to the presence of death at the very opening of his work, Lu Xun introduces an important distinction between death as the extinguishing of human life and death in the more general sense as the negative force that drives all temporal movement. This appearance of death at the beginning of the narrative is repeated at its end in the lyrical description of a day dying into its tomorrow. As Lu Xun suggests by this title, "tomorrow" is nothing other than this change. A long humanist tradition exists in Lu Xun scholarship that does not shirk from confidently declaring "tomorrow" the site of social progress and greater human happiness.[16] Certainly such possibility of advancement must be treated in all seriousness. However, even before "tomorrow" receives this particular determination, it is most rigorously seen as an opening. This opening represents both a chance and a threat.[17]

In this conception, the future exists in its barest aspect as a time whose singular difference from all other previous times makes it unknowable. The future may present itself as a site that favors life and

all that is held to be good. In order for this new time to open, however, it must contain within itself the possible unfolding of death and
all that is held to be evil. Here it is evident that Lu Xun's notion of
tomorrow (or rather the "*change* into tomorrow," as he specifies) must
impartially hold open both these possibilities at once. Viewed from the
perspective of time, life and death and good and evil give themselves
less as oppositions than as elements within an interlocking twofold.[18]
And this insight prepares us to think what must now be seen as the true
tragedy of Lu Xun's narrative: the death that is time and negativity acts
as the condition for all specifically human life and death. This is in no
way to diminish the importance of individual death and mourning. But
without the more general death that precedes these, there could be no
human life whatsoever.

In Lu Xun's writings, death comes to be generalized in an additional
manner, and this way bears intimately upon Takeuchi's notion of *mu*, or
nothingness. Although it should now be clear that Lu Xun's thinking of
death actively incorporates elements of a conceptual nature, the idea of
nothingness may nevertheless appear excessively abstract in light of his
more concrete and practical concerns as a writer. In order to show that
Takeuchi's analysis draws substantially on Lu Xun's own works, I would
like to quote a long passage from the latter's 1925 prose poem, "Zheyang
de zhanshi" (Such a fighter):

> He walks into the lines of nothingness, where all that meet
> him nod to him in the same manner. He knows that this nod
> is a weapon used by the enemy to kill without bloodshed,
> by which many fighters have perished. Like a cannon-ball, it
> renders ineffective the strength of the brave.
>
> Above their heads hang all sorts of flags and banners,
> embroidered with all manner of titles: philanthropist, scholar,
> writer, elder, youth, dilettante, gentleman . . . Beneath are all
> sorts of surcoats, embroidered with all manner of fine names:
> scholarship, morality, national culture, public opinion, logic,
> justice, Asiatic civilization . . .
>
> But he raises his javelin.
>
> Together they give their solemn oath that their hearts
> are in the centre of their chests, unlike the case of other
> prejudiced people. They hope to prove by their breastplates

that they themselves believe their hearts are in the centre of their chests.

But he raises his javelin.

He smiles and hurls his javelin to the side, and it pierces them through the heart.

All crumble and fall to the ground, leaving only a surcoat in which there is nothing. The nothingness has escaped and won the victory, because now he has become the criminal who killed the philanthropist and the rest.

But he raises his javelin.

He walks with great strides through the ranks of nothingness, and sees again the same nods, the same banners and surcoats . . .

But he raises his javelin.

At last he grows old and dies of old age in the lines of nothingness. He is not a fighter after all, and the nothingness is the victor.[19]

The term Lu Xun uses for "nothingness" in these lines is *wuwu* (無物), literally "no thing." Unsurprisingly, Takeuchi quotes this passage in *Lu Xun* as evidence of the importance of the notions of "nothingness" and "non-existence" (*hisonzai*) in the Chinese writer's thinking.[20] What is especially striking about this work is the fact that Lu Xun uses precisely the same nesting structure as in "Tomorrow" to call attention to the ultimate hollowness of the various achievements of human society, such as "scholarship, morality, national culture, public opinion, logic, justice, Asiatic civilization." These accomplishments are typically regarded as proof of mankind's ability to raise itself above the brute immediacy of nature in order to claim a position of superiority in the world. In this way, man easily forgets that his existence unfolds within a medium that is governed throughout by negativity, and that this negativity is responsible for all death and temporal change. This relation between the narrower world of human affairs and the more general element of negativity is one in which the former is essentially interlaid within the latter.

Both Takeuchi and Lu Xun exercise vigilance in insisting that this relation is not to be understood in the logical terms of oppositionality. In "Tomorrow," the site of death occupied by the mother and son is located directly next to the tavern and its ongoing rhythms of life, whereas in

"Such a Fighter" the warrior initially stands facing his opponents before advancing into their ranks. Lu Xun skillfully creates these spatial configurations in order to draw his readers into a kind of trap regarding the limits of oppositionality. Just as death is shown to resist any delimitation, demanding instead to be acknowledged in its proper generality, so too does Lu Xun reveal that the scope of nothingness is such as to contain within it not only the false advocates of civilization—"philanthropist, scholar, writer, elder, youth, dilettante, gentleman"—but ultimately even the warrior himself. Despite his immense ferocity and capacity for violence, the warrior, too, must eventually fall prey to nothingness and suffer the ignominy of aging and death. If Lu Xun merely indulged in the fantasy of oppositionality, then the pain of death could be restricted, for there could then be posited a space outside of it that would act as its foil. In this way, the world could be safely divided into two areas: an undesirable zone of death and negativity and a desirable one of life and presence, with the choice to be made purely by the subject on the basis of his reason and morality. For Takeuchi, however, such a scenario must be dismissed as a mere "illusion of liberation," as he scornfully called it, and much of Lu Xun's greatness lies in the fact that he consistently rejected this chimera.[21]

In Takeuchi's 1956 translation of "Such a Fighter," he preserves in exact form Lu Xun's original term for "nothingness," with its core character of *wu/mu* (無).[22] Grasping the decisive role played by negativity in Lu Xun's works, Takeuchi doubtless wanted to convey its presence in the Japanese language as faithfully as possible. This point can be confirmed by glancing at Lu Xun's other writings in which he utilizes this same character in particularly marked fashion. In for example the 1924 prose poem "Ying de gaobie" (The shadow's leavetaking), Lu Xun twice repeats the phrase "wander in nothingness," although here he renders the noun not as *wuwu* but rather as *wudi* (無地), literally the "place of nothing."[23] Just as in "Such a Fighter," Takeuchi elects to translate this term by maintaining it verbatim.[24] Lu Xun also makes conspicuous use of this *wu* character in his 1926 "Xie zai 'Fen' houmian" (Afterword to *Graves*), a piece much admired by Takeuchi. Reinforcing the link between "nothing" and the radical disappearance that is death, Lu Xun writes as follows:

> If one speaks of leading the way for others, that is even more difficult, inasmuch as I myself do not know which way to go.

China more than likely has enough 'elders' and 'advisers' to the young, but I am not one of them, nor do I trust them. I know for a fact only one destination, and that is the grave. This is, however, something everyone knows, and no one is needed to lead the way.[25]

Several lines after this passage we find the following statement: "Perhaps the best contribution I can give to those readers partial to me is simply 'nothing.'"[26] The term emphasized here by scare quotes is *wu suo you* (無所有)—"nothing in the site of being"—and, again, Takeuchi remains consistent in his translation practice by leaving these three characters untouched.[27]

Nonetheless, a notable exception can be seen in Takeuchi's treatment of Lu Xun's short story of 1924, "Zai jiulou shang" (Upstairs in the tavern). This work portrays a chance encounter between the narrator and his old friend, who engage in a long conversation over food and wine. The friend recounts that he has returned to Taiyuan in order to move the grave of his cherished younger brother, since the swelling of the river was threatening to destroy the boy's remains. As the friend relates:

The day before yesterday, I bought a little coffin in town, supposing the old one would be completely rotten by now. I hired four diggers and off we went into the countryside to move the grave, bringing extra cotton wool and bedding. I was suddenly glad: glad I was about to see the remains of a little brother I had once loved so much. It was a novelty. When we reached the burial site, we found the river had indeed been eating away at the bank, and was now less than two feet from the grave. . . . When they'd dug down to the coffin, I went over to take a look. As I'd thought, it had rotted almost completely away—leaving only a few chips of wood. My heart in my mouth, I began to clear it carefully away, hoping to see my little brother. But there was nothing below—no quilt, no clothes, no skeleton. It must have all crumbled away, I thought to myself. Remembering, from somewhere, that hair is meant to take the longest to decay, I bent down to see if there was anything in the mud where the pillow would have been. Nothing. Not a trace.[28]

Lu Xun describes this unnerving void of the final line with the phrase *zongying quan wu* (踪影全無), the precise meaning of which is "complete absence or nothingness of traces." Repeating Lu Xun differently on this occasion, Takeuchi translates the final part of the passage as *daga, kore mo nain da. kage mo katachi mo nain da* (だが、これもないんだ。影も形もないんだ), or "But there was nothing here either. There was neither trace (or "shadow") nor form."[29] While it is certainly true that the negative verb *nai* could be transcribed with the character *mu*, Takeuchi nevertheless decides in favor of the more common or "natural" usage with hiragana. In this case, it seems clear that Takeuchi breaks with Lu Xun's linguistic expression not because of any conceptual difference regarding negativity, but instead simply to make the sentence more mellifluous in Japanese.

It is significant here that Lu Xun associates the notion of nothingness with a loss now suffered twice, for the narrator's friend has lost his brother to death and then once again to the ravages of time. In the overall context of Lu Xun's generalization of death, this new aspect of negativity brings to light what might be called the death of death. As goes without saying, this expression does *not* imply an extinguishing of mortality in the attainment of eternal life and presence. On the contrary, the point is that the force of negativity is of such intensity that it captures in its sweep not merely all life, but indeed even the vestiges of death. The danger to the child's corpse, Lu Xun tells us, takes place simultaneously from the inside and outside. In its most overt form, the decrepitude of the flesh commences with death, but as the body gradually decomposes and returns to the soil the river continues to steadily rise.[30] This bilateral threat posed to the cadaver illustrates the ultimate futility of conceiving of the distinction between interiority and exteriority in any fixed sense. As Lu Xun suggests, death makes a mockery of the various attempts in life to hold these two realms apart. Wishing to be reunited with his beloved brother, even if it be only the barest traces of him, the narrator's friend discovers that negativity has worked so thoroughly upon the body that nothing of him now remains.

In order to gain a more nuanced understanding of Lu Xun's thinking of death, this scene in "Upstairs in the Tavern" must be compared with the many descriptions of funerals that appear in his works. In the latter, the deceased is still physically present. Negativity has taken life, but the flesh still bears enough resemblance to the living person as to facilitate the identification required for mourning. From the perspective of Lu

Xun, this represents yet an early stage of death when judged against the full range of effects that will in time be wrought by negativity. Indeed, the question of death as a violent erasure of traces can be said to have haunted Lu Xun with particular virulence. In the tale "A Cat among the Rabbits," for instance, the narrator contemplates the uncanny way in which death comes to be doubled by obliteration:

> Years ago, I remembered, when I was living in a guesthouse in Beijing, I'd got up one morning to discover, beneath a large locust tree, a scattered heap of pigeon feathers—the leftovers of a hawk's feast. By noon, the servant had swept the yard clean again, removing all traces of the massacre. Another time, passing by Xisi Arch, I saw a small dog close to death after being run over by a cart. But when I came back that way later, its body had been tidied away, with pedestrians passing unknowingly over the spot where a life had been ended. On summer nights, I would sometimes listen to the long whines of flies—bitten by spiders, I expect. But I soon forgot about them.[31]

In precisely the same way as "Upstairs in the Tavern," Lu Xun illustrates that negativity is in the first instance neither objective nor subjective. Three different cases of death are presented by the narrator—that of the pigeon, the dog, and the fly—but it is noteworthy that the first two specifically involve effacement by external factors. In the case of the pigeon, a servant has come to remove the remains of the bird; whereas for the dog, its corpse has been cleared away by unidentified strangers. In the final example of the fly, however, Lu Xun unexpectedly shifts attention away from the domain of empirical events to the delimited sphere of the individual psyche. Here the act of destruction is attributed to the subject's own forgetting, and yet this internal force reveals itself to be no less effective and violent than the erasures performed by the outside world. On each occasion, the loss of life is soon followed by the disappearance of all evidence of death. Regardless of whether traces come to be extinguished by physical (objective, external) or psychic (subjective, internal) means, they prove equally ruthless. If both object and subject alike can be placed in the service of negativity, however, then this indicates that negativity "itself" must exist even prior to this traditional distinction.

In concluding this section, it seems evident that conceptual scrutiny of Lu Xun's work reveals layers of remarkable subtlety and complexity. In demonstrating how his thinking of death exceeds the typical understanding of this phenomenon, I explore Takeuchi's claim that this movement of generalization must be conceived on the basis of negativity. In this regard, it is to Takeuchi's great credit that he uncovered this otherwise hidden facet of Lu Xun with such incisiveness. The presence of death in Lu Xun's writings is ultimately irreducible to such factors as his educational background in medicine, the personal morbidity or bleakness of his character, or the fact that his lifetime spanned a period of Chinese history marked by immense political upheaval and violence.[32] In the generalized sense of death that emerges from his works, Lu Xun attempts to more broadly determine the range of mortality beyond living forms to include such things as cities and rain. Similarly, he lends unusual prominence to the *si* character for "death," showing that oppositions that otherwise appear to structure his fiction and essays maintain no independent existence outside of the temporal realm of finitude. Lu Xun calls attention to this priority of death by provocatively reflecting upon the concept of "nothing" (*wu*), which influenced both Takeuchi's reading strategy and his practice of translation. Finally, consideration of this force of negativity leads Lu Xun to introduce a striking form of violence that I have called the death of death. Here negativity in its restlessness perceives the termination of life as a mere departure point, for it will then proceed to obliterate and return to nothing even the residual traces of death.

THE TRACE OF MEMORY

What happens when, as in "Upstairs in the Tavern," we ardently wish to return to someone or something and find only what Lu Xun calls *zongying quan wu*, or "Nothing. Not a trace," as it appears in the English translation? In this tale, the narrator's friend painfully discovers that the loss of his younger brother exceeds even the absence brought about by death. What is at stake here, I believe, is the Hegelian concept of interiorization, or *Erinnerung*, which involves a drastic shift from the sensible immediacy of the external world to the subjective and mediated domain of memory. The narrator's friend intends to move the boy's corpse to higher ground because it will be safer there, the risk of desecration reduced by reburying the body far from the river and its attendant danger of flooding. It gradually becomes clear, however, that the safest place to keep the dead sibling is located within the mind and memory of the older brother himself. It is in this regard that we must acknowledge the value of Lu Xun's insight in "A Cat among the Rabbits." In his musing on death, the narrator indirectly reveals that the only way to retain the dead is by remembering them. The killing of the fly by the spider is eventually forgotten by him, and in this way the narrator shows that his ability to destroy the remains of death is as formidable as those of the servant and stranger in the case of the other animals. But one forgets, of course, only by first remembering. The physical fly is dead, but the narrator continues to animate the insect each time he recalls the sonic image of its whines that have since been interiorized.

However, attention must be paid to the fact that Lu Xun frames this entire reflection on death and disappearance in "A Cat among the Rabbits" specifically as a matter of memory. "Years ago, I remembered" (*jiqi jiushi lai*, literally "I remembered something of old"), as the passage begins. Here one glimpses the extraordinarily convoluted nature of memory. The narrator is troubled by the fact that death itself comes to be negated in the extinguishing of remains: what should be remarked as the site of life's destruction is now forgotten, and the survivors continue to go about their everyday affairs with callous indifference. In this very recounting, however, the animals come to be returned to life in the form of language. Although the animals themselves are now lost, their existence can nevertheless be partially restored by means of a mnemonic image that remains in the minds of those who have survived them. In the final anecdote of the fly, the narrator confesses that he eventually forgot about the insect. But this forgetting is already contradicted by the narrator's own words, for the narrative present is for him that unique time in which the forgotten past may now be recalled. Hence the itinerary of the life and death of Lu Xun's fly can be seen to include five distinct stages: immediate life, death by the spider, commemorative resurrection by the narrator, a further death by the narrator in the form of forgetting, and finally the triple instantiation of life in the narrator's present remembrance of the past that had once been forgotten. Such an account of the insect's multiple reincarnations may perhaps seem amusing, but my point is that all memory operates in this fashion. The situation is essentially no different in "Upstairs in the Tavern," where the narrator's friend wishes to find his brother's remains so as to achieve what might be viewed as a double resurrection on the basis of what he believes will now be his first encounter with the decayed corpse.

In the previous section I examined the characters for "death" (*si/shi*) and "nothing" (*wu/mu*). These concepts are intimately related, but the nature of their relation goes beyond the contingent and historical and must rigorously be understood as intrinsic. Only in this way does death fully reveal its identity as a force of negativity. In this present section, I would like to focus on Takeuchi's use of the unusual character *yomigaeru* (甦), which brings together the radical *sei* (生) for "life" and the component *sara* (更) for "again" or "further" to form the set of interrelated meanings of "rebirth," "resurrection," and "recall." In the particular context of *Lu Xun*, Takeuchi appeals to this character when describing the impressions he received when returning to his first book several years after its publication. As he recalls, he wrote this text during the war in a state of considerable anxiety as to whether he would live to see its completion. Referring to that perceived threat of death, Takeuchi states: "That same tension is revived (*yomigaette kuru*) even when I reread the work now . . . Rereading this book now after such a long time, my face reddens at my immaturity, but at the same time there are parts that revive (*yomigaeraseta*) in my mind the location of questions that I had forgotten."[33]

The character *yomigaeru* calls attention to the curious way that life is able to suffer interruption and yet regenerate itself. Takeuchi acknowledges having experienced an increasing sense of strain while working on *Lu Xun*, but that feeling seemed to disappear after the manuscript was safely completed. It is only upon encountering the book years later that the initial tension returns. In similar fashion, he recalls that his writing was at least partly driven by the need to address problems that were then of significance. Once the book was finished, however, those issues apparently vanished from Takeuchi's mind. It is only when he happens to revisit that past effort that those same questions reappear. In these autobiographical comments, Takeuchi underscores how the self is never fully present to itself in the course of its own life. Feelings and ideas may arise at a certain moment only to disappear the next, and there is no guarantee that the subject will even be aware of that disappearance. Only at a later time when such mental content again announces its presence might the self retroactively become conscious of what had been lost to it.

Takeuchi expresses a related sentiment in his essay "The Discontinued Publication of 'Chinese Literature' and Myself." Explaining his decision to disband the Chinese Literature Research Association, he writes, "Through its dissolution, the Association will resurrect (*yomigaerasu*) the full range of activities of the past. It chooses death in order to live."[34] With this reference to life and death, Takeuchi merely reinforces the logic already contained within the *yomigaeru* character itself. Death is chosen not for itself but exclusively for the purpose of revitalizing that which is seen to have already reached its point of exhaustion. The explicit mention of death brings to the fore the destruction of life that is only implied in the use of the verb *yomigaeru*, for the sole reason why "life" must proceed "again" is because it has already experienced an interlude of death. In other words, there is a kind of alternating rhythm at stake in this character in which the repetition of presence is achieved strictly through the mediation of absence. The once vibrant energy of the Chinese Literature Research Association is now spent, Takeuchi declares, and the only way for that past glory to resurrect itself in the future is for the Association to be summarily put to death in the present.

In its everyday form, the discourse on resurrection plays a dominant role in religion, of course, but also in popular culture, where life that has somehow passed through the trial of death can take either the figural form of enhanced psychological awareness or the literal form of cinematic zombies and vampires. But this simplistic division of good and evil really points to the manner in which the notion of "life again" continues to disturb thought and elude easy answers. For Takeuchi, the challenge posed by this notion consists in understanding various kinds of life forms (the individual self, the Chinese Literature Research Association, etc.) as governed by a general movement made up of constantly changing degrees of presence and absence. Since all entities must submit to the radical difference of time in order to experience any life whatsoever, the sense of unity necessary for the experience of individual identity finds itself at each moment under attack. Here it becomes clear that the character *yomigaeru* signifies first and foremost the temporal nature of existence. The condition for there to be "life again" is death, but death is in turn conditioned by a prior life that is determined as essentially mortal. In the foregoing autobiographical passages, Takeuchi confesses to feeling a "revival" of a sensation that had otherwise been lost, just as the act of rereading brings about in him a "revival" of questions that had previously been forgotten. In analogous fashion, it is hoped that the event of terminating the Chinese Literature Research Association will trigger the "resurrection" of its past activities in the future.

It is against this larger conceptual background that Takeuchi introduces the *yomigaeru* character to Lu Xun—who of course by this time is already dead. At issue here is the translation of the final lines of Lu Xun's 1925 prose poem, "Fengzheng" (The kite). The passage reads as follows: "Now the spring of my home is in the air of these strange parts again. It carries me back to my long departed childhood, and brings with it an indefinable sadness. I had better hide in dread winter."[35] In Takeuchi's translation of the second sentence, the verbal phrases "carries me back" and "brings with it" are rendered as *yomigaerase* and *yomigaeraseta*, respectively.[36] In the original Chinese, Lu Xun uses two distinct verbal expressions: *gei wo huiyi* ("gives me memories") and *daizhe* ("brings"). Takeuchi's decision to use the verb *yomigaeru* in this context is doubtless motivated by the fact that Lu Xun insists on describing memory as something that is activated by external forces. It is not merely the solitary narrator who chooses to remember in the traditional form of spontaneity or subjective freedom. On the contrary, the immediate cause of memory is placed decisively outside the subject and in the world. What provokes the narrator's memory in the time of the present—and Lu Xun clearly marks this temporality in his use of *xianzai*, which then reappears in Takeuchi's *ima*—is the spring of his hometown when he was still a child. Now, when he is far removed from both his home and childhood, the favored season returns and draws him back to his desired place in the past.

Both Lu Xun and Takeuchi seem to be reflecting on the difference between man as the active agent of memory and man as a being who must passively suffer memory, regardless of whether the particular mnemonic content is regarded as desirable or undesirable. In this sense, the faculty of memory appears to point to something fundamental in man's relationship with the world. When Takeuchi rereads his own writing after the passage of several years, he does so primarily because he has made this conscious decision himself. While it is undeniable that various extrinsic factors were influential, the decision ultimately seems to be taken on the basis of his own free will. However, this subjective freedom abruptly finds itself curtailed upon the act of reading. As emphasized by the verb *yomigaeru*, Takeuchi experiences the visitation of feelings and ideas that appear to depart from the text itself. Internal tensions and questions are revived in him by an outside source, and he has no choice but to passively accept their presence. In similar fashion, the future resurrection of the past activities of the Chinese Literature Research Association is most immediately set in motion neither by the Association nor by Takeuchi himself. Rather, it is the specific act of dissolution experienced by the organization that is expected to trigger the return of its former vitality. These diverse instances of rebirth in Takeuchi's text seem to confirm Lu Xun's thinking of memory in "The Kite" as something that is to be passively suffered by the subject, no matter how defined.

In truth, Lu Xun can be said to have already hinted at this insight in his short story "Tomorrow." I have already quoted and discussed the work's conclusion, "Only the dark night, eager to change into tomorrow, was journeying on in the silence." However, my present examination of the character *yomigaeru* reveals yet another layer of meaning that now assumes particular relevance. In Lu Xun's stunning phrase, it is the night that actively expresses the desire for movement: literally, it "wants to become" (*xiang biancheng*) tomorrow, a phrase that Takeuchi faithfully renders as *nari kawarō to shite*.[37] In this narrative of life and death, Lu Xun suggests, subjective agency in its conventional sense of will and mastery must be forcefully displaced from the realm of man to that of the world. Yet the world's volition—if it is indeed possible to speak in these terms—is withdrawn from any particular content and directed solely to the constant opening of the future in the continuation of temporal change. The fact that man must both bear witness to and passively suffer the effects of this movement is signaled in the character *yomigaeru*. "Life again" means nothing other than that time has passed from one moment in the past to another moment in the future. In the revival that Takeuchi experiences, it is his past self that visits, demanding that he now accommodate it as host. In the case of the Chinese Literature Research Association, similarly, it is time itself that places the organization in a position of passivity, whereby it will be forced to receive the past in its future reincarnation. This death of the past that is reborn in the future is precisely what so fascinates Lu Xun in "The Kite." Time in its movement reminds the narrator that the past is forever closed to him, yet this very reminder, as bitter as it may be, nevertheless allows the vestigial sweetness of that period to be revived in him in the form of memory.

For both Takeuchi and Lu Xun, memory can only be rigorously understood in its relation to death. Regardless of whether the object of one's remembrance is alive or dead, memory operates strictly by resurrecting the otherwise dead past in such a way that it receives a second life at a later time. Given the radical negativity of time, however, the reappearance of what is recalled is never fully identical to its original appearance. This point, now widely accepted in theoretical discourse, must be lingered over so as to gain a sense of the devastation it wreaks on all historical reflection. No matter how well intentioned, there can be no "politics of memory" that does not take as its point of departure an investigation into the essential limits of commemoration.[38] These limits, it is worth underlining, are *essential* rather than merely contingent or accidental because the repetition of the past cannot be reduced to a question of man's subjective desire. Here one glimpses a momentous reversal in the relation between man and the world insofar as temporal movement is now forced to submit to the expansive powers of subjectivity.[39] In historiographic knowledge in general, the past can only be retrieved in the present because of the subject's capacity for objectivization. Such objectivization is based on the assumption that time is intrinsically repeatable. Only in this way can one establish a relation of identity between the past empirical event and the present reincarnation of it in the form of the object of inquiry. It should be evident, however, that such conception of time stands on very tremulous ground. By declining to interrogate the general possibility of historical objectivization, scholarship can be said to avoid confronting the fact that the return to the past necessarily proceeds by way of death.

For Takeuchi, death casts such a conspicuous shadow over the operation of memory that it is at times difficult for his readers to determine precisely who is dead and who is alive. This unusual blurring of borders can be seen in his essay "On the Death of Lu Xun." As he avers, "Just as Lu Xun has today certainly not died among his countrymen, he has not died among us [Japanese] either. It is both useful and necessary for us also to study and assess him, drawing out lessons on that basis. And this work continues to be done."[40] To avoid confusion, let me clarify that this text was composed in 1946, fully a decade after Lu Xun's death. Takeuchi of course realizes that he writes in the wake of that absence. His language is figural, but it would be wrong to overlook the manner in which pressure is applied to the fixed distinction between life and death. In his mourning of Lu Xun, Takeuchi wishes to avoid the trap of a dualist ontology in which the objective loss of an actually existing individual must now pave the way for our subjectively created mental representation of him. In such a framework, the world appears firmly divided between matter and mind. The faculty of memory is situated within the mind, which means that its contents possess merely a subjective reality. For Takeuchi, this basic distinction between matter (object) and mind (subject) is not in question. Rather, he simply inquires whether such conception is able to adequately account for the immense complexity involved in the acts of memory and mourning.

In this context, let me reiterate my earlier point that Takeuchi was not a philosopher and that at no time does he ever develop a systematic thinking of ontology. Nevertheless, his reflections on the nature of memory seem to have instilled in him an awareness of the power of absence. Memory fills with presence that which is otherwise absent and lost. Yet this supplementation of an original presence that is now forever gone ensures that this repetition of presence carries within it a kind of hollowness that voids that presence from within. In *Lu Xun*, Takeuchi expresses this uncanny relation between presence and absence in the explicitly ontological terms of being (*yū*) *and* nothingness (*mu*):

> To say that silence represents a critical attitude means that silence is an act. Silence is an act. Silence as criticism of acts is itself an act. This is to believe that not only words exist, but that a wordless space also exists. What makes words possible at the same time makes possible the non-existence of words. If being exists, then nothingness also exists. Nothingness makes being possible, but nothingness itself also becomes possible in being. This situation is one of originary chaos, as it were. Here we find the foundation that creates the present actant (*genzai no kōdōsha*), who carries as his shadow the 'permanent revolutionary.' This represents the ultimate place in which the writer Lu Xun infinitely brings forth the enlightenment thinker Lu Xun.[41]

In the specific terms of memory, Takeuchi appears in these lines to reject any dichotomous viewpoint that would pose the remembered as an objective or material presence against the remembrance as a subjective or mental representation. Ontological dualism is grounded on the distinction between material being and mental being, but Takeuchi claims here that *all* forms of being are in the final instance drawn forth from nothingness. This negativity, it is crucial to note, does not exist in any way apart from positive being. That is to say, the rejection of dualist ontology in favor of a more original conception of negativity does not then replicate the recourse to dichotomy as a structuring device. On the contrary, the withdrawal from oppositional forms of presence is achieved partly by abandoning the very notion of duality itself. As Takeuchi asserts, "Nothingness makes being possible, but nothingness itself also becomes possible in being." The effect produced here, as he repeats in *Introduction to Lu Xun*, "is like the nothingness that can only reveal itself through being."[42] In this view, the force of negativity is such as to breach even the borders between interiority and exteriority, with the result that positive being comes to find itself partially contaminated by nothingness. When seen through the lens of a dualist ontology, Takeuchi's description of Lu Xun as no longer alive and yet not entirely dead would naturally be judged as false, for this mental representation fails to correspond to material reality. From the more fundamental vantage point of what Takeuchi calls here "originary chaos" (*gensho no konton*), however, a certain ambiguity regarding the boundary between life and death remains at all times unavoidable.[43]

In reading Lu Xun, it is extraordinary how often memory appears as a way to mark the lives of those who have perished. Of course there is no necessity for memory to travel this path—its general scope far exceeds that object—but Lu Xun seems to find the present absence of the dead so disturbing that he feels compelled to supplement those destroyed lives through the medium of writing. Writing, then, as foremost an act of commemoration. This understanding of the unique power of writing to pay tribute to the deceased appears to be the motivation behind the creation of the 1920 short story "Toufa de gushi" (Hair). Here Lu Xun recalls the 1911 Xinhai Revolution, celebrated annually on October 10, as expressed by a character who remains traumatized by that historical violence:

> I too am someone who has forgotten to commemorate October Tenth. If I did commemorate it, I'd start thinking back over everything that actually happened in 1911. I can't bear it. All those old friends—young men, quietly finished off by bullets, after years of sacrifice. Or tortured in prison for weeks. Or just suddenly gone without a trace, along with their hopes and ambitions, their corpses thrown who knows where . . . Mocked, abused, persecuted, their graves forgotten. No—I don't want to remember any of that.[44]

The distinctive irony of Lu Xun's narrative voice is on full display in these lines. This aggrieved monologue on the importance of forgetting functions precisely to remind readers of the precious weight borne by memory. In this regard, attention must be directed to Lu Xun's particular use of the character "forget." The verb here is *wangque*, and this first character 忘 is composed of the radical "heart" (心) together with the component 亡, meaning "perish," "flee," or "lost." In its most literal meaning, then, what is at stake in this ideograph is a perishing or disappearing that takes place internally, within the delimited sphere of the heart or mind. This is significant because it allows us to achieve a more nuanced understanding of the intimate relation between death and forgetting. In a certain sense, the material fact of death finds its analogue in the mental destruction of the mnemonic image. In Lu Xun's tale, the desire to forget is provoked by the pain caused by remembering. While forgetting the deaths of those who were sacrificed during the 1911 Revolution would certainly help alleviate the present suffering of the survivors, Lu Xun is clearly urging his readers to resist that trap and somehow accept the grief of memory.

This work concludes by once again raising the question of forgetting. "My apologies for having disturbed you," the traumatized character tells the narrator while taking his leave. "Luckily, tomorrow is not October tenth, and we can forget all about this."[45] Significantly, this ending continues the earlier speech on the numerous victims of the 1911 Revolution in such a way as to call to mind the stories "Upstairs in the Tavern" and "Tomorrow." As I pointed out, Lu Xun describes the terrible absence of the younger brother's corpse in the former tale as *zongying quan wu* (踪影全無). In "Hair," he employs nearly the exact expression to represent the disappearance of the young revolutionaries: *zongying quan wu* (蹤影全無). This "complete absence or nothingness of traces" proves that death, radically determined as a force of negativity, does not rest once it has taken life. Rather, it continues its work of destruction by now applying itself to the lifeless corpse, eliminating anything that might recall its former status as living. In "Tomorrow," as I have noted, Lu Xun ends the tale by having the narrative gaze recede far from its invested hovering over human affairs to the indifferent expanse of the night sky, whose sole concern is to continue its movement into the future. "Hair" repeats this decision identically, thereby reminding the reader that these fictional endings are really no endings at all, since the flux of time contradicts any definitive notion of end. Time in "Tomorrow" evinces a desire to leave the present day and transform itself into the next day as if in sympathy with the misery suffered by the grieving widow and her dead son. In "Hair," however, time appears reluctant to change from October 10 to October 11 because the many deaths violently taken during the 1911 Revolution demand first to be honored. Yet Lu Xun's larger point is that, regardless of the human desire for time to proceed or for it to stop, time "itself" continues its itinerary entirely unmoved by such pleas.

By allowing these three works—"Upstairs in the Tavern," "Tomorrow," and "Hair"—to communicate with one another, an important question comes to emerge: what is the relation between memory in the sense of traces (zongying), negativity or nothingness (wu/mu), and temporal movement understood as the constant breaching of new futures? At first glance, the philosophical nature of such inquiry might seem very distant from the literary concerns of Lu Xun. Yet when one pauses to consider such vital elements of his work as the obsessive depiction of death, the contrast between the dead remains that are present and those that are absent, the representation of the past as now forever lost to us, and finally the focus on the future as the advent of the new, it becomes apparent that a neglect of conceptual attention merely does a disservice to Lu Xun's genius as a writer. With characteristic insight, Takeuchi perceived Lu Xun's value as a thinker, and the ideas that he gleaned from Lu Xun did much to contribute to his own formation as a critical intellectual. Despite the continuing force of disciplinary divisions—now even stronger in our own day, perhaps, than in Lu Xun's or Takeuchi's—it is worth acknowledging that such fundamental issues as death, memory, mourning, and time are the exclusive property of neither literature nor philosophy.

In his interpretation of Lu Xun, Takeuchi feels compelled at a certain point to appeal to the ontological relation between being and nonbeing. Since the question of memory bears directly on the distinction between the remembered being and the interiorized being of remembrance, it seems evident that memory draws profoundly on the resources of ontology in order to first claim its various objects as its own. All present memory must take as its object something from the past, no matter how minimally determined that past might be. The identification of that past object can be understood as a kind of reading, and in this sense it is revealed that the past presents itself to memory's gaze in the specific form of writing. The present act of remembering, in other words, appears as a reading of the writing of the past.

Nevertheless, the difference of time prohibits the journey from past to present to be conceived purely in terms of identity. In order to survive the destruction wrought by temporal difference at each passing moment, a thing must be capable of repeating itself in the form of a trace, whereby a minimal degree of identity is carried over from an earlier past moment to the moment that immediately succeeds it. Present memory does not read the past itself. Instead, it reads only a trace of the past, or that part of identity that has managed to survive the negativity of time. In order to retain that past trace that has now been presently remembered, however, it must be recorded or inscribed, either materially in some external way or mentally in an internal fashion. To remember something in the present means that the past has now been marked, and that marking can take multiple forms. The immense difficulty, however, is that this inscribed trace of the past must *itself* now submit to future acts of reading in order to be retroactively identified as such. Paradoxically, the capturing of time requires temporalization so as to discover what exactly has been captured. Only in this ceaselessly alternating movement of reading and writing can we remember anything from the past whatsoever.

In this account of memory, forgetting looms as a constant because intrinsic danger. Prior to any consideration of content, remembrance in its most formal sense involves a passage through time, but it is precisely the difference that exists between one moment and the next—a difference that is a necessary condition for all temporal movement—that ensures that the threat of forgetting can never be overcome. From the perspective of memory, forgetting appears purely as violence. This standpoint is certainly correct, but it is imperative that one distinguish between various types of violence to memory. In "Hair," Lu Xun begins by introducing two types: historical violence and psychological violence. As recalled by the traumatized character, historical violence appears in the random killings of young activists during the 1911 Revolution. These youths disappeared, the remains of their corpses and graves brutally erased: "Or just suddenly gone without a trace, along with their hopes and ambitions, their corpses thrown who knows where . . . Mocked, abused, persecuted, their graves forgotten," as Lu Xun's readers are told together with the narrator. For Lu Xun, psychological violence follows directly from this historical violence. The trauma inflicted by these events on the tale's protagonist is such that he is forced to repeat this same destruction of memory by an act of willful forgetting. "No," he resolves. "I don't want to remember any of that." And he reinforces this message at the story's closing: "Luckily, tomorrow is not October tenth, and we can forget all about this." Despite his genuine sympathy for the revolution, this character now finds himself acting in a way that reinforces the earlier violence perpetrated against the revolutionaries.

For both Lu Xun and Takeuchi, the effects of historical and psychological violence in the context of memory must be examined as sensitively as possible. There can be no easy solution to the problems posed by these twin dilemmas. Nevertheless, it would be unfair to overlook the third type of violence to memory as articulated in Lu Xun's works. In choosing to conclude both "Tomorrow" and "Hair" with a reflection on temporal movement, Lu Xun shows that the incessant renewability of the future is only brought about by the annihilation of what precedes it. Where time is concerned, the acts of creation and destruction are to be seen as inextricable. In order for a past trace to continue presenting itself, it must time and again expose itself to that possibility of destruction. And this erasure of the trace of the past is nothing other than forgetting. In Lu Xun, then, the violence to memory can now be seen to include the differential nature of time itself. Unlike the historical and psychological types of violence, however, this temporal violence to memory is an intrinsic part of all remembering. At each moment in time, a surviving trace of the past that has hitherto given itself to memory may suddenly meet with destruction and thus suffer forgetting. Conversely, traces of the past that were hitherto concealed and consigned to oblivion may at any time reappear and assume once again their tenuous status as memory. In this manner, it can be seen that the danger to memory is in fact carried within memory itself. Whereas the historical and psychological types of violence to memory are merely contingently related to the survival of the past trace—such violence, after all, either may or may not take place—the temporal violence to memory can only be eliminated at the cost of remembering anything at all.

Such a consideration of forgetting and the distinct types of violence posed to memory is necessary if we are to understand Lu Xun's strong attachment to this issue. As he famously writes in the opening lines of his "Preface" to *Nahan* (Outcry):

> When I was young, I too had many dreams, most of which
> I later forgot—and without the slightest regret. Although
> remembering the past can bring happiness, it can also bring

a feeling of solitude; and where is the pleasure in clinging on to the memory of lonely times passed? My trouble is, though, that I find myself unable to completely forget. And part of this inability to completely forget has now become the reason behind Outcry.[46]

In Lu Xun, an intriguing tension arises around the question of memory. On the one hand, there is a powerful impulse in his work to view memory from a narrow lens as the province of the human. To confess that "my trouble is, though, that I find myself unable to completely forget" is to imply that memory is best approached as a matter of individual psychology. From this perspective, it is Lu Xun's unique ability of recall—which he recognizes, significantly, as both a blessing and a curse—that distinguishes him from other people. On the other hand, however, his recurrent interest in time points to a more general conception of memory that certainly involves the human, but that is in the final instance grounded on temporal movement itself. In this account, it is above all the survivability of the trace that determines what will be remembered and what forgotten. Absolute forgetting would then be synonymous with what Lu Xun calls the "complete absence or nothingness of traces," although obviously this expression must now be hyperbolized in a way that goes beyond his explicit intentions. My point is that while Lu Xun is clearly committed to a notion of memory centered on the human individual, there are nevertheless moments in his text when he recognizes that memory is irreducible to that dimension and must instead be grasped from the broader perspective of time and death. At that level, memory no longer submits to human agency or subjectivity—for example, "I want to remember again" ("Upstairs in the Tavern"), "I want desperately to forget" ("Hair"), "I remember too much" ("Preface" to Outcry)—but is instead something that relentlessly haunts the subject, forcing this latter into the position of passive host who has no choice but to accommodate memory within.

The truth, however, is that few were more acutely aware of this problem of haunting than Lu Xun. He admits of his own encounters with ghosts quite openly in the essay "Afterword to Graves." As he confesses, "I am, however, pained by the fact that I cannot escape from these ancient specters (guihun) I carry on my back, and often feel a depressing weight on myself."[47] Here the question of memory as in any way governed by individual will, desire, or even ability gives way to another relation with time, one in which the boundary between the present self and the specters or ghosts of the past can no longer be drawn with any sense of certainty. Indeed, this experience of spectrality is something that was deeply shared by Takeuchi, who often spoke of his own haunting by Lu Xun:

> I myself am someone who is possessed by Lu Xun. From a certain moment in my life when I happened to come across his works by chance, I became obsessed and cannot free myself from them even now. Lu Xun's shadow will likely haunt me throughout my entire life. I cannot live without caring about him. And the more I care about him, the deeper he grows within me.[48]

As attested to by both Lu Xun and Takeuchi, memory seems to place the self in a highly unusual position. Lu Xun realizes that his sense of individual identity is indebted to certain ghosts of the past who have formatively shaped him as the person he has now become. Takeuchi, too, acknowledges that he would not be the same person he is without the influence of Lu Xun. However, these instances of self-reflection simultaneously point to the absence of unity required for any self-identity whatsoever. The presence of the ghost who resides within the self while nevertheless being irreducible to it reveals that alterity is paradoxically constitutive of all self-identity. In truth, however, this insight really does nothing more than confirm that the self's existence is primordially temporal. In the case of Lu Xun, these "ancient specters" are now dead, and yet they continue to inhabit his life in the present. For Takeuchi, similarly, Lu Xun's death in the past has little bearing on the fact that Takeuchi now continues to be haunted or possessed by the Chinese writer's "shadow" (kage), and he even conjectures that this shadow will keep trailing him in the future. Certainly the question of the identity of these phantoms is of considerable interest. Even prior to that, however, it is essential to recognize that the question of haunting testifies to the self's contamination by other times and places that are not its own.

I would like now to conclude this section with a discussion of two provocative works on Takeuchi and Lu Xun. Although shaped by different academic contexts, this scholarship nonetheless points to the ways in which these writers continue to challenge interpretive closure and engage thinking at its deepest level. The text on Takeuchi is written by noted scholar of French literature and thought, Ukai Satoshi, whose "Commentary" appears in the 2002 new edition of Takeuchi's *Lu Xun*. Ukai begins his discussion by reminding readers that Takeuchi wrote this work at the very height of the Japanese invasion of China during the Asian Pacific War. The political nature of Takeuchi's reading of Lu Xun was formidably influenced by this background, and this helps explain why the book must be regarded as a kind of "monument." As Ukai claims:

> Yet this book is a "monument," not a "classic." For like many actual monuments, and also in the same yet opposite sense of Lu Xun's essay, "Remembrance for the Sake of Forgetting," this book is a "monument" of slaughter, one that is moreover filled with scars. And these scars are not only open toward the past; they also remain open toward the future.[49]

These lines provide a sense of the complexity of Ukai's approach to Takeuchi in his relation to Lu Xun. On the basis of the temporal perspective adopted here, Takeuchi's investigation of Lu Xun and his past is simultaneously an opening of Lu Xun's text onto the future. Following Lu Xun, Ukai is concerned to show that memory contains a political valence that must be plainly underlined. Such memory represents "a politicality that is given through the rejection of politics," as he writes, quoting Takeuchi.[50] What Ukai calls a "classic" (*koten*) can be understood as an instance of inauthentic memory insofar as its status appears to be timeless. Takeuchi's *Lu Xun* is a "monument" rather than a classic because the marks or "scars" that it carries render visible the manner in which its constant relation to other times and places allows it to first come into itself. These scars include the historical violence then taking place in Asia, certainly, but they also point toward the acrimonious debates of Lu Xun's past, the even more distant past of the "ancient specters" so instrumental to his development as a writer, the future remarking actualized over a half-century later in Ukai's "Commentary," and beyond that our own attempt to unfold the various layers of the Lu Xun-Takeuchi relation today. Here it becomes clear that the notion of memory that Ukai discerns in Takeuchi's "monumental" work exceeds its traditional orientation to the past and extends, in the mode of possibility, to future times and places as well. This insight successfully develops the implications already contained within Lu Xun's and Takeuchi's conception of the phantom.

Ukai finds the specific term used to describe this phantom in Lu Xun's notion of "shadow" (影), as appears for example in the prose poem "The Shadow's Leavetaking." This same word, Ukai reminds us, is accorded a privileged status in Takeuchi's text on Lu Xun, and here Ukai quotes Takeuchi's claim that literature "sees its own shadow in politics." Explicating this strange concept that so attracted both Lu Xun and Takeuchi, Ukai writes:

> This "shadow," first of all, is reflected in the mind's "eye" of Takeuchi as reader and translator. This shadow is "always in the same place." It is not itself being, but rather the darkness or abyss from which all being and light appear and in which they disappear. However, it is not that Lu Xun stares at this "shadow" or darkness or abyss as if it were directly before his eyes. The Lu Xun as reflected in the mind's "eye" of Takeuchi is someone who doesn't *pursue* but rather "*bears* the shadow." Takeuchi "sees" a Lu Xun who "bears" this "shadow" or darkness or invisibility.[51]

The notion of shadow, Ukai suggests, must not be grasped as simply part of being, as if it were a thing akin to any other in the world. Rather, he perceives in the writings of Lu Xun and Takeuchi an attempt to conceive of this notion in a more general sense. By writing of the shadow that "it is not itself being (*sonzai*), but rather the darkness or abyss from which all being and light appear and in which they disappear," Ukai calls attention to the presence of a kind of ontological fold that lies at the heart of all things. The typical way that things appear to us in their identity represents merely a reified conception of existence. All things are shadowed in such a way that their unique mode of appearance before us is at each moment a disappearance. This is the secret behind Lu Xun's "wander[ing] in nothingness" that is so pivotal to "The Shadow's Leavetaking," and which Takeuchi later attempts to think in terms of a foundational negativity. As a result, even Lu Xun is unable to present the truth of this shadow as such, for it constantly "takes its leave" (*gaobie/kokubetsu*) before he can visually or theoretically fix it in place.

For many scholars of Lu Xun, Ukai's intervention will doubtlessly be seen as excessively abstract. In pursuing broader questions of being and negativity, however, he boldly reinforces Takeuchi's project of mining the conceptual resources already available within Lu Xun's text. Here the notion of shadow assumes particular significance, as it points to a manner of reconceiving things in the world in a specifically verbal sense. Rather than interpreting shadows in their particularity, Ukai suggests that anything that appears finds itself originally shadowed by that which remains irreducibly other to it. To speak of "wander[ing] in nothingness," then, is to in effect accept this internal exteriority. Ukai illustrates this point with a pun: Lu Xun "doesn't *pursue* (*ou*) but rather '*bears* (*ou*) the shadow,'" as he declares, again quoting Takeuchi. In this view, man can no longer be seen in accordance with tradition as the source of truth, the sovereign subject whose cognitive activity somehow exempts him from the world of time and death. On the contrary, the general scope of this shadowy being discovered by Lu Xun signifies that man is in the first instance a recipient, someone whose actions always take place as a delayed response to the world.

The second work I shall consider is Eileen J. Cheng's 2013 monograph entitled *Literary Remains: Death, Trauma, and Lu Xun's Refusal to Mourn*. This book, which includes mention of Takeuchi, represents an attempt to treat seriously Lu Xun's status as a thinker by studying his writings in the context of such important topics as, for example, ethics, trauma, representation, and historical transmission. What serves to unite these diverse analyses, however, is a steady focus on death. Here Cheng laudably goes beyond past examples of Lu Xun scholarship that sought to present death in a strictly symbolical sense as the disappearance in China of an obsolescent cultural era. Death is now determined more broadly to include, as she writes, "the deaths of others . . . the radically unknown, [and] his [i.e., Lu Xun's] own mortality."[52] In this sense, I believe, Cheng's work is instrumental in helping to free Lu Xun from the narrow confines of culturalism, forcing us to reread him more fundamentally along the lines Takeuchi suggested earlier.

Nevertheless, *Literary Remains: Death, Trauma, and Lu Xun's Refusal to Mourn* somewhat curtails the movement of reflection at a point that makes it difficult to grasp the precise manner in which death communicates with such concepts as "remains," "trauma," and "mourning." What is needed to forge that bond is a consideration of the question of time. Cheng provides a careful analysis of the gaze back from the present to the past, and her insights into the profound ambivalence with which Lu Xun regarded tradition are vital if one is to reevaluate his ideas on modernity and Chinese nationalism. However, time "itself" is connected to death in an even more intimate manner. This link emerges in full view, for example, in a work by Lu Xun that Cheng introduces in her epilogue. There she quotes from the 1925 prose poem "Mu jie wen" (Epitaph) as follows:

> . . . I tore out my heart to eat it, wanting to know its true taste. But the pain was so agonizing, how could I tell its taste? . . .
>   . . . when the pain subsided I savoured the heart slowly. But since by then it was stale, how could I know its true taste? . . .
>   . . . Answer me. Or, be gone![53]

These words appear as a weathered inscription on the back of a tombstone, beside which lies a corpse whose body has been torn open to reveal several missing organs. Cheng's reading of the scene is astute: "As the remains—the rotting corpse and fading tombstone inscriptions— suggest, the being they purportedly represent is marked much more by absence."[54] The accompanying analysis focuses on the limits of representation, but even prior to that one must recognize that the death and destruction everywhere present in "Epitaph" derive most primordially from the passage of time. The writing on the grave, Lu Xun sensitively notes, appears as "remaining," or *cancun* (殘存). This notion of "remaining" is inordinately complex, for it signifies a relation between an earlier and later moment of time whose interval is marked by destruction. As I have argued, this destruction that is intrinsic to the movement of time must be understood on the basis of negativity. In the specific context of the prose poem, the death on display exists as the bare "remains" of life, the violated corpse as the "remains" of a physical body that was once intact and animated, and the faded inscription as the "remains" of language that was once plainly legible.

These instantiations of remaining now come to be reinforced by Lu Xun in the very content of the inscription, where the failed achievement of presence is illustrated with regard to time by a logic of what can be called "neither before nor after." In wishing to know the real taste of his heart, the corpse discovers on its first attempt that the time is yet unripe. This temporal unreadiness directly affects the subject, whose sense of physical pain prevents it from determining the taste of the organ. On the second attempt, however, the corpse realizes that the time has ironically now grown overripe. Here the temporal delay touches upon the object, for the heart itself has since grown stale, making it once again impossible for the corpse to judge its true taste. Whether for subjective or objective reasons, knowledge of what is regarded as "true" (or "original": *ben*) is disrupted because the constant movement of time prevents any pure correspondence between the experience of the thing and the thing itself.

Time "is" only what remains after the occurrence of death under-stood in its most general sense as negativity. Cheng perceptively alerts us to the significance of "remains" in her account, but I believe that this notion must not be restricted to the merely physical. As she declares, Lu Xun's text contains two types of remains: the corpse and the tomb-stone inscription. Yet another form of remains must also be present, for indeed this form acts as the necessary condition for these two empirical remains to appear at all. This more essential form of remains is nothing other than time itself—time determined here as the residual marks that differentially survive the movement of negativity. Here one must grasp that the remains in "Epitaph" appear at fundamentally different levels, and that these levels are not to be conflated. It is strictly a matter of contingency whether the bodily and inscriptive remains appear, since there is no necessity at stake here. In contrast to these remains, the remains that allow for all temporal movement *must* be present in this narrative of death and decay. Lu Xun's point, in my reading, is that death can only be conceived as an issue of remains. Yet these remains exceed the immediately empirical level and demand sustained reflection on the differential nature of time itself.

THE ORIGINAL DARKNESS OF LIGHT

In their distinct ways, Ukai and Cheng help us better appreciate the complexity of the relation between Lu Xun and Takeuchi by stressing the need to think of death in its link to the notions of shadow and remains. At its most basic level, these concepts form part of a broader logic that is able to account for all instances of decline and disappearance. Such loss never occurs in isolation, however, but rather is at each moment bound together with the contrasting possibilities of regeneration and appearance. In this regard, it is the unusual nature of this jointure that requires attention in a way that faithfully explores the paths opened up by Lu Xun and Takeuchi.

From the perspective of Takeuchi, this jointure or twofold that brings together life and death as well as memory and forgetting must now be reconceived in the opposition between light and darkness in terms of the traditional relation of grounding. As he argues in *Lu Xun*:

> What Lu Xun saw was darkness. Yet he saw that darkness with wholehearted passion. And he despaired. For him, only despair was the truth. But eventually even despair ceased being true. Despair too was an illusion. 'Despair, like hope, is an illusion.' If even despair is an illusion, then what should one do? Those who despair of despair have no choice but to become writers. One must appropriate everything to oneself by neither depending on others nor using others as the self's support. In this way the writer Lu Xun came to be formed in a present sense. This formation of the writer Lu Xun makes possible the various appearances of the enlightenment thinker Lu Xun. What I have called Lu Xun's conversion and his lit-erary form of pure enlightenment (*shōgaku*) are brought forth in the same way that shadows bring forth light.[55]

In passages such as this, it must be said, Takeuchi's prose can seem unduly tortuous, obfuscating rather than clarifying the ideas that he seeks to express. But he appears to be making two chief claims. First, Lu Xun is a figure whose thought must be viewed in terms of negativity. This negativity, Takeuchi insists, only came about gradually as a result of certain formative experiences. Although Lu Xun's thinking was initially characterized by despair, he eventually comes to realize the inadequacy of that position. This leads him, in Takeuchi's resonant phrase, to "despair of despair," and from this experience he attains what appears to be a standpoint of more genuine negativity. Second, light exists not in and of itself but strictly as grounded upon darkness or shadow. Here Takeu-chi associates light with Lu Xun's status as an "enlightenment thinker" (*keimōsha*), in reference to the latter's ideas about social reform and his attendant critique of tradition. Yet these two forms of light are contrasted to the "pure enlightenment" that Lu Xun experiences in his vocation as writer, which exists at a more fundamental level than his identity as enlightenment thinker. Just as darkness and shadow ground light insofar as light derives from them, so too does the writer "make possible" the enlightenment thinker.

Why does Takeuchi decide to read Lu Xun from this unique perspective of light and darkness? Is this merely a psychological claim about
the alleged virtue of suffering in the pursuit of artistic achievement? At
first glance, it might certainly appear so. In this view, the "darkness" and
"despair" of which Takeuchi speaks are the necessary price the writer
must pay if he is to learn the painful secrets of existence and, above all,
the iniquity concealed within the human heart. Yet it must be borne in
mind that Takeuchi consistently attempts to raise his discourse beyond
the particularistic levels of psychological and cultural analysis.[56] As I
have argued, his introduction of the concept of nothingness as a key to
understanding Lu Xun is to be grasped in its most general ontological
sense, despite the fact that Takeuchi lacked the philosophical resources
required to develop this idea. The appeal to the interrelated notions of
light and darkness takes place at this same level of generality. For Takeuchi,
this appeal is motivated by the need to reconceive of man as essentially
an actant—what he termed, alternately, *kōisha* or *kōdōsha*—rather than a
knower or seer. Since man acts in the world without the aid of theoretical
vision, his deeds occur in a fundamental state of darkness. Light begins
to radiate upon the gradual attenuation of darkness, Takeuchi suggests,
but that darkness can never be fully overcome insofar as man's cognitive
gaze at the world remains ultimately an action.

Thus when Takeuchi concludes in the above passage that "shadows bring forth light," we can see that his point is *not* that existence is
composed uninterruptedly of darkness and shadows and that any recourse
to light and vision is to be condemned as false. On the contrary, the
emergence of light is to be valued in its fashion, but light can never exist
in and of itself in static form. Light is "brought forth" (*umidasareru*) from
a more elemental region that exists without light, which means that the
appearance of light is in truth an appear*ing*, that is, it is but an effect
of a larger movement that reveals the constant interplay between light
and darkness. Or as Takeuchi writes in *Lu Xun*, "Although the shadow
itself is not part of being, light is born from it and vanishes within it.
A certain point of darkness exists that hints (*anji* [暗示] *saseru*: literally,
'reveals darkly') at being through this process in which light is born
and vanishes."[57]

In philosophical language, we can say that Takeuchi's concern
lies in determining the precise epistemological consequences that are
brought about by the ontological insights he gleans from Lu Xun's text.
That is to say, if being together with the light required to identify being

both derive from a void that is as yet unilluminated, then how are we
to conceive of knowledge? For Takeuchi, the "nothingness" that plays
such a pivotal role in Lu Xun's thought cannot be understood as distinct
from man's experience of the world. As a general ontological claim, the
associated notions of nothingness, darkness, and shadow directly affect
the determination of man, leading us to rethink the dominant view
of man as sovereign subject. Since man does not exist outside of such
darkness, this latter must in some way point to man's intrinsic abilities
and limitations. In contrast to the standpoint of subjectivist philosophy,
which privileges man as capable of transforming darkness into light
through the power of reason, Takeuchi agrees with Lu Xun that man can
never definitively overcome darkness, within which he is forced to act
without any guarantee that his actions will be either rational or ethical.

In *Introduction to Lu Xun*, Takeuchi attempts to read the Chinese writer in such a way as to tie together these broader ontological
concerns with a narrower redetermination of man as actant given his
epistemological restrictions. He quotes from the 1933 collection *Liang
di shu* (Letters between two), which is a record of Lu Xun's correspondence with his lover Xu Guangping. As Lu Xun writes: "It seems you are
always reading my works, but my works are too dark, because I always
feel that only 'darkness and emptiness' (*heian yu xuwu*, 黑暗與虛無) are
'real' (*shiyou*, 實有), and yet I persist in waging a despairing battle of
resistance against them. . . . Actually, this may be a matter of my age
and experience, and is not necessarily true, because after all I can't prove
that only darkness and emptiness are real."[58] Takeuchi's discussion follows
directly from these lines:

> Darkness does not exist without the escape from it. Darkness
> appears only through resistance. There can be no despair
> where there is no hope. Consciousness of despair is born
> together with an awareness of reconstructing hope. In order
> for hope to be lost, it must first be sought. One cannot lose
> hope without seeking it. That is to say, despair appears at the
> place of action, not at the place of theoretical contemplation.
> To say that Lu Xun is someone who despairs is to say that
> he is an actant. It is to say that he is someone who lives
> (*seikatsusha*). "Where should I go?" "There is no place to go."
> Such anxiety reveals that he has walked and is still walking
> along a path. Those who don't walk can never lose their way

(see "Guoke" [The passer-by]). "I do not know what I am
doing. But I am doing something" ("Afterword to *Graves*").
Because one fumbles about in the darkness, the hands can
feel a response. It was precisely this self that fumbles about
in the darkness of which Lu Xun was certain. One wishes
to escape that darkness but cannot. Yet one must escape it.
This action, which Lu Xun named 'resistance' (*zhengzha* [挣
扎]) or struggle, assured him of the presence of darkness.[59]

Here we reach the very core of Takeuchi's treatment of Lu Xun.
In Lu Xun's letter to Xu Guangping, he expresses his belief that "only
'darkness and emptiness' are 'real'" by illustrating the destabilizing effects
that such void has on his own ability to make this claim. The immediate
qualification to that assertion—"because after all I can't prove that only
darkness and emptiness are real"—shows that there can be no position
available to the epistemological subject outside of this same darkness.
This double negation appears to be what Takeuchi is referring to when
he speaks of those who, like Lu Xun, even "despair of despair." According
to Takeuchi, Lu Xun responds to the question of ontology by conceiving
of a level of negativity that precedes that of being. Because man can
only exist within this negative being, however, the doubt inevitably
emerges as to man's ability to determine being in this manner. Without
turning full circle and posing this question to the subject who issues such
ontological claims, the danger arises of exempting subjective certitude
from that "darkness and emptiness." It is precisely to avoid this trap that
Takeuchi specifies that the standpoint occupied by Lu Xun is not that
of the "place of theoretical contemplation" (*kansō no ba*, 観想の場), as
he calls it, but rather the "place of action" (*kōi no ba*, 行為の場).

Takeuchi's use of this uncommon word *kansō* provides a vital clue
to understanding his interpretation of Lu Xun. This is a philosophical
term that translates the Greek *theōria*, and later the Latin *contemplatio*,
and contains the dual meanings of seeing and knowing.[60] Hence the
opposition that Takeuchi draws between the "place of theoretical contemplation" and "place of action" can be viewed as a repetition of the
classical distinction between theory and praxis. The excessive abstraction
of theoretical reflection, in Takeuchi's view, is soundly rejected by Lu Xun
in favor of the concreteness associated with practical action. And this
concreteness, moreover, comes to be determined on the basis of daily life
(*seikatsu*), which for both Lu Xun and Takeuchi is inextricably linked to

death. Takeuchi characterizes this state of everyday existence as one of anxiety, for individuals are constantly forced to act more or less blindly, without the insight required to guide their conduct and guarantee safe passage from one moment to the next.

Yet Takeuchi seems intent to regard this relation between theory/ abstract contemplation and praxis/concrete action as something other than a pure opposition. In the pages of *Lu Xun*, he turns once again to a specialized philosophical vocabulary to describe this nonoppositional division as a "contradictory unity that appears in the form of the simultaneous existence of antinomies" (*niritsu haihanteki na dōji sonzai toshite no ikko no mujunteki tōitsu*).[61] While this expression indeed appears abstruse, it is nonetheless important to realize that the concreteness Takeuchi finds in Lu Xun renders his work fundamentally incompatible with the terms of formal logic. In other words, if man as actant must exist in the world without the vision required to penetrate into the true nature of things, then the ability to distinguish things in binary fashion is necessarily lost to him. For Takeuchi, this is a general claim that encompasses distinctions in both epistemology and ethics, and thus the actant is denied any direct access to either what is true or what is just. In his language, the "despair" and "anxiety" that practical beings encounter as a result of this incapacity is total. Here antinomies only appear as contradictorily bound together, such that a subjective commitment to one (e.g., truth, justice) can never take place without the possible risk of contamination by the other (falsehood, injustice).

From Takeuchi's perspective, action can potentially give rise to knowledge "in the same way that shadows bring forth light." The notion of action or praxis in this sense contains two diverse if overlapping meanings: first, and more narrowly, it signifies what the history of thought has long determined as the opposite of theoretical contemplation; and second, the disruption of such oppositionality through the concept of "contradictory unity" reveals that practical action *also* signifies the general matrix in which that opposition first comes to appear. The "place of action," then, as the very medium in which the opposition between action and theoretical contemplation begins to unfold. Crucially, this generality ensures that the notions of theory and praxis are now considerably more elusive, for they no longer give themselves in any fixed sense.

In what way might these insights shape our reading of Lu Xun? In the works of this writer, a contrast frequently emerges between what Leo Ou-fan Lee has called, in his influential study *Voices from the Iron*

House: A Study of Lu Xun, "the loner and the crowd."[62] Here the "loner" typically takes the form of the alienated intellectual, who through a gesture of self-sacrifice is finally able to attain a sense of solidarity with the "crowd," composed of those who unjustly bear the weight of social oppression. In this framework, it would not be difficult to identify the intellectual as a figure of theoretical abstraction, whose sole means of redemption lies in overcoming the elitism of his class and approaching the position of praxis as conversely figured by the uncultivated collective. To be sure, there exist elements in Lu Xun's writings that appear to invite this line of interpretation as based on such contrasting figuration between theory and praxis. In its most radical sense, however, the theory-praxis relation possesses a degree of complexity that prevents any immediate application to particular figures strictly on account of their given social position. Following Takeuchi, the "place of action" is to be conceived as a threat to all attempts at identification and oppositional determination, and this creates problems for a literary criticism that might seek to make use of these notions.

In the above quotation from Takeuchi, two works of Lu Xun are explicitly mentioned while a third is merely suggested. After commenting on the metaphor of walking in the 1925 play "The Passer-by," Takeuchi briefly touches upon the relation between acting and knowing in the essay "Afterword to *Graves.*" No reference is given for the quotation, "Where should I go?" "There is no place to go," but Takeuchi immediately adds the remark that "such anxiety reveals that he has walked and is still walking along a path." Given the nature of these lines, it seems likely that Takeuchi is pointing here to Lu Xun's 1921 short story "Guxiang" (My old home), which concludes as follows: "I thought: hope originally cannot be said to exist, nor can it be said not to exist. It is just like roads across the earth. For actually the earth originally had no roads, but when many men pass one way, a road is made."[63]

I would now like to examine these texts more closely so as to gain a better sense of Takeuchi's thinking of theory and praxis as these notions operate in Lu Xun. "My Old Home" depicts the narrator's return to his birthplace after an absence of many years. Recounting his experiences in the first person, the narrator discovers with a sense of dismay that the home of his childhood no longer exists in the ideal way he remembered it, and he is at a loss to explain whether this difference derives from the object that is the place or the subject that is he himself. Initially he is convinced that the fault lies with the home: "As I remembered it, it was nothing like this; it was a much better place." Upon reflection, however, he considers the alternate possibility that the home remains unaltered but that he himself is now different: "Maybe it had always been like this, I told myself. . . . It was I who had changed, I reasoned; grown melancholy."[64] After selling the family house and experiencing the failed attempt to rekindle his friendship with a childhood acquaintance, the narrator sadly takes his leave while considering the strange link between hope and roads.

In his 1958 essay "Wasurerarenai kotoba" (Unforgettable words), Takeuchi explores this notion of road or path with which Lu Xun closes his story. As he writes:

> Roads exist together with the daily life of mankind. They can be found even in the mountains. The fact that we walk on those roads means that we have received the help of ancestors who lived thousands of years ago. However, there would be no new roads if we walked only on those that already existed. In that case, mankind would stop progressing. Surely there would be a need for someone to take a risk and boldly cross a roadless, thorn-filled field. First one must start walking. It is not that one walks because the road is already there; rather, one must make the road by walking. Or indeed, it is only a secondary matter if one makes a road or not; one must in any case endeavor to step forth.[65]

In this passage, Takeuchi decisively removes the question of roads from any facile association with individualism. The issue of "my path" as uniquely one's own in its distinction from the ways of others is ignored in favor of a thinking of multiple persons who belong to different times and communicate with one another by means of historical transmission. As Takeuchi notes, "The fact that we walk on those roads means that we have received the help of ancestors who lived thousands of years ago." In the broadest sense of the term, the paths of the present were created by those who existed in the past. I draw attention to this point because it bears intimately on one of Lu Xun's primary concerns in writing "My Old Home." Immediately before the narrator confronts the question of roads and hope, he finds himself dwelling on the alienation he currently feels with his former friend Runtu and the unexpected way in which

that friendship might now be reborn between his own nephew Hong'er
and Runtu's son Shuisheng:

> And even though Runtu and I were now completely estranged,
> our young successors still had things in common, for wasn't
> Hong'er just now thinking about Shuisheng? I hoped they
> would not be like us and become estranged: I didn't want
> them to drift like me, or to suffer numbly like Runtu—nor
> to anaesthetize themselves with self-indulgence, as others
> did. . . . They should have new lives, lives that we had not
> lived.[66]

What is essential here is the connection between Lu Xun's notion
of "successors" (or "younger generation" [*houbei*, 後輩]) and Takeuchi's
notion of "ancestors" (*sosen*, 祖先).[67] The relation between theory and
praxis that Takeuchi wishes to think in terms of Lu Xun's portrayal of
roads now reveals its fundamentally historical character. Encompassing
both abstract contemplation and concrete action, Takeuchi's generalized
concept of action eludes any identification in the present. On the contrary,
it extends simultaneously back to the time of ancestors and forward to the
time of successors. At every moment, the practical act of pathbreaking
consolidates one's belonging to history insofar as one must follow the
paths of predecessors while invariably tracing out new routes for future
generations. Both Takeuchi and Lu Xun underscore the intrinsic newness
involved in opening paths: "However, there would be no *new* roads if
we walked only on those that already existed" (Takeuchi) and "They
should have *new* lives, lives that we had not lived" (Lu Xun). Yet this
newness never exists in isolation from the past. All action, regardless
of its degree of originality or triteness, comes into being as variations
of past action. This gives rise to a seeming paradox. On the one hand,
the radical difference of time prohibits any pure repetition without the
incursion of difference, which means that each action performed is utterly
new and unprecedented. On the other hand, however, each new action
appears as in some way related to the past, thereby reminding all "successors" of their indebtedness to those "ancestors" who preceded them.

   In his reading of Lu Xun, Takeuchi asks us to think these apparently contradictory truths together as a kind of "simultaneous existence
of antinomies," as he calls it. When action is conceived in its historical

singularity, it appears as no longer fully present to its occurrence. Pointing both to what came prior (先) to it in its formative influence and to what will come later (後) in its retroactive identification, the act must be seen as lacking in all punctuality. In this regard, there can be no ultimate distinction between roads that already exist and roads that one actively creates. As Takeuchi remarks, "It is only a secondary matter if one makes a road or not," since even preexisting roads must be traveled differently, never completely identically to similar journeys of the past. This is no doubt why Lu Xun calls attention to the unusual ontological status of the road, which, as he writes, "originally cannot be said to exist, nor can it be said not to exist." To be sure, roads in "My Old Home" are created "when many men pass one way," as Lu Xun adds. Even then, however, these new roads are never fixed; they exist only to be followed differently by other travelers under other circumstances at other times.

Vanishing in its singularity and yet profoundly in communication with both the past and future, the act comes to be thought by Takeuchi in the specific terms of historical transmission. In his 1958 piece "Ro Jin sensei ni kawatte" (On behalf of Professor Lu Xun), Takeuchi reflects on the meaning of responding in place of the dead Lu Xun and comes to the surprising conclusion that "the history of mankind is a baton handoff." As he states:

> The idea that the history of mankind consists in the taking over of a baton, and the awareness that this baton has now been passed to oneself, is an experience that touches upon the very deepest meaning of the classics, and I believe that it is also the correct way to read Lu Xun's literary works. In this process the classics are reborn; while from the perspective of the reader, the individual thus comes into being as someone related to history. That is to say, you as a person become an irreplaceable existence in the world.[68]

Takeuchi ends this essay by confirming that he regards this baton relay as the form of general action when understood historically. Having already established the link between practical action and pathbreaking (i.e., walking, roads), he now extends that chain by adding the element of baton transfer. "In any case, I have thus far walked my own path carrying this baton," as he concludes.[69]

In these lines, Takeuchi stresses that the notion of action is to be grasped in terms of the essential difference of time. The act by which one receives past knowledge in the present is described in the unconventional terms of a baton relay. In this relation, what takes priority is neither the giver nor recipient but rather the fragile act of transmission itself. If the transmission of knowledge across time were to be conceived from the abstract "place of theoretical contemplation," then the dual acts of giving and receiving would be purely identical. No difference would intervene between Lu Xun's literary corpus and the various instances of its future reception. Ironically, this passage of textual identity from one time and place to another would obviate the need for any baton transfer altogether, for there is an inherent risk in this process that the baton may fall or the handoff be bungled.

Here Takeuchi's notion of "rebirth" (*yomigaeru*) comes prominently to the fore. The need for rebirth arises only from death, and indeed Takeuchi recalls from the very beginning of this essay that Lu Xun has now been dead for over two decades. In its most elemental sense, however, death occurs at each passage from a prior moment to a later moment. The constant destruction of the past can never be undone, but there can take place an honoring of the dead—what Takeuchi refers to here as acting "on their behalf" (*ni kawatte*)—that reanimates the corpse and allows the deceased to survive beyond the environment that appears to be most immediately their own. Insofar as this act of resurrection (i.e., the historical reception of a past baton) occurs at the "place of action," however, the new life that has thus been granted the dead takes them far from where they were and renders them irreducibly other to themselves. But as Takeuchi appears to suggest, the only way to pay tribute to the dead and extend their life is to in effect betray them in this manner.

Referring to Lu Xun's play "The Passer-by," Takeuchi comments laconically, "Those who don't walk can never lose their way." This work concerns a mysterious traveler who in his wanderings comes across a girl and an old man who offer him water and briefly speak with him before he departs. Here Lu Xun is especially sensitive to the arrangement of time and light: the passerby arrives while the sun is still setting and leaves after it has fully gone. This focus on the sun's descent as brought about by the movement of time is but one part of the overall sense of decline that pervades the spatial setting. In the vicinity there can be seen what Lu Xun describes as some "desolate and dilapidated" *congzang*

(叢葬). This word is translated as "scrub" by both Yang and Yang and Takeuchi, whereas Leo Ou-fan Lee renders it as "wasteland."[70] I call attention to this term because its literal meaning is "mass burial." This is significant for two reasons: (1) It functions as a kind of foreshadowing device that anticipates the appearance of graves, which the old man informs the passerby lie ahead in precisely the same direction he is walking, and (2) Lu Xun's use of this word at the very opening of his work recalls his deployment of the character *si* (death) at the outset of the short stories "A Passing Storm" and "Tomorrow." At issue here is the insight that death is not to be located simply at the terminal point of an individual's existence. By commencing his work with an allusion to death, Lu Xun can be seen to reinforce the message he also conveys in "On Expressing an Opinion": that death is to be understood less as an actual event than as an intrinsic possibility. This decisive shift from actuality to possibility means that death must be situated most essentially at the initial moment of man's appearance in the world. Regardless of whether that world is an empirical or fictional one, Lu Xun insists that death is that which indelibly marks all things from the very beginning.

Directly following this description of the "scrub" is a brief sketch of a road that has long fallen into disuse. Lu Xun represents this figure of the landscape as *si lu fei lu de henji* (似路非路的痕跡). In Yang and Yang, this phrase appears as "a faint track" while Takeuchi translates it more literally as "the trace of a road that barely had form."[71] Even more precisely, however, Lu Xun is referring here to "the trace of that which resembled a road but that was not a road." Why is such molecular attention important? As we saw earlier, Lu Xun concludes the short story "My Old Home" with a meditation on the uncanny nature of the road, which "originally cannot be said to exist, nor can it be said not to exist." "The Passer-by" now repeats this same logic by pointing to something that "resembled a road but that was not a road." It is true that the signifier of negativity undergoes a transformation in these two texts from 無 to 非, but what is crucial is that this privileged notion of roads in Lu Xun is determined as that which is somehow not fully present to itself. Roads are neither there nor not there, vaguely like themselves but not entirely themselves.[72] From Takeuchi's perspective, Lu Xun's description of people as forced to create these elusive roads by walking upon them is representative of his view that praxis or action must be considered fundamental.

Both Lu Xun and Takeuchi are intent to think the "place of action" in its unique association with death, time, and negativity. In

"The Passer-by," Lu Xun reveals what conclusions are to be drawn from this focus on action with regard to the question of subjective identity. Here the passerby responds to the old man's simple question, "What is your name?"

> My name? That I don't know. Ever since I can remember, I've been on my own; so I don't know what my name was. As I go on my way, people call me by this name or that as the fancy takes them. But I can't remember them, and I have never been called by the same name twice.[73]

This same pattern continues when the passerby is then asked where he is from and where he is going. "I don't know" is the reply given to both queries. The unusual repetition of these words "I don't know" (*wo bu zhidao*, 我不知道) in the span of three brief questions serves to defamiliarize this everyday verb, forcing the reader to assess these characters from a more mediated and alien perspective. In this play about walking, Lu Xun seems to foreground the question of roads (道) in their relation to knowing (知), and his conviction that this latter comes to be enabled only through the former reinforces Takeuchi's assertion of the generality of the "place of action" vis-à-vis the more restricted "place of theoretical contemplation." When conceived radically, acts are not performed by a subject whose identity may be determined outside of that very action. All forms of knowledge, including that of self-knowledge, are made possible by epistemological acts, and so the ignorance displayed by the passerby is in fact a universal trait that is shared by the girl and old man alike.[74] Acts can only take place in time, but the incessant difference of time is such that each act must be succeeded by another if it is to maintain its efficacy in the world. This succession invariably alters the identity of the act, precluding any pure repetition. This is why Lu Xun's passerby has "never been called by the same (*xiangtong de*) name twice." Indeed, even the same name is uttered in circumstances that inevitably differ, however minimally, from those of the past. Such difference is not extraneous; it does not remain outside the propriety of the name itself. Just as each new step must differ from the last in order for walking to occur, so too do all matters of self-identity require constant confirmation if that self is to remain intact.

In his reference to Lu Xun's "Afterword to *Graves*," Takeuchi writes, "I do not know what I am doing. But I am doing something." As I stated, this remark appears to be a paraphrase of Lu Xun's confession that despite many years of hard work, "Even now, however, I still do not understand just what I have been doing all this time." Significantly, Lu Xun proceeds to develop this thought of knowing and doing through a sustained meditation on death. As he writes:

> It is like someone who digs for a living, who keeps working and working without understanding whether he is building a platform or digging a hole. Even if he knew it was in fact a platform, it would be just something he can fall off from or display himself on as he dies of old age. If it were digging a hole, then of course it would be for no other reason than to bury himself. In short, things pass away and pass away, every and all things pass away quickly like time; they are passing away and will pass away—that is all there is to it.[75]

The notion of death that Lu Xun presents here is not a simple one. At first glance, it appears that he is primarily concerned with the issue of human death, and perhaps specifically that of his own. Following this interpretation, Lu Xun might be seen to be wryly commenting on the absurdity involved in engaging in such arduous labor when death is ultimately the only thing that awaits. The work that one so diligently performs may eventually be realized in the form of literary works, but the comparison of such work with platforms and holes suggests that the writer is merely working himself to death, with the sole consolation being that he might use the fruits of those labors for narcissistic self-display. At the conclusion of this passage, however, Lu Xun suddenly broadens both the nature and object of such perishing. Death is now redetermined along vastly more general lines as a "passing away" (*shiqu*, 逝去), and what suffers such passing is not only people but "every and all things" (*yiqie yiqie*, 一切一切). Essential to this generalization of death is the notion of time with which Lu Xun compares the rapid disappearance of things. The word used in this context is not the more common *shijian* but rather *guangyin* (光陰), literally "light and shadow." Time, then, as the total movement brought about by the unceasing strife between light and darkness. In this conception, the phenomenon of passing away that happens to all things is not to be unilaterally reduced to the passage from light to darkness, for darkness itself must also pass away in order for light to be born. Here we return to the crucial issue of ghosts in Lu Xun, since the enigmatic transition that is "passing away" enables the occurrence of a certain survival of death that is nothing other than the memory of the dead that remains to haunt those in the present.

With the constant incursion of time, each act must be repeated if it is to continue producing effects in the world. This gives rise to a need to reconceptualize death as primarily affecting not the individual actant but rather these multiple acts themselves. If death only comes to Lu Xun's digger at the moment he falls from the platform or buries himself in his hole, then a lifetime of labor can be said to gain exemption from the "passing away" that otherwise affects all things. Yet Lu Xun firmly states that the scope of this passing is a general one. "Afterword to *Graves*" represents an attempt to recover those acts in order to make sense of their current meaning. Here Lu Xun gives the name "traces," which he writes alternately as *chenji* (陳迹) and *yuhen* (餘痕), to describe those remnants of a prior time that have somehow lived on into the present in an altered but still identifiable form. These near synonyms appear three times in "Afterword to *Graves*," as follows:

> I recall having said that these essays are nothing more than a few traces (*chenji*) of my life. If the things that have occurred in my past can be counted as actual living, then it can also be said that I have done some work.

> Yet, as long as I am still breathing, and as long as they are mine, I like gathering up the traces (*chenji*) from the past from time to time, knowing full well they are worthless; yet I can't help feeling some attachment to them.

> But for myself, I cannot firmly and decisively destroy them [i.e., my present collection of writings], wishing for the time being to use them to observe the remaining traces (*yuhen*) from a life that has passed by.[76]

In his turn back to the past, Lu Xun recognizes that the past actions performed by himself and others have now irrevocably passed away. From the vantage of the present, those actions possess the same status as the "graves" that Lu Xun uses as the very title of his book. In this regard, "Afterword to *Graves*" repeats the message so movingly conveyed in "My Old Home" that the past is a site from which one has been forever exiled. Just as the narrator in that short story realizes that his ability to survive the loss of his own past has come at the cost of part of himself, so too does the individual actant discover that each action he performs is immediately lost to him, thereby jeopardizing his identity as source of those actions. These deeds are now claimed by the past, where they exist merely as "traces" that are no longer purely identical to their original mode of appearing. It is because those actions are no longer precisely what they were that Lu Xun, as he confesses, "know[s] full well they are worthless." In their very disappearance, however, those acts can always possibly survive in a different form that nevertheless retains something that approximates their original identity. It is this effect of resemblance that incites in Lu Xun the desire for return: "Yet I can't help feeling some attachment to them." The ambivalence that he displays toward these traces of his own past is less proof of his own psychological complexity than a reflection of the very nature of the trace itself. For like the figure of the road at the conclusion of "My Old Home," the trace "originally cannot be said to exist, nor can it be said not to exist." Once they have "passed away," the traces of past action become worthless because they are not fully present, not fully our own. And yet insofar as they retain a modicum of sameness that allows us in the present to recognize them in their difference, they continue to provoke feelings of attachment.

In considering this division between his past self and present self and acknowledging that he belongs to neither, Lu Xun memorably identified himself as an "interstitial thing" (*zhongjian wu*, 中間物). As he proceeds to argue:

> But probably in large part out of laziness, I often take comfort in the fact that in all things as they change there are always a number of interstitial things. There are interstitial things between plant and animal life, and between invertebrates and vertebrates; actually, one can simply say that along the evolutionary chain, everything is an interstitial thing.[77]

In these lines we find Lu Xun enlarging the scope of his argument in a way that recalls his earlier remarks on death and "passing away." Just as destruction invariably goes beyond the level of individual humans to encompass "every and all things," so too does interstitiality exceed even the range of plant and animal life, invertebrates and vertebrates, to include "everything" (*yiqie*). And yet Lu Xun can be seen to pull back from this generality by restricting his claim to the "evolutionary chain," thereby focusing more narrowly on material things in their apparent objectivity. As he himself shows, however, the logic of the past trace must possess a greater generality if it is to bridge the gap between past and present, a preceding material or objective reality and its subsequent repetition in spiritual or subjective form. Here it is the trace that reveals itself to be the true "interstitial thing." Instead of being limited to the more or less fixed world of things, the trace allows events of the past to possibly survive their own demise and continue forward in time where they may be remarked and remembered otherwise. Released from its biologistic prejudice, the interstitial thing that is the trace puts into relation the past and the future, providing the chance for all things, events, and ideas to continue the differential trajectory of their lives. The desire for preservation that Lu Xun expresses in "Afterword to *Graves*" can be seen to apply to all of his texts. The traces that he wished to rescue from the past and transform into written traces in his own present can only appear to us now, in their futurity, by virtue of our own act of reading those writings and thus retracing them anew.

CONCLUSION

For Takeuchi, a conceptual focus on action does not seek to locate its presence in the here and now. While action can only take place in a now, that moment is fundamentally divided from itself. This leads to a seeming contradiction, Takeuchi realizes. On the one hand, each act performed must be singular since no other act can be identical to it. On the other hand, however, no act is ever performed in a vacuum, closed off from both the past and future in a hermetically sealed present. By putting into dialogue Takeuchi's privileged notion of the "place of action" with his thinking of history in the unorthodox terms of a "baton handoff," I seek to call attention to the conundrum of what might be called practical singularity. Whether performed consciously or not, each present act harkens back to a past that has shaped it, thereby creating a lineage in which its status is merely that of the most recent variation. In order to recognize this lineage and so understand the act in its contextual meaning, however, there must be a corresponding projection into a future in which the act may be determined retroactively.

Lu Xun confronts a similar temporal complexity when he reflects on the question of the trace. In his essay "Afterword to *Graves*," for example, one finds a powerful meditation on the ubiquity of death. Yet Lu Xun appears to generalize the notion of death beyond its biological meaning to include time itself. With each event of its demise, time passes away in the form of the past. Driven by the desire to recapture what was once his, however, Lu Xun perceives that the dead past can yet be accessed through its fossilized remains as traces. The past itself is destroyed, but remnants exist through which he may nevertheless animate what is otherwise permanently lost. The ardent wish to rescue that past from oblivion is what defines Lu Xun as a "writer," in the specific sense given this term by Takeuchi. By presently retracing those vestiges of the past, Lu Xun invariably alters what he aims to keep. As revealed with great poignancy in his fiction, however, Lu Xun recognizes that it is impossible to return to a time that has already passed. By inscribing that past, one necessarily changes it—and here we see that violence is inescapable from any act of commemoration. Paradoxically, however, time once captured in writing now comes to claim its revenge by demanding that legibility depend strictly on other times in the future. Despite Lu Xun's wish that his past be truthfully reproduced in the present, he is forced to acknowledge that the future now holds sway over those writings, and that at any moment they are vulnerable to misinterpretation and even destruction. Without this essential possibility of errancy, however, there can be no chance of reading Lu Xun at all.

The unsettling effects of time appear most vividly in Lu Xun's figure of the road, which, as he describes, "originally cannot be said to exist, nor can it be said not to exist." These words, which bore such a profound effect on Takeuchi's thinking, point to an instability that lies at the heart of all being. At issue here is not simply roads in their unique difference from other things. On the contrary, I interpret Lu Xun as endowing roads with a kind of exemplarity such as to disclose not a particular but rather general trait possessed by all things. Insofar as something exists, then, it experiences being strictly as an attenuated state that is at all times interlaced with nothing. However, such state, riven by negativity, is not to be opposed to a higher form of being characterized by the plenitude of presence. Both Lu Xun and Takeuchi insist that the only possible instance of being is one that is finite, and this finitude marks the individual thing throughout the course of its existence. Roads disappear, Lu Xun reminds us, but such disappearance must be grasped less as an actual event than as an intrinsic possibility that haunts that path from its initial appearance. Roads were created in the past, but at each new moment their use can be either continued or discontinued, and these decisions inevitably shape the existence of future generations. Through this privileged example of the road, Lu Xun and Takeuchi seek to guide their readers to a more historicized, and thus elusive, thinking of existence.

NOTES

INTRODUCTION

1. Jacques Derrida, *Aporias*, trans. Thomas Dutoit (Stanford, CA: Stanford University Press, 1993), 25; italics in the original. These same lines are quoted by Ethan Kleinberg in his important challenge to conventional historiographical practices in *Haunting History: For a Deconstructive Approach to the Past* (Stanford, CA: Stanford University Press, 2017), 8.

2. This would represent an additional difficulty of Ariès's research given that he appears to take for granted this notion of Western identity. See his *Western Attitudes towards Death: From the Middle Ages to the Present* (Baltimore: Johns Hopkins University Press, 1974).

3. *Before Identity: The Question of Method in Japan Studies* (Albany: State University of New York Press, 2021).

CHAPTER 1

1. Akira Kurosawa, *Something Like an Autobiography*, trans. Audie E. Bock (New York: Vintage, 1983), 96.

2. *Zenshū, Kurosawa Akira* [Complete works: Kurosawa Akira] (Tokyo: Iwanami shoten, 1988), 3:150. For an English translation of the screenplay, see *Modern Film Scripts: Ikiru, a Film by Akira Kurosawa*, ed. Donald Richie (New York: Simon and Schuster, 1968).

3. *Zenshū, Kurosawa Akira*, 3:150.

4. *Zenshū, Kurosawa Akira*, 3:149.

5. The significance of this action is aptly noted by Donald Richie in *The Films of Akira Kurosawa* (Berkeley: University of California Press, 1996), 232.

6. *Zenshū, Kurosawa Akira*, 3:185, 364.

7. *Zenshū, Kurosawa Akira*, 3:196.

8. This series of cuts clearly anticipates that of the six pan cuts that Kurosawa famously uses two years later in *Seven Samurai*. In the particular context of death, the major difference between the two series can be detected in the clear sense of dread experienced by the bureaucrats, which contrasts with the active confrontation with death as shown by the individual samurai running toward (what they mistakenly believe to be) battle.

9. *Zenshū, Kurosawa Akira.*, 3:153, 162.

10. *Zenshū, Kurosawa Akira*, 3:166.

11. See, for example, Nishimura Yūichirō's discussion of the Gondola Song in *Kurosawa Akira: oto to eizō* [Kurosawa Akira: Sound and image] (Tokyo: Rippū shobō, 1998), 144–146.

12. *Zenshū, Kurosawa Akira*, 3:360–361.

13. Such interpretation of individual death is attributed to Kurosawa by Damian Cox and Michael P. Levine in *Thinking through Film: Doing Philosophy, Watching Movies* (Chichester, UK: Wiley-Blackwell, 2012), 172.

14. G. W. F. Hegel, *Phenomenology of Spirit*, trans. A. V. Miller (Oxford: Oxford University Press, 1977), 271.

15. As James Goodwin notes, "Rather than use stressed optical or editing devices, however, Kurosawa accents the emotional and visual stimuli that prompt Watanabe's memories. The memorial altar and the photograph of his wife leads to recall of the funeral procession following the hearse." *Akira Kurosawa and Intertextual Cinema* (Baltimore: Johns Hopkins University Press, 1994), 151–152.

16. *Zenshū, Kurosawa Akira*, 3:159.

17. In this regard, Mitsuo's fears clearly bear comparison with those of little Ernst, whose repeated playing of the *fort/da* game as a way of coping with the painful absence of the parent is analyzed by Freud in *Beyond the Pleasure Principle*, trans. James Strachey (New York: W.W. Norton, 1961).

18. Maureen Turim provides a penetrating discussion of the flashback technique in general as well as its specific role in *Ikiru* in her *Flashbacks in Film: Memory and History* (New York: Routledge, 1989).

19. *Zenshū, Kurosawa Akira*, 3:157, 181. Visually, this presence of Japan is signaled most clearly in the collective waving of the Rising Sun flag when Mitsuo and the other soldiers are being sent off to war.

20. *Zenshū, Kurosawa Akira*, 3:149.

21. Mitsuhiro Yoshimoto, *Kurosawa: Film Studies and Japanese Cinema* (Durham, NC: Duke University Press, 2000), 201.

22. *Zenshū, Kurosawa Akira*, 3:174.

23. With regard to the director's depiction of Watanabe, it is perhaps noteworthy that this fall does not appear in the earlier version of the screenplay but was only subsequently added. *Zenshū, Kurosawa Akira*, 3:362.

24. Tadao Satō, *Currents in Japanese Cinema*, trans. Gregory Barrett (Tokyo: Kodansha, 1982), 116. This viewpoint was subsequently reinforced by Stephen Prince, who argues that "Watanabe will come to represent a powerfully subver-

sive example to established society" "by separating from, rebelling against, and rejecting the institutional frameworks of modern Japanese society." *The Warrior's Camera: The Cinema of Akira Kurosawa* (Princeton, NJ: Princeton University Press, 1991), 103, 107.

25. *Zenshū, Kurosawa Akira*, 3:184.

26. *Zenshū, Kurosawa Akira*, 3:183.

27. Watanabe's memorable words in this scene when dismissing the protests of his subordinates—"If you just have the will to do it" (*yaru ki ni nareba*)—points to a similar core or subjectivity. Just as the Citizens Section occupies the position of subject in the context of the municipal government, so too is the faculty of the will implicitly regarded in *Ikiru* as the defining factor in human subjectivity.

28. *Zenshū, Kurosawa Akira*, 3:184.

29. *Zenshū, Kurosawa Akira*, 3:154. The importance of this connection between succession and death is also signaled by the fact that Kurosawa reworks this line from an earlier version, which read, "Fifteen or sixteen people would need to die first before you two get a turn!" (see p. 356).

30. This point may be related to Satō Tadao's reading that, through *Ikiru*, Kurosawa was "attempting to send an ethical message to his contemporaries." *Kurosawa Akira no sekai* [The world of Kurosawa Akira] (Tokyo: San'ichi shobō, 1969), 166.

31. Shimura Takashi's mystified expression here reveals untold emotions, as he finds himself suddenly caught between two different times. As Kurosawa describes it, "This small act of caring reverberated within Watanabe's frozen heart with unexpected force." *Zenshū, Kurosawa Akira*, 3:172.

32. Akira Mizuta Lippit, *Cinema Without Reflection: Jacques Derrida's Echopoiesis and Narcissism Adrift* (Minneapolis: University of Minnesota Press, 2016), 44.

33. *Zenshū, Kurosawa Akira*, 3:158.

34. From a different standpoint, Michael Lucken offers a nuanced reading of the visual effects involved in this transition in his *Imitation and Creativity in Japanese Arts: From Kishida Ryūsei to Miyazaki Hayao*, trans. Francesca Simkin (New York: Columbia University Press, 2016), 108.

35. *Zenshū, Kurosawa Akira*, 3:181.

36. *Zenshū, Kurosawa Akira*, 3:181, 193, 195.

37. Nöel Burch points to an important line of inquiry in linking this shot of the deceased wife with the later close-ups of Watanabe's altar photograph. See Burch, *To the Distant Observer: Form and Meaning in the Japanese Cinema* (Berkeley: University of California Press, 1979), 306.

CHAPTER 2

1. Michael Berry, *Speaking in Images: Interviews with Contemporary Chinese Filmmakers* (New York: Columbia University Press, 2005), 387.

2. This question of resurrection in the context of Tsai's works is also underscored by Sun Songrong in *Rujing chujing: Tsai Ming-liang de yingxiang yishu yu kuajie shijian* [Frame in/frame out: Tsai Ming-liang's art of the image and transgressive practice] (Taipei: Wunan Tushu, 2014), 88–125.

3. Jiao Xiongping, *Heliu: Cai Mingliang de dianying* [The river: A film by Tsai Ming-liang] (Taipei: Huangguan, 1997), 140. The published script is at slight variance with the dialogue actually presented in the film. I am indebted to Ivy Chang and Li Chengfeng for their help in procuring a copy of this part of the script.

4. Rey Chow detects a similar link between past and future in Tsai's visual compositions. See Chow, *Sentimental Fabulations, Contemporary Chinese Films: Attachment in the Age of Global Visibility* (New York: Columbia University Press, 2007), 188–189.

5. Zhang Jingbei, *Bujian busan: Cai Mingliang yu Li Kangsheng* [The missing/goodbye, dragon inn: Tsai Ming-liang and Lee Kang-sheng] (Singapore: Bafang wenhua chuangzuo shi, 2004), 62. The published script is at slight variance with the dialogue actually presented in the film.

6. For a reading of such devolution that emphasizes the effects of urban demolition, see Gary G. Xu, *Sinascape: Contemporary Chinese Cinema* (Lanham, MD: Rowman & Littlefield, 2007), 89–110.

7. Jean-Pierre Rehm, Olivier Joyard, and Danièle Rivière, *Tsaï Ming-liang* (Paris: Dis Voir, 1999), 104–105.

8. Rehm, Joyard, and Rivière, *Tsaï Ming-liang*, 107–108.

9. This point does not appear to be uniformly accepted in the secondary literature on Tsai Ming-liang. For instance, Fran Martin, who is otherwise a gifted reader of Tsai, formulates the notion of "temporal dysphoria" in such a way as to divorce time from space: "a disorientation in relation to time rather than space." See Martin, "The European Undead: Tsai Ming-liang's Temporal Dysphoria," in *Senses of Cinema* (website), accessed May 2020, http://sensesofcinema.com/2003/feature-articles/tsai_european_undead/. By way of contrast, Andrea Bachner seems closer to Tsai when she writes of "the impossibility of conceiving of space and time as two distinct categories." See Bachner, "Cinema as Heterochronos: Temporal Folds in the Work of Tsai Ming-liang." *Modern Chinese Literature and Culture* 19, no. 1 (Spring 2007), 61.

10. Erin Y. Huang devotes a chapter to Tsai's work from the perspective of the notion of precarity in *Urban Horror: Neoliberalism, Post-Socialism, and the Limits of Visibility* (Durham, NC: Duke University Press, 2020), 184–217.

11. Here a reference to the well-known passage in Derrida appears unavoidable. As he writes in reply to Lacan: "A letter does *not always* arrive at its destination, and from the moment that this possibility belongs to its structure one can say that it never truly arrives, that when it does arrive its capacity not to arrive torments it with an internal drifting." See Jacques Derrida, *The Post-*

card: From Socrates to Freud and Beyond, trans. Alan Bass (Chicago: University of Chicago Press, 1987), 489.

12. Léaud performed this role of Antoine Doinel over the next twenty years, appearing in one short (*Antoine and Colette* [1962]) and three features (*Stolen Kisses* [1968], *Bed and Board* [1970], and *Love on the Run* [1979]).

13. Although there can be no question of direct influence between Tsai and his predecessors in the New Taiwan Cinema movement, it nevertheless bears remarking that Edward Yang's 1986 *Kongbufenzi* (*Terrorizers*), a film that focuses on the similar themes of ghosts and return, includes a virtually identical scene in which the protagonist papers over all the external light from his apartment window.

14. Rehm, Joyard, and Rivière, *Tsaï Ming-liang*, 113.

15. One of the most scandalous aspects of *Visage* can be seen in the diligence with which Tsai performs his role as agent of death vis-à-vis his cast. As Salome, Laetitia Casta's violence is limited to her decapitation of Hsiao Kang (who is thus equated with John the Baptist). In various forms, however, Tsai subtly stages the death of nearly all of his major actors throughout the film. The message conveyed is clear: neither fame nor wealth can safeguard one from death.

16. Berry, *Speaking in Images*, 387.

17. The films in which this paternal relationship is presented include *Rebels of the Neon God*, *The River*, and *What Time is it There?*

18. In his fine essay, "'Nezha Was Here': Structures of Dis/placement in Tsai Ming-liang's *Rebels of the Neon God*," Carlos Rojas provides an alternative reading of this tool that emphasizes the physical sense of the protagonist's enclosure: "For Xiaokang, the compass not only symbolizes the math homework for which he is presumably using it (and, by implication, the parental and institutional strictures by which he clearly feels confined), but also, more abstractly, suggests the physical boundaries of his bedroom, his home, and even of the Taipei neighborhood through which he moves—all of which both delimit his physical movement and define his identity (that is, specifying his own figurative radius and point of origin)." See Rojas, *Modern Chinese Literature and Culture* 15, no. 1 (Spring 2003): 73.

19. This vigilance, notably, does not preclude the possibility of humor. Thus we listen to the comical exchange between Chen Shiang-chyi and the restaurant waitress in *The Skywalk is Gone* about the various items that have disappeared from the menu. In *Visage*, similarly, comedy pervades the scenes in which Fanny Ardant loses a shoe and a deer while Nathalie Baye misplaces an earring.

20. Song Hwee Lim reads this pivotal scene from the perspective of Buddhist-Taoist symbolism in *Tsai Ming-liang and a Cinema of Slowness* (Honolulu: University of Hawai'i Press, 2014), 107–108.

21. Jean Ma describes Léaud here as a "doubled presence across the two cities, a virtual phantom of history confined to the television screen in the one

and an actual living presence in the other." See Ma, *Melancholy Drift: Marking Time in Chinese Cinema* (Hong Kong: Hong Kong University Press, 2010), 75.

22. While it seems undeniable that Tsai's primary interest lies in the filiative relation between father and son, there can nevertheless be seen important instances of filiation and following between figurative mothers and daughters in, for example, *The Skywalk is Gone, Visage,* and the 2013 film *Jiaoyou (Stray Dogs).*

CHAPTER 3

1. "Wuchang," in *Lu Xun zuopin quanji* [Complete works of Lu Xun] (Taipei: Fengyun Shidai, 1996), 4:53; "Wu Chang, or Life-is-Transient," in *Selected Works of Lu Hsun,* trans. Yang Hsien-yi and Gladys Yang (Peking: Foreign Languages, 1957), 1:385.

2. See here above all the 1948 essay "Kindai toha nanika (Nihon to Chūgoku no baai)" [What is modernity? (The case of Japan and China)], in *Takeuchi Yoshimi zenshū* [Complete works of Takeuchi Yoshimi] (Tokyo: Chikuma shobō, 1980), 4:128–171; Richard F. Calichman, trans., *What is Modernity? Writings of Takeuchi Yoshimi* (New York: Columbia University Press, 2005), 53–81.

3. *Takeuchi Yoshimi zenshū,* 1:172.

4. *Takeuchi Yoshimi zenshū,* 1:172.

5. *Takeuchi Yoshimi zenshū,* 1:3. For a succinct account of Lu Xun's sickness and death, see Cao Juren, *Lu Xun de yisheng: Zhongguo jindai wenxueshi de ceying* [Lu Xun's Lifetime: A profile in modern Chinese literary history] (Taipei: Xinchaoshe, 1987), 144–157.

6. See, for example, Kan Takayuki, *Takeuchi Yoshimi ron: Ajia he no hanka* (On Takeuchi Yoshimi: An envoy to Asia) (Tokyo: San'ichi shobō, 1976). As Kan writes, "Having encountered Lu Xun, Takeuchi did not so much research him as *live him* . . . Takeuchi tried to see Lu Xun as a writer instead of viewing him in the context of his ideas (as a conceptual system) or his literature (in the form of his individual works), and clearly this standpoint corresponds to the very nature of Lu Xun's life. By regarding Lu Xun in this manner, Takeuchi was in no way merely the subject of analysis. If Takeuchi's study of Lu Xun consisted of actually living him, then the flesh and blood Takeuchi also had to live like Lu Xun" (p. 62; italics in the original).

7. *Takeuchi Yoshimi zenshū,* 1:3–4. In his essay "Displacing Japan: Takeuchi Yoshimi's Lu Xun in Light of Nishida's Philosophy, and Vice Versa," Christian Uhl quotes and provides a rigorous analysis of this same passage in its connection to the thought of the Kyoto school philosopher Nishida Kitarō. *Philosophy and the Political in Wartime Japan, 1931–1945,* special issue of *Positions: East Asia Cultures Critique* 17, no. 1 (Spring 2009): 218–220.

8. *Takeuchi Yoshimi zenshū*, 1:180–181.

9. In a similar vein, the critic Yoshimoto Takaaki characterizes Takeuchi's thought as Hegelian in "Jōkyō he no hatsugen—Takeuchi Yoshimi ni tsuite," *Shikō*, #50, June 30, 1978, p. 5 (cited in Lawrence Olson, *Ambivalent Moderns: Portraits of Japanese Cultural Identity* (Lanham, MD: Rowman and Littlefield, 1992), 163, n. 64).

10. See here the remarkable work by Françoise Dastur, *How Are We to Confront Death? An Introduction to Philosophy*, trans Robert Vallier (New York: Fordham University Press, 2012). As Dastur claims on p. 6, "Disposing of the corpse in order to allow for the reestablishment of a virtual relation with the deceased is the profound meaning of funeral rites."

11. This appeal to the notion of spirit in the attempt to find meaning in Lu Xun's death is continued several years later in Takeuchi's 1953 work *Ro Jin nyūmon* [Introduction to Lu Xun]: "Lu Xun's death appeared suddenly and meaningfully. The occurrence of his death was such that it is appropriate to use the word 'appeared.' It wasn't that his life was lost, but rather that his lost life was reborn. His spirit (*seishin*) lived on in the hearts of thousands of people. It produced a force that sustained the eight-year war of resistance." See *Takeuchi Yoshimi zenshū*, 2:74–75.

12. *Lu Xun zuopin quanji* 19:195–196; Eileen J. Cheng and Kirk A. Denton, trans. and eds., *Jottings Under Lamplight: Lu Xun* (Cambridge, MA: Harvard University Press, 2017), 66.

13. *Lu Xun zuopin quanji* 9:95; *Jottings Under Lamplight: Lu Xun*, 72.

14. "Yi Wei Suyuan jun" [In memory of Wei Suyuan] and "Lun 'renyan kewei' " [On "Gossip is a Fearful Thing"], in *Lu Xun zuopin quanji* 17:75–84 and 18:149–153; *Jottings Under Lamplight: Lu Xun*, 90–94, 95–98.

15. *Lu Xun zuopin quanji*, 9:111–118 and 14:85–100; *Jottings Under Lamplight: Lu Xun*, 74–78, 79–89.

16. *Lu Xun zuopin quanji*, 2:105; Julia Lovell, trans., *The Real Story of Ah-Q and other Tales of China: The Complete Fiction of Lu Xun* (London: Penguin, 2009), 232. The particular term for "funeral" that Lu Xun uses here is *song lian*, literally a "sending off to the coffin."

17. *Lu Xun zuopin quanji*, 2:106; *The Real Story of Ah-Q and Other Tales of China: The Complete Fiction of Lu Xun*, 233.

18. *Lu Xun zuopin quanji*, 2:108; *The Real Story of Ah-Q and Other Tales of China: The Complete Fiction of Lu Xun*, 235.

19. *Lu Xun zuopin quanji*, 2:131; *The Real Story of Ah-Q and Other Tales of China: The Complete Fiction of Lu Xun*, 252. Translation slightly modified.

20. After describing the narrator's lupine howl of grief, Lu Xun ends the story by showing how the narrator now experiences a sense of psychological ease or relief. In his well-known study *The Limits of Realism: Chinese Fiction in the Revolutionary Period* (Berkeley: University of California Press, 1990), Marston Anderson suggests that this conclusion represents a significant moment of catharsis:

"The narrator of 'The Misanthrope' [i.e., 'The Loner' (this title was originally given to the work in *Selected Works of Lu Hsun*, 1:212)] unexpectedly cries out in 'anger and sorrow mingled with agony' upon seeing his friend Wei Lianshu's corpse laid out, but 'then my heart felt lighter, and I paced calmly on along the damp cobbled road under the moon.' These passages can only represent the cathartic moment in which the narrator's weighty sense of identification with a victimized friend or acquaintance is exorcised" (see pp. 89–90).

My reading departs from Anderson's in that the logic of spectrality that I develop renders impossible any notion of purity, as appears in the above reference to catharsis and exorcism. Because of the constancy with which the dead spectrally inhabit the living, any moment of psychological cleansing or purgation must be seen for essential reasons to be already undercut from within.

21. *Takeuchi Yoshimi zenshū*, 1:105–106.

22. *Takeuchi Yoshimi zenshū*, 2:55.

23. *Takeuchi Yoshimi zenshū*, 2:55. Upon concluding these lines, Takeuchi immediately introduces a vital difference between Lu Xun and Lianshu: "However, Lu Xun does not affirm the 'loner's' philosophy. The 'loner' is destroyed. (He destroys himself.)"

24. This identification is repeated by William A. Lyell Jr. in *Lu Hsün's Vision of Reality* (Berkeley: University of California Press, 1976): "Wei is perhaps the closest to a self-portrait of all the intellectuals in Lu Hsün's stories" (see p. 187).

25. *Lu Xun zuopin quanji*, 2:117; *The Real Story of Ah-Q and Other Tales of China: The Complete Fiction of Lu Xun*, 242. Translation slightly modified.

26. Takeuchi's attempt to think of negativity in its status as foundational clearly echoes Lu Xun's own conception in "The Loner." At issue here is a discussion between Lianshu and the narrator regarding the nature of evil in children. For Lianshu, children are by nature good, and it is only through the fault of nurturing that they subsequently become evil. The narrator vigorously disagrees with this opinion: "But if children don't have the roots of evil already in them, how come they go on to produce the fruits and flowers of evil? A seed produces branches, leaves, or fruit or flowers of a certain sort because it carries them inside as embryos." *Lu Xun zuopin quanji*, 2:111; *The Real Story of Ah-Q and Other Tales of China: The Complete Fiction of Lu Xun*, 237–238.

Takeuchi would certainly side with the narrator in this argument. From the standpoint that he shares with Lu Xun, Lianshu's view can only be seen as a desperate wish to "seek salvation from the outside."

27. *Lu Xun zuopin quanji*, 19:147; *Selected Works of Lu Hsun*, 1:429.

28. *Lu Xun zuopin quanji*, 19:196; *Jottings Under Lamplight: Lu Xun*, 67.

29. *Lu Xun zuopin quanji*, 19:196; *Jottings Under Lamplight: Lu Xun*, 67.

30. *Takeuchi Yoshimi zenshū*, 1:136, 192.

31. Hence, for example, the very title of the 1949 essay "Shisōka toshite no Ro Jin" (Lu Xun as thinker). See *Takeuchi Yoshimi zenshū*, 1:158–163.

32. The reference is of course to Hegel: "Spirit has won the pure element of its existence, the Notion. The content, in accordance with the *freedom* of its *being*, is the self-alienating Self, or the immediate unity of self-knowledge . . . The distinct content, as *determinate*, is in relation, is not 'in itself'; it is its own restless process of superseding itself, or *negativity*." *Phenomenology of Spirit*, trans. A. V. Miller (Oxford: Oxford University Press, 1977), 490–491 (italics in the original).

33. *Takeuchi Yoshimi zenshū*, 1:6. Nakagawa Ikurō provides a thoughtful reading of this passage in his *Takeuchi Yoshimi no bungaku to shisō* [Takeuchi Yoshimi's literature and thought] (Tokyo: Orijin, 1985), 108–110.

34. *Lu Xun*, in *Takeuchi Yoshimi zenshū*, 1:7–8.

35. *Introduction to Lu Xun*, in *Takeuchi Yoshimi zenshū*, 2:73.

36. "On 'Diary of a Madman,'" in *Takeuchi Yoshimi zenshū*, 1:225.

37. For a thorough examination of Lu Xun's relation to evolutionary theory, see James Reeve Pusey, *Lu Xun and Evolution* (Albany: State University of New York Press, 1998).

38. See the following passage from "Lu Xun as Thinker": "Lu Xun is not a systematic thinker. He has neither a theory of literature nor a literary history. . . . His fiction is poetic and his criticism based on sensibility (*kanseiteki*). Even temperamentally, he is distant from conceptual thinking." *Takeuchi Yoshimi zenshū*, 1:158. I undertake a reading of these lines in *Takeuchi Yoshimi: Displacing the West* (Ithaca, NY: Cornell East Asia Series, 2004), 99–105.

39. From a different standpoint, Rey Chow offers a perceptive analysis of guilt in the work of Lu Xun in *Woman and Chinese Modernity: The Politics of Reading Between West and East* (Minneapolis: University of Minnesota Press, 1991), 107–112.

40. For a recent study of this problem, see Ethan Kleinberg's important book *Haunting History: For a Deconstructive Approach to the Past* (Stanford, CA: Stanford University Press, 2017).

41. *Lu Xun zuopin quanji*, 3:67–68; *Selected Works of Lu Hsun*, 1:345. Translation slightly modified.

42. Martin Heidegger, *Being and Time*, trans. John Macquarrie and Edward Robinson (New York: Harper & Row, 1962), 354. Italics in the original.

43. My reading of "On Expressing an Opinion" in its aspect of the pathos of finitude differs considerably from the conclusion reached by Bonnie S. McDougall, who finds the tale "aggressively sarcastic." *Love Letters and Privacy in Modern China: The Intimate Lives of Lu Xun and Xu Guangping* (Oxford: Oxford University Press, 2002), 38.

44. And not only the question of when, Lu Xun reminds us, but also that of where. As he writes in the 1925 prose poem "Sihou" (After death): "'Why should he die *here*?' I heard someone ask. The voice was so near that the speaker must be bending over me. But where should a man die? I used to think although a man could not choose where he would live, he could at least

die wherever he pleased. Now I learned this was not the case." *Lu Xun zuopin quanji*, 3:71–72; *Selected Works of Lu Hsun*, 1:348. Italics in the original.

From a very different tradition, albeit one that was also decisive for Takeuchi, the philosopher Tanabe Hajime argues as follows: "That is to say, the fact of our living is the fact of our dying. Just as in the case of good and evil, life and death are intrinsically linked. Since we think we are simply living, we fear death; but death is always connected with life. If death did not enter into life at all, and if one just came to die after the flow of life has been interrupted, then death would be no problem. Death becomes a problem precisely because life and death are intertwined. I may die tomorrow or die next year. The fact of my dying is indeed already decided; it is simply uncertain now as to when I will die." See "A New Stage in Historical Reality," in *Sourcebook for Modern Japanese Philosophy: Selected Documents*, trans. and ed. David A. Dilworth et al. (Westport, CT: Greenwood, 1998), 114.

Takeuchi notes his reading of Tanabe at several points in his diary, and on one occasion remarks upon the importance of Tanabe's ideas for his own thought. See *Takeuchi Yoshimi zenshū*, 16:12.

CHAPTER 4

1. "Qisi," in *Lu Xun zuopin quanji*, 5:156; "Bringing Back the Dead," in *The Real Story of Ah-Q and Other Tales of China: The Complete Fiction of Lu Xun*, 394.

2. *Takeuchi Yoshimi zenshū*, 2:35.

3. *Takeuchi Yoshimi zenshū*, 14:448. As Christian Uhl rightly points out, much of the philosophical terminology in this essay reflects the influence of Nishida Kitarō, whose works Takeuchi was assiduously reading at the time. See *Positions: East Asia Cultures Critique*, 216–217.

4. In his review of the Chinese Literature Research Association, Samuel Guex describes Takeuchi's well-known severity of judgment as "the refusal of all compromise, a desire for integrity that was not devoid of a certain naiveté." *Entre nonchalance et désespoir: Les intellectuels japonais sinologues face à la guerre (1930–1950)* (Berne: Peter Lang, 2006), 45.

5. Heidegger, *Being and Time*, 294.

6. See here Derrida's meticulous reading of Aristotle and Hegel in "*Ousia* and *Grammē*: Note on a Note from *Being and Time*," in *Margins of Philosophy*, trans. Alan Bass (Chicago: University of Chicago Press, 1982), 29–67.

7. *Takeuchi Yoshimi zenshū*, 1:61.

8. In these two chapters, I have chosen not to pursue the specific question of the death of animals. Perhaps the most famous example of such death in Lu Xun's work can be seen in his 1922 short story "Tu he mao" (A cat among

the rabbits), where the narrator finds himself unexpectedly distraught by the killing of two baby rabbits. As he reflects, "Then who is to blame? The Creator, perhaps: for generating, then destroying life with such irresponsible excess." *Lu Xun zuopin quanji*, 1:182; *The Real Story of Ah-Q and Other Tales of China: The Complete Fiction of Lu Xun*, 143.

   9. *Lu Xun zuopin quanji*, 2:40; *The Real Story of Ah-Q and Other Tales of China: The Complete Fiction of Lu Xun*, 188. Translation slightly modified.

   10. *Lu Xun zuopin quanji*, 3:30; *Selected Works of Lu Hsun*, 1:325. Takeuchi quotes these lines in *Lu Xun*, in *Takeuchi Yoshimi zenshū*, 1:102.

   11. *Lu Xun zuopin quanji*, 1:66; *Selected Works of Lu Hsun*, 1:52–53. The subtlety with which Lu Xun incorporates these references to death can be seen in the fact that this pivotal word "death" does not appear in either of these passages in Julia Lovell's otherwise excellent newer translation. See *The Real Story of Ah-Q and Other Tales of China: The Complete Fiction of Lu Xun*, 62.

   12. *Introduction to Lu Xun*, in *Takeuchi Yoshimi zenshū*, 2:126. Takeuchi also refers to the tale's critique of traditional Chinese medicine, a point that is frequently raised in the secondary scholarship on Lu Xun.

   13. *Lu Xun zuopin quanji*, 1:41; *Selected Works of Lu Hsun*, 1:40; *The Real Story of Ah-Q and Other Tales of China: The Complete Fiction of Lu Xun*, 46.

   14. *Lu Xun zuopin quanji*, 1:49; *Selected Works of Lu Hsun*, 1:48. Translation slightly modified.

   15. As Lu Xun specifies, this opening onto the future must be understood in the sense of radical contingency and the accompanying loss of subjective certitude. As he writes at the conclusion of "Upstairs in the Tavern": " 'So what are your plans for the future?' 'The future? . . . I've no idea. Have any of the dreams we once had come to anything? Right now I don't know anything, not even how tomorrow will be nor even the next minute.' " In *Lu Xun zuopin quanji*, 2:106; *The Real Story of Ah-Q and Other Tales of China: The Complete Fiction of Lu Xun*, 187. Translation slightly modified.

   16. See, for example, Huang Sung-K'ang, *Lu Hsün and the New Culture Movement of Modern China* (Westport, CT: Hyperion, 1975), 69. In Huang's view, it was the force of Lu Xun's "great humanitarianism" that "not only offset the negative aspects of reality which he had placed before the eyes of his readers but also summoned them to shoulder their heavy and yet glorious responsibility as heralds of a new age."

   17. This insight, I believe, lies at the very center of Derrida's thinking. See, among many other texts, "My Chances/Mes Chances: A Rendezvous with some Epicurean Stereophonies," in *Taking Chances: Derrida, Psychoanalysis, and Literature*, eds. Joseph H. Smith and William Kerrigan, trans. Irene Harvey and Avital Ronnell (Baltimore: Johns Hopkins University Press, 1984), 1–32.

   In the scholarship on deconstruction, Martin Hägglund has above all mined this aspect with the greatest rigor and clarity. See his *Radical Atheism: Derrida and the Time of Life* (Stanford, CA: Stanford University Press, 2008) and *Dying for Time: Proust, Woolf, Nabokov* (Cambridge, MA: Harvard University Press, 2012).

18. See, for example, Takeuchi's "Lu Xun as Thinker": "Lu Xun could not believe in a good that existed in opposition to evil." In *Takeuchi Yoshimi zenshū*, 1:162.

19. *Lu Xun zuopin quanji*, 3:75–76; *Selected Works of Lu Hsun*, 1:351–352.

20. *Takeuchi Yoshimi zenshū*, 1:103–104.

21. *Takeuchi Yoshimi zenshū*, 1:162.

22. *Ro Jin, Mu Jun: sekai bungaku taikei 62* (Lu Xun, Mao Dun: The system of world literature 62), trans. Takeuchi Yoshimi et al. (Tokyo: Chikuma Shobō, 1958), 180. For a study of Takeuchi's notion of translation, see Leo Tak-hung Chan, "Japanization and the Chinese 'Madman': Triangulating Takeuchi Yoshimi's Philosophy of Translation," in *Translation Studies* 9 (2016): 1–16, n. 1.

23. *Lu Xun zuopin quanji*, 3:6; *Selected Works of Lu Hsun*, 1:316–317.

24. *Ro Jin, Mu Jun: sekai bungaku taikei 62*, 164–165.

25. *Lu Xun zuopin quanji*, 6:326; *Jottings Under Lamplight: Lu Xun*, 32.

26. *Lu Xun zuopin quanji*, 6:326; *Jottings Under Lamplight: Lu Xun*, 32–33.

27. *Ro Jin, Mu Jun: sekai bungaku taikei 62*, 202.

28. *Lu Xun zuopin quanji*, 2:30; *The Real Story of Ah-Q and Other Tales of China: The Complete Fiction of Lu Xun*, 182.

29. *Ro Jin, Mu Jun: Sekai bungaku taikei 62*, 76. It should be noted that Takeuchi slightly revises this phrase in the retranslation of Lu Xun he conducted in his later years. There the expression is rendered more simply as *nain da, kage mo katachi mo. Ro Jin bunshū* (Collected writings of Lu Xun) (Tokyo: Chikuma shobō, 1979), 1:234.

30. As Henry Staten argues, "More primordial than the thought of the body of pleasure or of the 'body in pain' is that of the body of dissolution." See Staten's astonishing *Eros in Mourning: Homer to Lacan* (Baltimore: Johns Hopkins University Press, 1995), 59.

31. *Lu Xun zuopin quanji*, 1:181–182; *The Real Story of Ah-Q and Other Tales of China: The Complete Fiction of Lu Xun*, 142.

32. For a recent study that attempts to situate Lu Xun's literary work within its era of historical brutality, see Gloria Davies, *Lu Xun's Revolution: Writing in a Time of Violence* (Cambridge, MA: Harvard University Press, 2013).

33. *Takeuchi Yoshimi zenshū*, 1:172–173.

34. *Takeuchi Yoshimi zenshū*, 14:450. Several pages earlier in this essay (p. 446), Takeuchi disassembles this character to its component parts to form the compound *kōsei* (更生), which functions as a synonym of *yomigaeru*: "I merely wanted two things: to withdraw myself and for the journal to be reborn."

35. *Lu Xun zuopin quanji*, 3:35–36; *Selected Works of Lu Hsun*, 1:328.

36. *Takeuchi Yoshimi zenshū*, 1:103. In the later translation in *Ro Jin, Mu Jun: sekai bungaku taikei 62*, Takeuchi renders these verbs in hiragana as opposed

to the earlier use of kanji (see p. 170). This practice is continued in the final *Ro Jin bunshū* (2:28), although there the second appearance of the verb is given in the present rather than past tense.

37. *Ro Jin bunshū*, 1:59.

38. The literature on this topic is vast, encompassing a wide range of geographic regions and historical periods. But see, for example, Franziska Seraphim, *War Memory and Social Politics in Japan, 1945–2005* (Cambridge, MA: Harvard East Asia Monographs, 2006). Let me stress that I am very much in agreement with the progressive politics that inform this type of research. My reservation springs solely from my conviction that research on memory cannot continue to ignore the long history of philosophical reflection on time.

39. In an extremely rare passage, Lu Xun issues a veiled critique of the notion of subjectivity by means of an opinion delivered by a fatuous government official: "The common people, after all, exist in the most benighted state of ignorance and emotional superficiality, possessing not a scrap of the profundity that wiser minds project on to them. Subjectivity (*zhuguan*) is the key to judging men and their times." See "Lishui" (Taming the floods), in *Lu Xun zuopin quanji*, 5:49; *The Real Story of Ah-Q and Other Tales of China: The Complete Fiction of Lu Xun*, 329.

In Takeuchi, by contrast, the attack against subjectivity is explicit and frequent. In its most distilled form, however, it can be seen in the opposition that Takeuchi draws between what he calls the "place of contemplation" (*kansō no ba*) and the "place of action" (*kōi no ba*). *Introduction to Lu Xun*, in *Takeuchi Yoshimi zenshū*, 2:58. I return to this distinction later in the chapter.

40. *Takeuchi Yoshimi zenshū*, 1:180.

41. *Takeuchi Yoshimi zenshū*, 1:152.

42. *Takeuchi Yoshimi zenshū*, 2:38.

43. In a more humorous vein, Takeuchi's apparent confusion as to whether Lu Xun is actually alive or dead might be seen to derive from this same ambiguity in Lu Xun himself. In his 1951 article "Kodoku naru henrekisha" (The lonely pilgrim) (*Takeuchi Yoshimi zenshū*, 1:264), Takeuchi recounts the famous anecdote told by a dying Lu Xun in his essay "Death": "Probably because my illness had dragged on for so long and my health seemed so precarious, a few friends secretly came up with a plan to ask Dr. D, an American citizen, to examine me. He is the only European tuberculosis specialist in Shanghai. After tapping my body and listening to my heart and lungs, he praised me as a typical specimen of the Chinese, with a most remarkable resistance to disease. Yet he also pronounced that my death was near at hand, adding that had I been European, I would have died five or six years ago. This verdict made my more sensitive friends shed tears. I didn't ask the doctor for a prescription because I thought that since his medical training had been done in Europe, he would surely not have learned to write a prescription for a patient who had already been dead for five years." *Lu Xun zuopin quanji*, 19:194–195; *Jottings Under Lamplight: Lu Xun*, 65–66.

44. *Lu Xun zuopin quanji*, 1:56; *The Real Story of Ah-Q and Other Tales of China: The Complete Fiction of Lu Xun*, 56–57. Translation slightly modified.

45. *Lu Xun zuopin quanji*, 1:61; *The Real Story of Ah-Q and Other Tales of China: The Complete Fiction of Lu Xun*, 60. Translation slightly modified.

46. *Lu Xun zuopin quanji*, 1: i; *The Real Story of Ah-Q and Other Tales of China: The Complete Fiction of Lu Xun*, 15. Translation slightly modified.

47. *Lu Xun zuopin quanji*, 6:327; *Jottings Under Lamplight: Lu Xun*, 34.

48. *Introduction to Lu Xun*, in *Takeuchi Yoshimi zenshū*, 2:3–4.

49. Takeuchi Yoshimi, *Ro Jin (shinpan)* (Lu Xun [new edition]) (Tokyo: Miraisha, 2002), 220.

50. See also on this point Okayama Asako, *Takeuchi Yoshimi no bungaku seishin* (Takeuchi Yoshimi's literary spirit) (Tokyo: Ronsōsha, 2002), 96–102.

51. Takeuchi Yoshimi, *Ro Jin (shinpan)*, 226. Italics in the original.

52. Eileen J. Cheng, *Literary Remains: Death, Trauma, and Lu Xun's Refusal to Mourn* (Honolulu: University of Hawai'i Press, 2013), 220.

53. *Literary Remains: Death, Trauma, and Lu Xun's Refusal to Mourn*, 224–225; *Lu Xun zuopin quanji*, 3:62.

54. *Literary Remains: Death, Trauma, and Lu Xun's Refusal to Mourn*, 225. For a recent examination of this issue of inscription in the context of China, see Andrea Bachner, *Beyond Sinology: Chinese Writing and the Scripts of Cultures* (New York: Columbia University Press, 2014).

55. *Takeuchi Yoshimi zenshū*, 1:113. The quotation "Despair, like hope, is an illusion" is originally taken from the Hungarian poet Sándor Petöfi, whom Lu Xun quotes to this effect in several places.

56. At the same time, however, we must recognize that Takeuchi's thinking contains an undeniable element of cultural particularism, as for example when he attempts to present Chinese literature as the simple converse of Japanese literature. See on this point the 1948 essay "Seiji to bungaku no mondai (Nihon bungaku to Chūgoku bungaku I)" (The question of politics and literature [Japanese literature and Chinese literature I]), in *Takeuchi Yoshimi zenshū* 4:102–115; *What is Modernity? Writings of Takeuchi Yoshimi*, 83–92. For the most sophisticated discussion of this problem both within and beyond Takeuchi, see Naoki Sakai, *Translation and Subjectivity: On "Japan" and Cultural Nationalism* (Minneapolis: University of Minnesota Press, 1997), 153–176.

57. *Takeuchi Yoshimi zenshū*, 1:47.

58. *Takeuchi Yoshimi zenshū*, 2:38–39; *Lu Xun zuopin quanji*, 30:18–19; *Love Letters and Privacy in Modern China: The Intimate Lives of Lu Xun and Xu Guangping*, 131. Translation slightly modified.

59. *Takeuchi Yoshimi zenshū*, 2:39. Two points need to be added here: (1) Takeuchi's quotation of Lu Xun's "Afterword to *Graves*" appears to be a paraphrase of the lines "A portion of my life has been spent this way, that is, on doing this sort of work. Even now, however, I still do not understand just what

I have been doing all this time" (*Lu Xun zuopin quanji*, 6:324; *Jottings Under Lamplight: Lu Xun*, 31); and (2) Takeuchi retains here the original Chinese in his use of the term *zhengzha*, which he otherwise famously translates as *teikō*.

60. *Iwanami tetsugaku shisō jiten* (The Iwanami dictionary of philosophy and thought), ed. Hiromatsu Wataru et al. (Tokyo: Iwanami shoten, 1998), 283–284.

61. *Takeuchi Yoshimi zenshū*, 1:13. In her powerful book *Takeuchi Yoshimi to iu toi* (The question of Takeuchi Yoshimi) (Tokyo: Iwanami shoten, 2005), Sun Ge concurs that Takeuchi's thinking must be characterized by this disruption of binarity (xxv).

62. Leo Ou-fan Lee, *Voices from the Iron House: A Study of Lu Xun* (Bloomington: Indiana University Press, 1987), 69–88.

63. *Lu Xun zuopin quanji*, 1:90; *Selected Works of Lu Hsun*, 1:75. (Here I have used the earlier Yang and Yang translation rather than the Lovell because it follows more closely the original Chinese.) Translation slightly modified.

64. *Lu Xun zuopin quanji*, 1:77–78; *The Real Story of Ah-Q and Other Tales of China: The Complete Fiction of Lu Xun*, 70.

65. *Takeuchi Yoshimi zenshū*, 2:360–361. In the secondary scholarship on Lu Xun, it is not uncommon to find this figure of roads used as a symbol for his life and work. See, for instance, in the collection *Lu Xun* (Taipei: Guangfu shuju, 1990) the essay by Zhou Yushan is entitled "Lu Xun zouguo de lu" (The road traveled by Lu Xun), 13–30.

66. *Lu Xun zuopin quanji*, 1:89–90; *The Real Story of Ah-Q and Other Tales of China: The Complete Fiction of Lu Xun*, 78. Translation slightly modified.

67. This particular word *houbei* appears to have given Takeuchi some pause when translating Lu Xun. In *Ro Jin, Mu Jun: Sekai bungaku taikei 62* (p. 32), he renders it as *watashi tachi yori wakai mono* ("those younger than us") but then changes this to *wakai sedai* ("younger generation") in the later *Ro Jin bunshū*, 1:96.

68. *Takeuchi Yoshimi zenshū*, 2:356–357.

69. *Takeuchi Yoshimi zenshū*, 2:358.

70. *Lu Xun zuopin quanji*, 3:42; *Selected Works of Lu Hsun*, 1:332; *Voices from the Iron House: A Study of Lu Xun*, 101; *Ro Jin, Mu Jun: sekai bungaku taikei 62*, 171. The specific word Takeuchi uses here is *yabu*.

71. *Lu Xun zuopin quanji*, 3:42; *Selected Works of Lu Hsun*, 1:332; *Ro Jin, Mu Jun: sekai bungaku taikei 62*, 171. Takeuchi's Japanese reads *katachi bakari no michi no ato*.

72. This negativity that Lu Xun wishes to think in connection with roads or paths can be fruitfully contrasted to the ideas of the philosopher and social reformer Hu Shi. Trained in pragmatism under John Dewey, Hu Shi conceives of negativity strictly as a problem to be resolved through the aid of reason. As he writes in the 1919 essay "Shiyanzhuyi" (Experimentalism): "This type of thinking contains two characteristics: 1. It requires the existence of a state of perplexity, hesitation or doubt as its starting point; and 2. It requires an act

of search or investigation in which new facts or knowledge are sought out so as to resolve these perplexities, hesitations, and doubts. For instance, in the example given above of the man lost in a forest, he goes east and west but has lost the direction and is unable to find his way. The situation therefore is one of perplexity and hesitation. This is the first condition. The man climbs atop a tree and gazes out into the distance. Through perhaps the use of his binoculars he is able to locate running water, which he then follows as a way out. It is this act of search or investigation which fulfills the second condition." *Hu Shi zuopin ji* (Collected works of Hu Shi) (Taipei: Yuanliu chuban, 1986), 4:93–94.

73. *Lu Xun zuopin quanji*, 3:43; *Selected Works of Lu Hsun*, 1:333.

74. This type of primordial ignorance is another name for what Avital Ronell calls "stupidity." See Ronell, *Stupidity* (Champaign: University of Illinois Press, 2002).

75. *Lu Xun zuopin quanji*, 6:324; *Jottings Under Lamplight: Lu Xun*, 31.

76. *Lu Xun zuopin quanji*, 6:324, 329; *Jottings Under Lamplight: Lu Xun*, 30, 31, 35. In *Ro Jin, Mu Jun: sekai bungaku taikei 62*, Takeuchi translates these important words as *iseki* (遺跡) and *nagori* (なごり), respectively (see pp. 201, 203).

77. *Lu Xun zuopin quanji*, 6:327; *Jottings Under Lamplight: Lu Xun*, 34. (I have substituted this expression "interstitial thing" for the translator's own choice of "intermediate form.")

BIBLIOGRAPHY

Anderson, Marston. *The Limits of Realism: Chinese Fiction in the Revolutionary Period.* Berkeley: University of California Press, 1990.

Ariès, Philippe. *Western Attitudes towards Death: From the Middle Ages to the Present.* Baltimore: Johns Hopkins University Press, 1974.

Bachner, Andrea. *Beyond Sinology: Chinese Writing and the Scripts of Cultures.* New York: Columbia University Press, 2014.

———. "Cinema as Heterochronos: Temporal Folds in the Work of Tsai Ming-liang." *Modern Chinese Literature and Culture* 19, no. 1 (Spring 2007).

Berry, Michael. *Speaking in Images: Interviews with Contemporary Chinese Film-makers.* New York: Columbia University Press, 2005.

Burch, Nöel. *To the Distant Observer: Form and Meaning in the Japanese Cinema.* Berkeley: University of California Press, 1979.

Calichman, Richard F. *Before Identity: The Question of Method in Japan Studies.* Albany: State University of New York Press, 2021.

———. *Takeuchi Yoshimi: Displacing the West.* Ithaca, NY: Cornell East Asia Series, 2004.

———. *What is Modernity? Writings of Takeuchi Yoshimi.* New York: Columbia University Press, 2005.

Cao Juren, *Lu Xun de yisheng: Zhongguo jindai wenxueshi de ceying* [Lu Xun's lifetime: A profile in modern Chinese literary history]. Taipei: Xinchaoshe, 1987.

Cheng, Eileen J. *Literary Remains: Death, Trauma, and Lu Xun's Refusal to Mourn.* Honolulu: University of Hawai'i Press, 2013.

———, and Kirk A. Denton, trans. and eds. *Jottings Under Lamplight: Lu Xun.* Cambridge, MA: Harvard University Press, 2017.

Chow, Rey. *Sentimental Fabulations, Contemporary Chinese Films: Attachment in the Age of Global Visibility.* New York, Columbia University Press, 2007.

———. *Woman and Chinese Modernity: The Politics of Reading Between West and East.* Minneapolis: University of Minnesota Press, 1991.

Cox, Damian, and Michael P. Levine, eds. *Thinking through Film: Doing Philosophy, Watching Movies.* Chichester, UK: Wiley-Blackwell, 2012.

Dastur, Françoise, *How Are We to Confront Death? An Introduction to Philosophy*. Translated by Robert Vallier. New York: Fordham University Press, 2012.

Davies, Gloria. *Lu Xun's Revolution: Writing in a Time of Violence*. Cambridge, MA: Harvard University Press, 2013.

Derrida, Jacques. *Aporias*. Translated by Thomas Dutoit. Stanford, CA: Stanford University Press, 1993.

————. *Margins of Philosophy*. Translated by Alan Bass. Chicago: University of Chicago Press, 1982.

————. "My Chances/*Mes Chances*: A Rendezvous with Some Epicurean Stereophonies." Translated by Irene Harvey and Avital Ronnell. Edited by Joseph H. Smith and William Kerrigan. *Taking Chances: Derrida, Psychoanalysis, and Literature*. Baltimore: Johns Hopkins University Press, 1984.

————. *The Postcard: From Socrates to Freud and Beyond*. Translated by Alan Bass. Chicago: University of Chicago Press, 1987.

Dilworth, David A., trans. and ed. *Sourcebook for Modern Japanese Philosophy: Selected Documents*. Westport, CT: Greenwood, 1998.

Freud, Sigmund. *Beyond the Pleasure Principle*. Translated by James Strachey. New York: W.W. Norton, 1961.

Goodwin, James. *Akira Kurosawa and Intertextual Cinema*. Baltimore: Johns Hopkins University Press, 1994.

Guex, Samuel. *Entre nonchalance et désespoir: Les intellectuels japonais sinologues face à la guerre (1930–1950)*. Bern: Peter Lang, 2006.

Hägglund, Martin. *Dying for Time: Proust, Woolf, Nabokov*. Cambridge, MA: Harvard University Press, 2012.

————. *Radical Atheism: Derrida and the Time of Life*. Stanford, CA: Stanford University Press, 2008.

Hegel, G. W. F. *Phenomenology of Spirit*. Translated by A.V. Miller. Oxford: Oxford University Press, 1977.

Heidegger, Martin. *Being and Time*. Translated by John Macquarrie and Edward Robinson. New York; Harper & Row, 1962.

Hiromatsu Wataru. *Iwanami tetsugaku shisō jiten* [The Iwanami dictionary of philosophy and thought]. Tokyo: Iwanami shoten, 1998.

Huang, Erin Y. *Urban Horror: Neoliberalism, Post-socialism, and the Limits of Visibility*. Durham, NC: Duke University Press, 2020.

Huang Sung-K'ang. *Lu Hsün and the New Culture Movement of Modern China*. Westport, CT: Hyperion, 1975.

Hu Shi. *Hu Shi zuopin ji* [Collected works of Hu Shi]. Taipei: Yuanliu chuban, 1986.

Jiao Xiongping. *Heliu: Cai Mingliang de dianying* [The river: A film by Tsai Ming-liang]. Taipei: Huangguan, 1997.

Kan Takayuki. *Takeuchi Yoshimi ron: Ajia he no hanka* [On Takeuchi Yoshimi: An envoy to Asia]. Tokyo: San'ichi shobō, 1976.

Kleinberg, Ethan. *Haunting History: For a Deconstructive Approach to the Past.* Stanford, CA: Stanford University Press, 2017.

Kurosawa Akira. *Something Like an Autobiography.* Translated by Audie E. Bock. New York: Vintage, 1983.

———. *Zenshū, Kurosawa Akira* [Complete works: Kurosawa Akira]. Tokyo: Iwanami shoten, 1988.

Lee, Leo Ou-fan. *Voices from the Iron House: A Study of Lu Xun.* Bloomington: Indiana University Press, 1987.

Leo Tak-hung Chan. "Japanization and the Chinese 'Madman': Triangulating Takeuchi Yoshimi's Philosophy of Translation." *Translation Studies* 9, no. 1 (2016).

Lim, Song Hwee. *Tsai Ming-liang and a Cinema of Slowness.* Honolulu: University of Hawai'i Press, 2014.

Lippit, Akira Mizuta. *Cinema without Reflection: Jacques Derrida's Echopoiesis and Narcissism Adrift.* Minneapolis: University of Minnesota Press, 2016.

Lovell, Julia, trans. *The Real Story of Ah-Q and Other Tales of China: The Complete Fiction of Lu Xun.* London: Penguin, 2009.

Lucken, Michael. *Imitation and Creativity in Japanese Arts: From Kishida Ryūsei to Miyazaki Hayao.* Translated by Francesca Simkin. New York: Columbia University Press, 2016.

Lu Xun, *Lu Xun zuopin quanji* [Complete works of Lu Xun]. Taipei: Fengyun Shidai, 1996.

Lyell, William A., Jr. *Lu Hsün's Vision of Reality.* Berkeley: University of California Press, 1976.

Ma, Jean. *Melancholy Drift: Marking Time in Chinese Cinema.* Hong Kong: Hong Kong University Press, 2010.

Martin, Fran. "The European Undead: Tsai Ming-liang's Temporal Dysphoria." *Senses of Cinema* (website), http://sensesofcinema.com/2003/feature-articles/tsai_european_undead/

McDougall, Bonnie S. *Love Letters and Privacy in Modern China: The Intimate Lives of Lu Xun and Xu Guangping.* Oxford: Oxford University Press, 2002.

Nakagawa Ikurō. *Takeuchi Yoshimi no bungaku to shisō* [Takeuchi Yoshimi's literature and thought]. Tokyo: Orijin, 1985.

Nishimura Yūichirō. *Kurosawa Akira: oto to eizō* [Kurosawa Akira: Sound and image]. Tokyo: Rippū shobō, 1998.

Okayama Asako. *Takeuchi Yoshimi no bungaku seishin* [Takeuchi Yoshimi's literary spirit]. Tokyo: Ronsōsha, 2002.

Olson, Lawrence. *Ambivalent Moderns: Portraits of Japanese Cultural Identity.* Savage, MD: Rowman and Littlefield, 1992.

Prince, Stephen. *The Warrior's Camera: The Cinema of Akira Kurosawa.* Princeton, NJ: Princeton University Press, 1991.

Pusey, James Reeve. *Lu Xun and Evolution*. Albany: State University of New York Press, 1998.

Rehm, Jean-Pierre, Olivier Joyard, and Danièle Rivière. *Tsaï Ming-liang*. Paris: Dis Voir, 1999.

Richie, Donald, ed. *Modern Film Scripts: Ikiru, A Film by Akira Kurosawa*. New York: Simon and Schuster, 1968.

———. *The Films of Akira Kurosawa*. Berkeley: University of California Press, 1996.

Rojas, Carlos. "'Nezha Was Here': Structures of Dis/placement in Tsai Ming-liang's *Rebels of the Neon God*." *Modern Chinese Literature and Culture* 15, no. 1 (Spring 2003).

Ronell, Avital. *Stupidity*. Champaign: University of Illinois Press, 2002.

Sakai, Naoki. *Translation and Subjectivity: On "Japan" and Cultural Nationalism*. Minneapolis: University of Minnesota Press, 1997.

Satō Tadao, *Currents in Japanese Cinema*. Translated by Gregory Barrett. Tokyo: Kodansha, 1982.

———. *Kurosawa Akira no sekai* [The world of Kurosawa Akira]. Tokyo: San'ichi shobō, 1969.

Seraphim, Franziska. *War Memory and Social Politics in Japan, 1945–2005*. Cambridge, MA: Harvard East Asia Monographs, 2006.

Staten, Henry. *Eros in Mourning: Homer to Lacan*. Baltimore: Johns Hopkins University Press, 1995.

Sun Ge. *Takeuchi Yoshimi to iu toi* [The question of Takeuchi Yoshimi]. Tokyo: Iwanami shoten, 2005.

Sun Songrong. *Rujing chujing: Tsai Ming-liang de yingxiang yishu yu kuajie shijian* [Frame in/frame out: Tsai Ming-liang's art of the image and transgressive practice]. Taipei: Wunan Tushu, 2014.

Takeuchi Yoshimi. *Ro Jin bunshū* [Collected writings of Lu Xun]. Tokyo: Chikuma shobō, 1979.

———. *Ro Jin, Mu Jun: sekai bungaku taikei 62* [Lu Xun, Mao Dun: The system of world literature 62]. Tokyo: Chikuma Shobō, 1958.

———. *Takeuchi Yoshimi zenshū* [Complete works of Takeuchi Yoshimi]. Tokyo: Chikuma shobō, 1980.

Turim, Maureen. *Flashbacks in Film: Memory and History*. New York: Routledge, 1989.

Uhl, Christian. "Displacing Japan: Takeuchi Yoshimi's Lu Xun in Light of Nishida's Philosophy, and Vice Versa." *Philosophy and the Political in Wartime Japan, 1931–1945*, special issue of *Positions: East Asia Cultures Critique* 17, no. 1 (Spring 2009).

Ukai Satoshi. "Kaisetsu" [Commentary]. Takeuchi Yoshimi, *Ro Jin (shinpan)* [Lu Xun (new edition)]. Tokyo: Miraisha, 2002.

Xu, Gary G. *Sinascape: Contemporary Chinese Cinema*. Lanham, MD: Rowman & Littlefield, 2007.

Yang Hsien-yi and Gladys Yang. *Selected Works of Lu Hsun*. Peking: Foreign Languages Press, 1957.

Yoshimoto, Mitsuhiro. *Kurosawa: Film Studies and Japanese Cinema*. Durham, NC: Duke University Press, 2000.

Yoshimoto Takaaki. "Jōkyō he no hatsugen—Takeuchi Yoshimi ni tsuite," *Shikō* 50, June 30, 1978.

Zhang Jingbei. *Bujian busan: Cai Mingliang yu Li Kangsheng* [The missing/goodbye, dragon inn: Tsai Ming-liang and Lee Kang-sheng]. Singapore: Bafang wenhua chuangzuo shi, 2004.

Zhou Yushan. "Lu Xun zouguo de lu" [The road traveled by Lu Xun]. In *Lu Xun*. Taipei: Guangfu shuju, 1990.

INDEX

Absence, 15, 19–20, 27, 39, 45–50, 54, 59, 73, 90, 112, 114, 117, 120–123, 127–128, 132, 139, 154

Actuality, 18, 31, 103, 144

Anxiety, 1, 15, 28, 31, 66, 116, 136, 138–139

Ariès, Philippe, 3, 153

Chen Shiang-chyi, 34–37, 40, 53, 56–57, 157

Cheng, Eileen J., 131–133, 159, 166

Circularity, 53–55, 57–59

Community, 10, 18–26, 80

Contingency, 14, 28, 46–47, 50, 82, 90, 94, 96, 133, 163

Culturalism, 131

Darkness, 8, 47, 79, 81–82, 84, 87, 91, 100, 130, 133–137, 146

Derrida, Jacques, 3, 153, 155–156, 162–163

Dialectics, 71, 102

Exteriority, 4, 7, 13, 49, 82–83, 92–93, 96, 112, 122, 131

Family, 6, 10, 18–20, 26–29, 51, 77, 93, 105, 140

Finitude, 7, 10, 14–16, 18, 31, 63, 68, 70, 77, 81, 94–95, 97–98, 103, 105, 114, 150, 161

Forgetting, 8, 73–74, 100, 113, 115, 123, 125–127, 129, 134

Funerals, 20, 68–69, 71–72, 74–77, 80–81, 83, 85, 105, 112, 154, 159

Future, 1–2, 6, 17, 26–27, 29–30, 37–38, 42–43, 47, 50–51, 55, 61, 73, 85, 96, 98, 101, 104, 107, 117–119, 123–126, 128–129, 141–143, 149–151, 156, 163

Ghosts, 26, 29–30, 35–36, 47, 60, 98, 105, 127–128, 146, 157

Haunting, 7, 29–30, 36, 70, 75, 77, 80, 85, 90, 93–95, 97, 100, 113, 127–128, 147, 150

Hegel, Georg Wilhelm Friedrich, 5, 19, 114, 154, 159, 161–162

Heidegger, Martin, 94–95, 103, 161–162

Hu, King (aka Hu Jinquan), 41

Identity, 3–5, 18, 23, 25, 27, 30, 42, 44, 48–52, 54–55, 64–67, 94–96, 104, 116–117, 120, 125, 128, 130, 134, 143, 145, 148, 153, 157

Inheritance, 28, 30, 77, 81

Interiority, 4, 7, 49–51, 82–83, 91–93, 96, 112, 122

Keeping, 6, 35, 73, 106

175

Kurosawa Akira, 5–6, 9–31, 33,
    153–155

Léaud, Jean-Pierre, 7, 44–46, 49–52,
    58–60, 157
Lee Kang-sheng (aka Hsiao Kang), 7,
    34–40, 44–59, 157
Lee, Leo Ou-fan, 138, 144, 167
Li Changzhi, 86–89, 92, 97, 105
Light, 8, 47, 79, 82, 100, 130,
    133–136, 138, 143, 146, 157
Line, 6, 9, 26–29, 38, 52–53, 81
Lippit, Akira Mizuta, 29, 155
Loss, 4–6, 8, 21, 27, 31, 34–36, 39,
    41, 46–48, 53–57, 59, 61, 64, 67,
    72–74, 80, 112–114, 120, 133,
    148, 163
Lu Xun, 5, 7–8, 63–151, 158–168

Memory, 8, 10, 19–20, 35, 60, 73–75,
    77, 90, 97–98, 100, 105, 114–115,
    118–129, 134, 147, 154, 159, 165
Methodology, 3, 5, 92, 97
Miao Tien, 33, 38–39, 41, 47, 51–53,
    56–57, 59
Mortality, 6, 9–10, 15, 18, 33, 38,
    46, 50, 68, 72, 77, 81, 93–97, 112,
    114, 117, 131
Mourning, 18–19, 36, 39, 47, 58, 73,
    75–76, 80, 85, 105, 107–108, 112,
    120–121, 124, 131, 164, 166

Nation-state, 10, 63
Necessity, 46, 93–94, 96, 122, 133
Negativity, 2–5, 7–8, 17, 24, 27,
    37, 39–40, 43, 55, 57, 65, 67,
    71, 77–78, 80–85, 88, 96–104,
    108–110, 112–114, 116, 119, 121,
    122–125, 130, 132–134, 137, 144,
    150, 160–161, 167
Nothingness, 4–5, 7–8, 15, 37, 53,
    78, 88, 97, 99, 102, 104, 108–112,

114, 116, 121–124, 127, 130–131,
    135–136, 150

Object, 3–4, 19, 21, 49–50, 68, 83,
    91, 97, 113, 119–122, 124, 133,
    139, 146
Ontology, 3, 79, 120–122, 124, 130,
    135–137, 142
Opposition, 2, 10, 24, 49, 65, 68–71,
    82–83, 134, 137–138, 164–165

Particularism, 4, 166
Past, 1, 3, 6, 19–20, 26, 29–31,
    34–39, 41–42, 44, 46–47, 49–53,
    55–56, 60–61, 90–92, 97–98, 101,
    104, 107, 115–120, 124–126, 128–
    129, 131, 140–143, 145, 147–151,
    153, 156, 161, 165
Possibility, 2–3, 7–9, 14, 17–18, 28,
    31, 41, 43–44, 46–47, 52–53, 55,
    66–67, 72, 77, 80, 85, 91, 94–95,
    103, 107, 120, 126, 129, 140, 144,
    150, 156–157
Praxis, 8, 100, 137–139, 141, 144
Presence, 2, 4, 7, 15, 17, 20, 27,
    29–31, 36, 39, 42, 46–47, 49–50,
    52–53, 55, 57, 59, 64, 66–67,
    72–75, 77, 80–82, 85, 88, 90,
    92, 97–103, 106–107, 110, 112,
    116–118, 121–122, 128, 130, 132,
    149–150, 157–158
Present, 1, 3–4, 6, 17, 19–20, 26,
    29–31, 34–36, 39, 42, 45–46,
    49–50, 52–53, 56, 60, 65, 67, 74,
    78, 82, 85, 90–92, 97–99, 104–105,
    107, 112, 115–118, 120–126, 128,
    131, 133, 140–144, 147–150,
    165
Preservation, 1, 7, 10, 18, 26, 40–44,
    46–47, 61, 73, 89, 110, 149
Psychology, 26, 59, 79, 85, 87,
    90–94, 96–97, 127

Reading, 37, 116–118, 124–125

Rebirth, 7, 31, 36, 51, 53–55, 57–60, 116, 119, 143

Remains, 50, 60, 111–113, 115, 124–125, 131–133, 150, 166

Renoir, Jean, 44–45

Repetition, 12, 30, 34, 37–39, 51, 57–58, 60, 74, 76–77, 117, 120–121, 137, 141, 145, 149

Resurrection, 20, 31, 35–36, 47, 53, 57, 60, 73, 80, 95, 100, 104–105, 107, 115–119, 143, 156

Retroactivity, 50, 65, 116, 125, 142, 149

Rivière, Danièle, 40, 42, 49, 55, 156–157

Satō Tadao, 24, 154–155

Science, 3, 64–65, 86, 88

Sending, 44, 75, 77, 159

Shadow, 97, 100, 110, 112, 120–121, 128, 130–131, 133–136, 138, 146

Shih Jun, 38–42

Space, 5, 7, 20, 29–30, 40, 42–44, 46–50, 57–58, 73, 75, 97–99, 101, 110, 121, 156

Spectrality, 74–75, 77, 80, 97, 127–129, 160

Subject, 4, 19, 25, 54, 68, 85, 91–92, 95–96, 100, 105, 110, 113–114, 116, 118–121, 127, 131–133, 136–139, 145, 149, 155, 158, 163, 165

Succession, 6, 13, 17, 26–30, 51–53, 77, 81, 104, 107, 145, 155

Survival, 3, 6–7, 10, 17–18, 26–27, 29–31, 33, 35–36, 40, 42, 54, 60, 69, 73–74, 77, 86, 89–90, 97–98, 105, 115, 123, 125–127, 133, 143, 147–149

Takeuchi Yoshimi, 5, 7–8, 63–151, 158–168

Time, 1–8, 11–14, 16–18, 30, 33, 35–44, 46–51, 53, 55–57, 60, 73, 75, 82, 85, 95, 97–98, 100, 103–104, 106–108, 112, 116–120, 123–129, 131–133, 141–147, 149–150, 155–156, 165

Trace, 8, 26, 31, 42, 100, 111–114, 122–127, 144, 147–150

Transmission, 77, 131, 140, 142–143

Truffaut, François, 7, 44–45, 50–51, 58–60

Tsai Ming-liang, 5–7, 33–61, 156–158

Ukai Satoshi, 129–131, 133

Unity, 13, 21–24, 49, 51, 55, 66, 69–71, 97, 117, 128, 138, 161

Violence, 6, 9–10, 12–14, 18, 21, 40, 63, 100, 106, 110, 114, 122, 125–126, 129, 150, 157

Vulnerability, 1, 5, 10, 17, 22, 52, 65–67, 98, 100, 106, 150

Writing, 40, 43–44, 73–74, 122, 124–125, 147, 149–150

Yoshimoto, Mitsuhiro, 22, 154